Paddling Alabama

Help Us Keep This Guide Up to Date

Every effort has been made by the authors and editors to make this guide as accurate and useful as possible. However, many things can change after a guide is published—regulations change, techniques evolve, facilities come under new management, etc.

We would love to hear from you concerning your experiences with this guide and how you feel it could be improved and kept up to date. While we may not be able to respond to all comments and suggestions, we'll take them to heart and we'll also make certain to share them with the authors. Please send your comments and suggestions to the following address:

The Globe Pequot Press
Reader Response/Editorial Department
P.O. Box 480
Guilford, CT 06437

Or you may e-mail us at:

editorial@globe-pequot.com

Thanks for your input, and happy travels!

A **FALCON** GUIDE®

Paddling Alabama

Joe Cuhaj and Curt Burdick

FALCON®

GUILFORD, CONNECTICUT
HELENA, MONTANA

AN IMPRINT OF THE GLOBE PEQUOT PRESS

Library of Congress Cataloging-in-Publication Data

Cuhaj, Joe.
    Paddling Alabama/Joe Cuhaj and Curt Burdick.—1st ed.
        p. cm.—(A Falcon Guide)
    Includes bibliographical references.
    ISBN 0-7627-2192-8
        1. Canoes and canoeing—Alabama—Guidebooks. 2. Alabama—Guidebooks. I. Burdick, Curt.
    II. Title. III. Series.
    GV776.A2 C84 2002
    797.1'22'09758—dc21

                                                                    2002072070

Contents

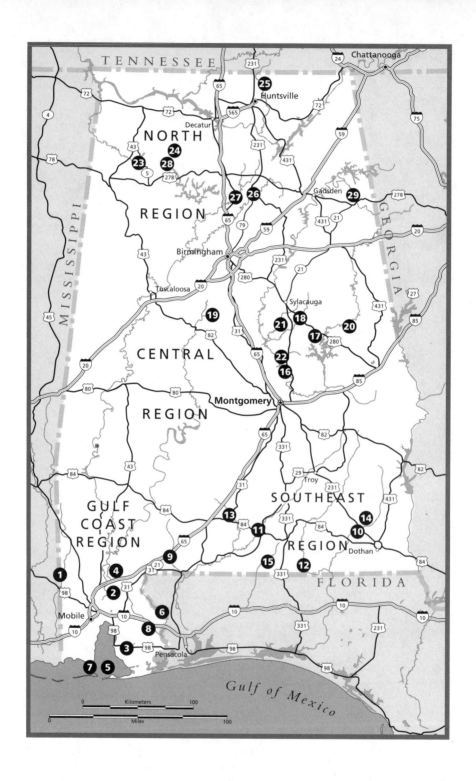

Central Region

North Region

Map Legend

～～	Stream
⬭	Lake, ocean
≈≈≈	Marsh
◣	Put-in
⟹	Route
3.2	River mileage
◤	Takeout
◐	Gaging station

	Dam
	Obstruction
	Rapids
	Shoal
	Bluffs
	Sandbar or beach
	Rock
	Pilings, bridge foundation
	Bridge
	Waterfall
	Pool

—〔36〕—	US Highway
—(108)—	State Highway
—[89]—	County road
= = = = =	Gravel road
= = = = = = =	Dirt road
- - - - - - -	Hiking trail
— · — · —	Pipeline
•——————•	Powerline
⊢⊢⊢⊢⊢⊢	Railroad

■	Building
⌘	School
†	Church
⁙	Steps
▲	Campground
⊞	Picnic area
🅿	Parking area
▲	Summit

Acknowledgments

Once again there are loads of people I need to thank for helping to make this book possible. First and foremost, there's my wife, Maggie, and daughter, Kellie. Thanks for putting up with another adventure and for the shuttles! Also, thanks to Jeff Serena at Falcon for guidance and the chance to put this book together. And of course, thanks to my buddies, affectionately known as the "Usual Bunch of Idiots, Inc.," Kevin, Jay, Debbi, Terri, Mark, Gary, and Tom, for the inspiration to continue writing, getting on the rivers, and having fun.

And finally to Curt for going along with this adventure, doing a great job with the manuscript, and keeping our spills to a minimum!

—Joe Cuhaj

For her continued support and patience with me on this great adventure, I'd like to thank my wife, Liz. And to my two boys, Aaron and Cary, thanks for giving me those long weekends away from the house. Also, many thanks to Jeff Serena at Falcon, without whom we would not have even been able to begin. Joe, thanks for the great writing and for having me along on the grand journey.

And to the scores of other people of Alabama who made this book possible, thanks for your help and expertise on the many different topics required to bring the book to fruition. It's been fun.

—Curt Burdick

Finally, both of us would like to thank the canoe clubs around the state who gave us a hand, including the Mobile Bay Canoe and Kayak Club (they have some great parties), Huntsville Canoe Club, Birmingham Canoe Club, and the Stroker's Paddling Club (Tuscaloosa).

Introduction

What's more fun, reading or canoeing? OK, we have to agree with you. We wrote this book for several reasons. One of those reasons is that any experience is almost always more fun and interesting when you have some relevant background and know-how, which we hope you will obtain by reading this book. Heck, it was fun writing the book for the knowledge *we* gained (all right, and the fact that it required lots of canoeing).

We've gained a real appreciation for nature and for the range of feelings invoked by being part of it. Floating some of the tranquil waters of Alabama elicits calm, a feeling that is not easy to come by these days. Many times on the same trip, and within minutes, you can go from cascading down 3-foot falls and bubbly shoals to a spot where the water slows, even stops, and you can just lie back and take in the wonder . . . priceless.

And talk about quality family time! Bring along the kids, and you'll instill the love of nature in them early. Too often these days our children (and we adults, too) find it easy to relax by plopping down in front of the TV or video game for hours on end. Before long our very lives become virtual reality.

We already know that there will be critics out there whining about "their" river not being included in the book. Heck! We hear it at our day jobs now: "When are you doing the Mobile River?" "Why aren't you paddling Chickasabogue Creek?"

The main goal of this book is to present the diverse paddling adventures in Alabama. We tried to include something for everyone. If you're a beginning white water, sea-kayak, or canoe paddler in general or an expert, we have it in here for you. We've also tried to give a balance to the state to show some of the best trips in the different regions and to not focus on one particular area.

We have also tried to cover rivers that have easy access. There is nothing more frustrating than trying to find a shuttle when you're out in the wilderness. We have tried to keep the trips to areas where you can either rent a shuttle or it's easy for two vehicles to access.

Keep in mind that the twenty-nine rivers we cover in this book are only the tip of the iceberg. There are hundreds of other opportunities waiting for you. Talk with the locals. Contact area canoe clubs. They're all eager to tell you about other adventures awaiting you on Alabama's rivers. So get outdoors, get paddling, and enjoy!

Alabama the Beautiful

Here are some interesting river statistics provided by Alabama Rivers Alliance:

- Alabama ranks seventh in the United States for its number of stream miles— 77,242 miles of river and stream channels.
- Alabama has 3,627,600 acres of wetland and 563,000 acres of ponds, lakes, and reservoirs.
- There are 33.5 trillion gallons of water withdrawn annually from streams, rivers, and reservoirs to supply drinking water to 56 percent of the population in Alabama.

- There are sixteen hydroelectric power dams and sixteen navigational dams (five of which are also hydroelectric) in Alabama.
- The southeastern United States has the world's greatest diversity of temperate freshwater fishes. Alabama has 303 freshwater species of fish, 20 of which are endemic to Alabama.
- Alabama's rivers are amongst the most biologically diverse waterways in the world. Among the natives of Alabama's rivers are 38 percent of North America's fish species, 43 percent of its freshwater gill-breathing snails, 51 percent of its freshwater turtle species, and 60 percent of its freshwater mussel species.
- There are more species of fish in the Cahaba River alone than in the entire state of California!
- Consider the economic value of clean waters. The Alabama Fisheries Association estimates that Alabama's water-based recreation industry brings more than $1 billion per year into the state's economy.

Weather

Weather in Alabama varies, of course, but is perfect almost any time of the year for paddling in one form or another. In the northern regions temperatures average around forty-six degrees F in January to eighty degrees in July. Of course colder temperatures can occur in the north with significant snowfall accumulations possible.

To the south temperatures average fifty-two degrees F in January to eighty-five degrees in July. Combined with the high humidity, the climate is best described as being subtropical. Don't get us wrong. Cold snaps of below thirty degress, even below zero, do occur in the southern regions, but they are few and far between and only last a day or two.

The southeast United States is prone to heavy late-summer rains. The warm, moist gulf air causes afternoon rainstorms to pop up unexpectedly and with ferocity. The storms are short in duration, but rainfall amounts can be significant. Severe lightning usually accompanies these storms. And don't forget about the high humidity of late summer in the south, which can make outdoor activity of any kind impossible.

The best white water runs in the state can be found in the north and central regions. Anywhere from a Class I to VI run can be found, but these rivers tend to dry up in the summer. The best times to visit these rivers would be in the winter and spring.

This is not to say that doing some white water in the northern half of the state is out of the question during the summer. As mentioned, the south is prone to sudden and severe summer thunderstorms. Keep an eye on the USGS (United States Geological Survey) and TVA (Tennessee Valley Authority) flow gauges for spikes in flows for some excellent summertime trips. Several rivers (see the individual trips for more information) are controlled by dams by the TVA or U.S. Army Corps of Engineers, who release flows during the summer to provide plenty of recreational white water.

In the Gulf Coast and southeastern regions, the subtropical climate is perfect weather for taking on a nice float trip down one of the blackwater rivers in the region. These are long, lazy rivers with beautiful white sandbars and plenty of pools to swim in. Or check out the many sea-kayaking opportunities in Mobile and Baldwin Counties in the Gulf of Mexico and Mobile Bay. And there are some nice Class I rapids along the rivers of the southeast. The beauty of the trips in these regions is that the summer heat doesn't bother the flow terribly, and you can float them year-round.

Of course, some precautions are necessary when dealing with the weather. Summer-time thunderstorms are severe and pop up out of nowhere. This is especially dangerous if you are kayaking the gulf or the Tensaw River Delta. Watch the weather forecast *before* heading out.

Don't forget that May through November is hurricane season. Although Alabama has only a small amount of real estate directly on the Gulf Coast, some very severe storms have wreaked havoc in the state—not only on the coast, but as far north as Huntsville as they moved inland. During this time of year, check the weather before you head out for any tropical disturbances. If there are any reported, keep an eye on their progress to determine if venturing out is a good idea at that time or not.

Flora and Fauna

Alabama is truly blessed with outdoor beauty. Botanists tell us that more than two-thirds of Alabama is covered in forest. While you float down the many rivers of the state, you are apt to see southern yellow, red, white, loblolly, and slash pine forests, with a good smattering of deciduous trees as well, including hickory, sweet gum, and several varieties of oaks. Time and again your senses will be filled with the fragrant aroma of flowering trees that line the rivers as well including magnolia and dogwood.

When it comes to wildflowers, Alabama is second to none in varieties, and most can be seen along the paddling excursions we cover in this book. Some of the unique varieties include merry bells, which bloom in the spring throughout the state. These flowers are part of the lily family and bloom from April to June. The plant has very thin and delicate stems topped with hay-yellow bells.

You are likely to see cardinal flower blooming into bright scarlet colors in late summer along the riverbanks. In early March the vines of the Carolina jessamine will be found clinging to fences and trees. These vines with yellow flowers can be found throughout the state.

A common wildflower is the yellow orchid, which blooms in late summer through early fall and can be found just about anywhere in the state. From late July through September, the yellow-fringed orchid can be found in bogs along the river ways.

Alabama has a varied wildlife population as well. Although you are more apt to find white-tailed deer than anything else, the state plays home to many different species of animals. Black bear can be found from one end of the state to the other, with the largest population being found in the Mobile-Tensaw River Delta of the Gulf Coast (refer to the Hurricane Creek and Rice Creek/Mound Island trips in the Southeast Region section). Bobcat or lynx are also quite common throughout the state, again many in the Mobile-Tensaw River Delta, but these are nocturnal animals and are only rarely seen in the day.

The American alligator, one of only two species of alligators in the world, also calls Alabama home and will be found in the trips in the southeast and Gulf Coast regions. It is important to remember that alligators feed on fish, frogs, snakes, turtles, birds, and mammals and are naturally afraid of humans, but feeding them or harassing them in any manner changes the rules. You really have to look to find them sometimes while paddling. They tend to hide behind logs or other obstructions and just sit back and keep an eye on what you're doing.

In 1967 the American alligator was declared an endangered species as a result of over-hunting, but the species has made a strong comeback, and some states have again allowed the hunting of them (Alabama is not one of them).

Several other endangered species of wildlife can be found in Alabama, including some you may encounter in your water excursions. If you sea kayak around south Baldwin County, you will be in prime nesting areas for the loggerhead sea turtle. And throughout the southeast and Gulf Coast regions, you will see the brown pelican.

Because of the number of lakes, rivers, and wetlands in the state, Alabama is a popular stop for migratory birds, especially ducks and geese. And when it comes to birds, hundreds of species will be found dispersed throughout the state, too many to name here. Please refer to Appendix A for some excellent resources that describe the wildlife and plant life to be found in Alabama.

Blazing New Trails: The Canoe Trails of Alabama

We think we've pretty well made the point that Alabama has an abundance of rivers, creeks, lakes, and ocean waterways that provide unlimited exploration and outdoor activity, and that support more species of amphibians, mammals, birds, insects, and wildlife than any other place in the world. Many states would not recognize a fact such as this, and even fewer would take an active role in promoting and developing these resources. Thankfully that's not the case in Alabama.

The Alabama Department of Conservation and Natural Resources, along with various other state, local, and volunteer organizations, have taken on the task of developing these waterways for canoers, kayakers, and outdoor lovers in general.

The project is known as Alabama River Expeditions. What does it involve? Well, first of all, it's one big canoe trip! Members of the expedition will use nonmotorized boats (canoes and kayaks, whatever the river conditions require) and travel more than 2,500 miles of waterways in 12 months. It is quite an ambitious project to say the least.

Which waterways will they float? If you look at the Alabama state seal, you will see on it a picture of the state and the major rivers and tributaries that were vital in its development. The expedition will float all of the rivers depicted in the seal and document them for posterity through films, photos, and writings. The expedition will be conducted not only by state employees, but also by volunteers from the public sector, and representatives of the media.

The three main objectives of the project are to ". . . make Alabama citizens more aware of our state's rivers and streams, and their significance to our quality of life; encourage public involvement in state programs directed at the conservation of Alabama's aquatic natural resources; and promulgate support of a Scenic Rivers Act by our State Legislature."

In addition to the stated objectives, the group will also study and create new canoe trails, such as the statewide Blue Trail and the Lloyd Owens Canoe Trail. They will also investigate, promote, and build overnight canoe trails. For example, in the 300,000-acre Mobile-Tensaw River Delta, they will be studying where to place and eventually install several floating camping platforms that will allow paddlers to visit the fragile delta environment for extended periods without disturbing it.

Photos and journals of the expedition may be found online at www.dcnr.state.al.us. If you would like to volunteer to help out or just get more information, send an e-mail to project coordinator Greg Lein at glein@dcnr.state.al.us.

Alabama's Watery Crown Jewel: The Mobile-Tensaw River Delta

Statistics cannot do the Mobile-Tensaw River Delta justice, but they are necessary to put its significance into perspective. In all the delta encompasses more than 400 square miles—that's 300,000 acres—of wilderness that ranges from swampland to river bottom to marshes. This makes it the second largest delta in the country, after the Mississippi River Delta. It is also one of the largest intact wetland ecosystems left in the United States. These statistics led Congress to declare the delta a National Natural Landmark.

The history, sights, and sounds of the delta create a spectacular story. Early Native Americans called the delta home as far back as 1500 B.C. On Mound Island (see the Rice Creek/Mound Island trip), eighteen separate mounds have been discovered that are believed to be the home of the aristocracy of the Mississippian Period Indians. Many state names came from the tribes who eventually called the delta region home, including the Alabamous, Mobile, and Tensaw.

Europeans arrived in the region in 1559, calling the river the "River of the Holy Spirit." It wasn't until 1778 that botanist to the Queen William Bartram made the first detailed expedition through the delta and uncovered its vast wealth of wildlife and plant life.

Amazingly what Bartram found in 1778 for the most part still exists in the delta today. Fed by dozens of freshwater rivers, creeks, and streams from what is called the Mobile Drainage Basin (the largest such basin in the world, with runoff from four states), and mixed with tidal flows of salty gulf water, the ecosystem of the delta is truly astounding, with multitudes of rare and exotic plant life and wildlife to be found.

Trees to be found within the delta include bald cypress, tupelo, sweet gum, swamp privets, and American elm, to name only a few. Of course Spanish moss hangs thick among the branches of most of the trees in the delta, and trumpet creeper flowers along branches. Rare plants that call the delta home include the greenfly orchid and the buckthorn, which blooms in the fall with a beautiful aromatic smell.

As for wildlife, the delta plays host to more than 300 species of birds, 70 percent of all of Alabama's reptiles, and 40 species of mammals. In the bird department the delta is the home of many formerly endangered species, including brown pelicans, osprey, and bald eagles.

In the reptile category, eighteen different species of turtles can be found here, ranging from common box turtles to gopher tortoise. There are also forty types of snakes, and the American alligator is prevalent throughout the bayous and feeders of the delta.

As you float through the delta, you may come across Florida black bear. The delta is the last refuge in the state for the bear, and which is currently being protected through the efforts of the Alabama Black Bear Alliance. There are also beaver, marsh rabbits, and so many other mammals that we couldn't possibly name them all here.

Of course, the Mobile-Tensaw River Delta provides plenty of outdoor activities as well, the chief one being fishing. National tournaments are becoming big business along the river. Currently the Mobile-Tensaw Canoe Trail is under construction (find out more by contacting the Mobile Bay Canoe and Kayak Club online at baykayaker.blogspot.com).

For canoe and kayakers looking for adventure and a true wilderness experience, there is none better than the Mobile-Tensaw River Delta, the last great untouched wilderness of the south.

So Who *Really* Owns the Rivers?

The days are long gone when a person can get out on a river in their canoe on a Friday afternoon and paddle its distance over the course of a weekend, picking and choosing camping spots along the way. As a matter of fact, in this book, with few exceptions, you will notice we don't even mention camping on the river.

Development in Alabama—and in every other state in the country, for that matter—along the waterways has taken away the freedom to paddle and camp. That's understandable. After all, many of the river's banks are private property. But what about the river itself? Just because someone owns land on both sides of a river, does that mean the property owner owns the river?

This very subject was presented to various state supreme courts around the country and even to the U.S. Supreme Court. Each case was to decide who had rights to use a river. In nearly every decision the courts stated that the use of a river is for everyone; that is, a river is held in trust by each state for the public, and if a river is navigable, it can be used by anyone. The only limitation was that the river could be used up to its natural high-water mark.

Right off the bat, property owners interpreted these decisions as meaning that if you can use motorboats on the river, then it is navigable; otherwise, it belongs to the property owners. Wrong again. The courts ruled that even canoes and kayaks could be used in determining if a river is navigable, and if you can maneuver down a river in any fashion, it is a public river.

Then the issue of waterfalls and rapids came up, with property owners saying that they make the river unnavigable. Again, the court ruled against property owners, saying that for the most part, falls and rapids are still runnable by kayaks and canoes. The National Organization for Rivers cites Niagara Falls as an example. Although it is the largest series of falls in the country, and no one in their right mind would paddle over them, it is still a viable river for commercial use, using the tour boat *Maid of the Mist* as an example.

Put-ins and takeouts are another story altogether. Many times these are located adjacent to bridges where private property butts right up against the perfect access point. In this case, the property owner has the right to boot you out if you use it. But talking with the owners and carefully using the property goes a long way to providing access to the waterways. Unfortunately carelessness and some strong-willed property owners can cause problems in this area. Take Hurricane Creek in Tuscaloosa, for example. This wonderful white water trip has been continually shrinking in length of runnable water because of property owners cutting off access. According to the Stroker's Paddling Club, the lower takeout is currently in jeopardy of being lost, and the entire run may no longer be available to float because you just can't get to it.

We have never had an experience with irate landowners for using nearby property as a takeout or for floating past (as a matter of fact, everyone we have met in these journeys was quite happy to help us), but that is not to say that there aren't some who would just as soon take a shot at a passing canoe. While the law is on your side when it comes to paddling any river in the United States, be a neighborly paddler and help change the landowner's perception of canoers and kayakers. Minimize the impact of your visit by carrying out all of your trash and maybe picking up some extra you might find in the area and taking it with you. Be friendly and courteous to everyone, and in the long run, the relationship between paddlers and property owners will be much better.

How to Use This Guide—Or, Using This Guide for Everything but Kindling

What's Covered

First and foremost, we have tried to include something for everyone. Alabama has an unbelievable number of paddling opportunities. We have tried our best to include trips that beginners through expert paddlers would enjoy, as well as the entire family.

Our main goal is to present a look at the wide variety of paddling opportunities available in the state. In the southern regions you will find long, lazy float trips along beautiful blackwater rivers with white sandbars and plenty of swimming holes. In the Gulf Coast region, you can venture out and do some sea kayaking in the gulf or along the shores of Mobile Bay. For the more adventurous, an outing in the 300,000-acre Mobile-Tensaw River Delta would be in order.

Moving inland to the central and northern regions, white water is the fare. Everything from Class I to Class III rapids are covered in this book. Most of the Class I and II trips are easy enough for beginners through intermediate paddlers. Class III trips may be a bit daunting. If you feel the least bit squeamish about trying them, there are usually easy portage areas around the rapid. Of course every river and situation is different, so make sure you read the trip information completely before heading out.

The Trips

We have broken down the trips more or less into the four regions identified by the Alabama Bureau of Travel and Tourism. These include the Gulf Coast, southeast, central, and northern regions. We have covered twenty-nine trips in this book, but don't get the impression that this is all there is to paddling in Alabama. We encourage you to get out and explore the regions. Talk with the locals. You will find most of them more than happy to talk with you about other trips. Use the references in Appendix A and scattered throughout the book to make contacts. And, of course, you can e-mail us!

As we said, we tried to include trips for folks with a wide range of abilities and interests. But besides writing a guide to the flatways of the state, we have also tried to write a travel guide of sorts to the regions so you can discover the magic of Alabama for yourself.

Each trip is divided into five distinct sections. The following is an overview of what you can expect:

River Specs

The River Specs section gives a quick at-a-glance overview of the trip, including the following information:

County: The name of the county(s) the trip flows through.

Start/End: A general description of where the trip begins and ends (details on how to get there can be found in the "Getting There" section).

Length: The total length of the trip in miles.

Approximate float time: The approximate time to paddle the trip. We say "approximate" because everyone's abilities are different, plus there are lots of views, play spots, and swimming holes to explore.

Difficulty rating: We try to give you an idea of the level of difficulty involved in paddling a trip. Our ratings are Easy, Moderate, Difficult, and Extreme. Remember, this is a subjective rating. Consider all aspects of the trip (i.e., miles, class rapids, etc.), as well as this rating to determine your ability to paddle the trip.

Rapids: We use the internationally recognized white water classifications (their definitions follow). Remember, if there is a + or - sign after the rapid, it means that the rapid is either just slightly above or below the class (i.e., II- is a light Class II rapid). Don't forget that the flow also affects the classification of a river.

- **Class I:** Easy, small waves, little, if any, maneuvering. Few obstructions.
- **Class II:** Medium, a few more obstructions and more maneuvering. Faster flow.
- **Class III:** Difficult, numerous waves with large irregular rocks, eddies, and drops. Passage is generally through narrow chutes between rocks and obstacles, requiring maneuvering.
- **Class IV:** Very difficult, has long rapids, powerful waves, irregular and potentially dangerous rocks, boiling eddies. Requires considerable experience.
- **Class V:** Extremely difficult, long and violent rapids are present without interruption. Large drops, violent current, steep grade. Paddlers must have extensive experience and training before attempting.
- **Class VI:** Unrunnable. Need we say more? Portage is *mandatory!*

River type: There are three specific river types covered in this book: white water (which includes rapids and shoals), float (usually long wide rivers perfect for just floating or tubing), and sea kayak.

Current: We give a *general* idea of a river's flow, from none to swift to fast. Don't forget that rain plays an important part in revising the current rating given here.

Minimum level: The minimum level of the river to be floatable. If this category isn't listed, then you can assume the river is runnable all year (see Season under Trip Information). Generally, the rivers in the north and central regions tend to dry up in the summer months. This category—along with the Other Resources section, which tells you where to go online for hourly river flow reports from the USGS—can help you plan your trips and determine if the river is runnable. Even though a river may be low, heavy summer thunderstorms can spike the flow, and you can catch some great summertime paddling. The information given is either feet (stage) or cfs (cubic feet per second).

Environment: An overview of the landscape around the trip, such as the type of trees and plants you will encounter and the geology.

Elevation drop: The total elevation drop from beginning to end of the trip.

Land status: Describes the land around the trip, whether it's private property, national forest, state park, or unincorporated.

Nearest town (or city): This is given to provide you with a reference so that you can easily locate the river on maps and make other arrangements for your visit.

Other users: If other people use the river, we will point it out here. Other uses include motorboats, jet skies, and fishing.

Getting There: Put-in and Takeout Information

This section is a detailed description of how to get to and from the put-ins and takeouts. We describe road directions from the nearest city to the takeout or shuttle point, and from there to the put-in. We also describe the condition of the put-in and takeout so you know what to expect when you get there.

Trip Summary

This section provides you with a *short* description of the trip and what you can expect.

Trip Description

This is the heart of the matter—the complete description of the trip with some interesting history and tidbits thrown in for good measure.

Trip Information

This section gives you pertinent information about a trip so that you can visit the area and experience all that it has to offer. In this section you will find the following information.

Contact(s): Who to contact for information about the trip.

Season: The best times to run the trip.

Fees/Permits: Special permits or fees required.

Local Information: The names of organizations that can help you plan your visit to an area, such as tourist councils and chambers of commerce.

Local Events/Attractions: You don't want to spend all of your time on the water, now do you? Here we spotlight some of the wonderful events and attractions that occur around the area of the trip, plus give you phone numbers and other contact information.

Accommodations: We try to provide you with our picks for local accommodations in case roughing it isn't to your liking.

Restaurants: Here we list some fine establishments to give you a taste—literally—of the local cuisine.

Guided Tours: If there are any tour guides for the trip, we list them here.

Organizations: There are hundreds of outdoor organizations in the state dedicated to preserving the rivers and environment, and we list some of them here.

Other Resources: Any additional resources that can help with the trip, such as where to find the river gauges online, will be included here.

Local Outdoor Retailer(s): If you need equipment, wherever possible, we will list local retailers who can help. This includes companies who provide shuttles and rentals.

Maps: Finally, we detail where you can get brochures on the areas the trips travel through, the relevant USGS topographic maps, and the DeLorme *Gazetteer* coordinates for the trip.

The Maps

Falcon and The Globe Pequot Press pride themselves in having the most accurate and informative maps available in their guides. Based on USGS topographic maps, the master cartographers painstakingly take our sketched and detailed trip maps and convert them into GPS (global positioning system) quality maps. On these maps, we have tried to give as much detail as possible to shoals, outcroppings, bluffs, boulders, obstructions, and so on. The maps are conveniently located in the guide on single pages so that you can make a copy to bring with you instead of the entire book.

We have also included a locator map for all of the trips covered in the book to give you a general idea of where they are in the state.

Preparing for That "Three-Hour Cruise"

More and more people are taking to the waterways whether in a canoe, kayak, or sea kayak. While the basics of canoeing and kayaking can take up volumes, there are some considerations that we would like to focus on to help get you started in the right direction. If you are already a more experienced paddler, maybe we'll touch on some information that can enhance your experience.

Lions and Tigers and Canoes—Which One?

So many types of canoes, so much information—where do you begin? How do you determine what boat is right for you? We could write book upon book about canoes and kayaks and materials but there are folks who've already done this in several excellent references (see Appendix C). Our goal is to show you what would be appropriate when paddling Alabama waters.

There is no perfect canoe that can handle all conditions. We've seen paddlers using aluminum with ease in the flat water and white water that we cover. Aluminum canoes are resilient, but reminders of all the rocks that you ram stay with you.

The most popular types of canoes being used in the state are polyethylene canoes. Developed by the Coleman Company and enhanced by the Old Town Canoe Company, these canoes feature formed plasticlike shells reinforced with ribs, keels, and thwarts. The combination makes the boats highly durable. Stories of these boats wrapping around a rock in white water and simply popping off and back into shape are countless.

For both canoes and kayaks, the shape of the bottom is important. The shape determines how water is displaced when you're paddling, and thus how the boat handles.

There are several different types of bottoms (Figure 1). The first is your basic flat bottom. This design displaces water evenly and is very stable. Rounded bottoms have less material actually below the surface. Therefore, they are faster than those with bottoms deep in the water because there is less drag. Then there is the V bottom. The V acts like a keel,

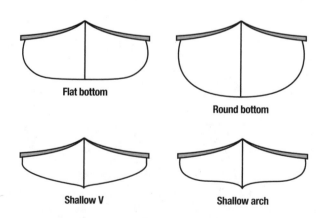

Figure 1. Canoe bottoms

and the boat tends to go straight through the water. Another advantage is that when you lean to one side, the side and the point of the V form an almost flat bottom, so leaning into turns is more stable.

All of this also applies to kayaks, whether a white water kayak or sea kayak. You must remember, however, that in a kayak you are able to roll over if you flip upside down—thus the bottom becomes the top and the top becomes the bottom. You need to consider the roundness of the top as well to make flipping it back over easier.

Keep in mind that the longer the boat, the faster it is. The wider the boat, the more stable it is. Personally, for all of the float trips and white water runs we describe in this book, we found the Coleman 15½-foot Ram X Journey a good all-purpose choice. It's wide and long enough to give plenty of room, and the construction has proven very durable (we acted as crash-test dummies a few times on some large boulders). The main drawback is that it's a bit sluggish in the maneuverability category, but overall it seemed to work well. The Colemans are inexpensive but unfortunately getting hard to find.

Old Town has a nice line of canoes in their sporting category that also are good general-use canoes. Check out their Web site at www.oldtowncanoe.com, and take a look at their line of Osprey and Discovery canoes.

There are plenty of sea-kayaking opportunities along the Alabama Gulf Coast and Mobile Bay. Canoes are nice, but do not venture out into open waters (such as the Gulf of Mexico) in one! They are not made for the type of environment you will encounter, and the consequences are not pleasant. Sea kayaks are the only way to go.

Because we only briefly touch on one or two sea-kayak trips in this book, we invite you to head to Appendix C for some excellent references on the subject of getting started in that sport. If you are a novice and do not want to buy a sea kayak, there are several outfitters we recommend in the book who rent them and can give you all of the necessary information and guidance in using them safely.

Up the Creek with the Right Paddle

Just as important as selecting the proper canoe or kayak is the selection of the proper paddle. There are three things you need to keep in mind when purchasing a paddle: your personal size, your style of paddling, and what you plan to paddle on.

The proper paddle should be efficient—there should be no wasted movement. It should not flutter as you take a stroke and should not make a splashing sound (or kerplunk) when it enters the water.

For canoes consider these four characteristics before buying: length, blade size, grip, and diameter.

The length depends on your torso size and whether you are using a bent-shaft or standard paddle. The depth of your boat also affects the length needed. Here is a general rule for measuring: For a bent-shaft paddle, which is shorter than a standard paddle, sit in a kitchen chair or any chair with a hard back, sit up straight, and measure from the seat to eye level. That is the shaft length you need for this type of paddle. Add an additional 5 to 6 inches for a standard straight paddle.

Equally as important as length is the size of the blade. The smaller the blade, the more strokes it takes to pull you through the water. Larger blades, however, are harder to paddle quickly. Most solo paddlers carry both a small-blade bent-shaft paddle for quickness and a large-blade straight paddle for those long stretches of flat water.

One overlooked area is the grips. There's nothing worse than getting blisters while on a long paddle. Some paddlers describe the grip as the steering wheel of the canoe. Get a grip that is comfortable for you. As a rule of thumb, most white water paddlers use T-grips for a more firm grasp on the paddle.

Finally, look at the diameter of the shaft. This is important. Grip it with your hands to find a size that is right for you. You don't want a shaft that's too wide to grasp. It will be cumbersome and very tiring to use.

When it comes to kayak paddles, there are two main types: touring and white water. Both are sized in generally the same manner.

Remember that the blade size and shaft diameter work the same as for canoe paddles. For length, use your height to determine the appropriate length, not precise measurements. The rule of thumb is to use a small paddle if you are shorter than 5 feet, 5 inches; a medium paddle if you are between 5 feet, 5 inches and 6 feet tall; and a large paddle if you are taller than 6 feet. Also factor in the size of the beam of your kayak: 22 inches calls for a short paddle, 24 inches for a medium, and wider for a large.

Feathering is how the blades of the paddle are angled in relation to each other. Unfeathered blades are not angled at all, which is rough on your wrists. Standard feathering is between eighty and eighty-five degrees. The upshot is that feathering doesn't require turning the blade of the paddle as you switch strokes from one side to another.

Accessorize: Accessories to Die For

Visit any outdoor outfitter and you'll find a plethora of accessories to use on the water. Some of these items are essential for safety (more on those in the Safety section), and others are for comfort or simply to enhance a paddler's experience on the water. Depending on the length of the planned trip, you'll want to make sure you come equipped with the correct accessories.

Long trips call for comfort items. First and foremost, and as described in the previous section, select a suitable paddle. The paddle can make all the difference in the world.

Kneeling is actually the safest and most stable method for positioning your body in a canoe, but long stints on your knees can take a toll (as you may have noticed the last time you spent time crawling through those big plastic tubes that kids love). Inexpensive knee pads can help. Most are made of closed-cell foam that will not absorb water. You may also choose a nonskid flat pad about one-half-inch thick that may be placed on the boat's bottom. Some of these even extend far enough back to pad your feet behind you, making it comfortable for bare feet. Occasional kneeling is also a good way to give your body a break from the standard sitting position.

Consider buying a seat with a back support. Many different brands and styles are available. Most of these require no drilling or bolts for fastening; they simply strap and buckle underneath the existing seat, and the angle of the back rest is adjustable. The less expensive types are made of nylon with a metal frame; for some more cash, you can get a wooden-framed model with a webbed cane mesh for comfort and style. Make sure you get a seat that is narrow and low enough so it won't get in the way as you paddle.

As for apparel, you have lots of choices. There are many different types of sandals available, most a rugged version of flip-flops with tough, grippy rubber soles that work well when walking over jagged or slippery rocks. Some fasten with Velcro, whereas others come with a more secure buckle. You may also choose a simple thong design, which simply slips over your feet. There are models that completely cover your feet, thus protecting your toes. These look much like tennis shoes but are meshed so as to prevent water from being trapped inside. Whichever type you choose, find a pair comfortable for you.

Hats range from traditional styles to downright trend-setting ones. The best sun protection comes from the wide-brimmed types with a brim that completely encircles the hat so that the sun's direct rays are blocked from your face and neck on all sides. These are made of straw, duck twill, or other materials and provide great ventilation. There are many styles of specially designed caps and visors or, you might just plop on your favorites Yankees cap. As everyone is aware, protecting your skin from the sun's damaging rays is vital.

You might even consider a bug mesh to fit over your hat. They may look a little silly, but they are quite inexpensive and can be real handy when the mosquitoes and other annoying insects are out in force.

If your hands are prone to blistering, there are gloves available to help. These specially designed water gloves are meant to reduce fatigue by conforming to the paddle and are waterproof while remaining breathable. They are also good for cold-water paddling and are used by kayakers mainly to keep their hands warm.

As mentioned numerous times in other sections of the book, weather should play a significant role in how you plan for your trip. Always check weather conditions before leaving, and be prepared for the unexpected by bringing along some type of rain gear. Air temperature is pretty easy to predict, so just bring along appropriate clothing. Cool weather may call for a drytop, which is a long-sleeved jacket meant to keep your upper body warm and dry. In warm weather, a simple hooded waterproof nylon rain jacket to pull over your head will be sufficient. These are very light and easy to pack in a bag because they can be folded into a very small space. Make one of these a standard take-along item.

Paddlers are a diverse group and have many different interests. Lots of people enjoy fishing from a canoe. Bring along a fishing rod and some tackle if you're inclined. If you're an angler without a rod in a canoe, you'll wish you had one when the fish start jumping.

Nature is another love common to many paddlers, and many are fond of capturing the outdoors on film. Bring along a camera, and you'll likely grab some beautiful images. Birders prefer canoes and kayaks on the water because of their stealthy qualities; often you can approach birds and take photographs at close range. The same goes for other wildlife.

The mention of cameras and other electronics calls for a method to protect them from water damage. A variety of dry bags are available in different sizes and type for this purpose. Definitely invest in a dry bag of some sort to keep your electronics and other expensive items dry. Some use a simple Velcro fastener to keep water out, whereas others use a plastic zip strip, like a sandwich bag. These bags are usually clear and made of thick, tough plastic. Taking one of these along can save you a lot of money in electronics repair or replacement costs.

On the Road Again: Traveling with Your Boat

The key to carrying your canoe or kayak on your car is, first of all, the vehicle itself. Although you can get away with single anchors in the front and rear (which I have on my car), double is better to create an upside down V shape with the tie-down ropes (Figure 2). It is also important to use a center tie-down rope or, better yet, an adjustable tie-down strap.

Canoes should be loaded on a car upside down (Figure 3). This reduces drag from wind, and they will not fill up with water if it rains hard while you're on the road. If you don't have a luggage rack on your car, make sure you use foam pads to protect your roof.

Kayaks can be carried in one of two ways: Place them on their right side in a "cradle" on the roof of your car, or stack them by tying them to an upright post and resting them

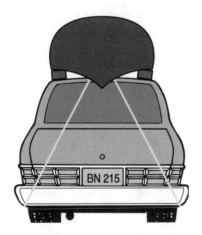

Figure 2. Car tie-down: the inverted "V."

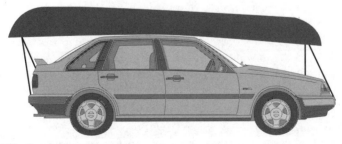

Figure 3. Profile of car tie-down.

on their sides. The latter method has a nasty habit of catching crosswinds and shifting the load. If you're using the stacking method, remember not to overload your car. Refer to your owner's guide for weight restrictions when loading items on the roof.

As for the ropes themselves, make sure they are at least ¼-inch nylon or Dacron line. You may also want to use pads under the edges of the boat and where lines touch the boat to protect not only the lines from excessive rubbing but your car as well. Most canoe and kayak retailers sell inexpensive tie-down kits with everything—including these foam pads —that you'll need to get the job done.

Once the boat is on your car, make sure it's tight. A rule of thumb is to grab either the bow or the stern of the boat and try to shift it side to side. The car, not the boat, should rock.

Once on the road, after the first 10 to 15 minutes, stop and check the ropes, make sure nothing has shifted, and then be on your way. We recommend on long trips to stop every once and awhile and check it again.

The Art of Shuttling

Canoeing and kayaking are great sports but unfortunately one of the most inconvenient when it comes to getting from the takeout back to the put-in. What's a body to do?

The easiest answer is to become a member of a paddling club and network with other clubs. Each week these clubs plan outings of all types and work together to help shuttle back and forth from end to end.

Of course on various rivers there are outfitters who provide shuttle service for a nominal fee, normally between $5.00 and $10.00. They will either carry your boat to the put-in and you leave your car at the takeout or vice versa. Wherever available we indicate these outfitters in the trips.

We have heard of some boaters who lock a bicycle at the takeout, or even take a small bike with them in the boat, to get back to the put-in. This isn't a bad idea, but remember that a long bike trip might be the last thing on your mind after an exhausting day on the river.

The alternative to all of this is to take two vehicles, parking one at the takeout and the other at the put-in.

Storing Your Boat

It's always best to keep your canoe or kayak off the ground and out of the sun when storing it. Excessive sunlight fades and weakens the material. Damp ground can cause all sorts of nasty problems with mildew and rotting.

The best bet is to tie your boat to the rafters in your garage or shed. Many people use winches or pulley systems to hoist the boat up. Some are lucky enough to have enough clearance in their garage door that they can hoist the canoe over the area where the car parks. When they are ready to hit the water, they just lower it onto the car, tie it down, and off they go.

If you are like us and the garage doesn't have any space whatsoever, sawhorses do the trick. Two of them keep the boat high and dry. If you have to store boats outside, invest in an inexpensive tarp and tie-downs to cover it and protect it from the elements.

Safety

Attend any paddlers' group meeting, and you'll quickly see that safety is essential on any paddling trip. No matter how slow or shallow a river, there are always potential hazards. Paddling is a water sport, and water in itself poses an inherent danger to humans. Entire books and courses are available on safety and first aid. A complete discussion is beyond the scope of this book, but here are a few quick tips.

First off, take a course. Classes are offered at various skill levels. Experts teach basic safety skills: how to handle a boat properly, select the right gear, and recognize common river dangers. Join a local canoe club. Knowledgeable groups are aware of local dangers and can show you how to minimize risk. Members share stories and safety information.

Familiarize yourself with the surroundings that you'll be covering. Maps are often available at county and state parks. Mapping out an intended route will give you a general idea of how long you'll be on the water.

Always check the river conditions ahead of time. A very low water level means that you'll have to drag your boat, slowing your progress. Make sure that you leave early in the morning, allowing plenty of daylight at trip's end. Being on a river as the sun is setting and the light is fading is an uncomfortable feeling if you are unprepared for night paddling. It's a good idea to bring along a flashlight in case you get caught on the river after dark.

Leave an itinerary with somebody, with a planned route and arrival time. If it comes down to it, authorities will know where to look. You should also place a note behind the windshield of your vehicle with your party's names outlining your route and scheduled arrival time. If you have a cell phone, take it along. Just make sure you keep it dry, as cell phones are highly sensitive to water. Write down and bring along the phone number of local authorities, just in case.

There is safety in numbers. It is recommended that you never paddle alone. Even calm waters can conceal rocky crevices and other lurking dangers. A partner can help you to escape should you become stuck in a fallen tree or between rocks.

The single most important safety item is a PFD (personal flotation device). Many places (and many states, such as Florida) require that every person traveling the waterway wear a PFD. Even the strongest swimmers will tire in deep water with strong current. A blow to the head on a rock may render a person unconscious and unable to swim on his own. Wearing a PFD increases one's chance of survival should this occur.

In white water, wear a helmet. Protecting your coconut is essential when floating down rocky water. Obviously being unconscious in the water is not a state in which you'd want to place yourself.

Hypothermia is a condition most often linked with cold climates, but it does get cold in Alabama. Combine cold weather with cold water, and the risk of hypothermia increases greatly. If you are wet, cold, and shivering, your body may be starting to go into a hypothermic state. If this happens, drink sweet warm liquids (not alcohol), remove wet clothes, and dry the body. Get into warm, dry clothes as soon as possible.

Carry a first-aid kit, and keep it dry in a dry bag. Make sure the bag is securely tied so that it is not lost should the boat capsize.

Carry a whistle or other attention-getting device. An inexpensive (about $5.00) and waterproof whistle/compass combination can be bought and attached to your PFD.

Know your skill level. It's tempting to travel rapid waters beyond your ability, and it's also dangerous. Never test your limits in unfamiliar waters.

Camping

There are currently twenty-four state parks scattered around Alabama, many of which are located within a few minutes of the rivers covered in this book. Thousands of modern and primitive campsites are available within these parks. From the mountainous areas of Cheaha and DeSoto State Parks to the beaches of Gulf State Park, there is a variety of fun and relaxing activities to enjoy. Most facilities include tables, grills, and picnic shelters complete with bathhouses, laundries, and dump stations. Many have refreshment stands, bait and tackle shops, boat rentals, and fishing piers.

Alabama's state park vacation cottages are furnished and most equipped with kitchen facilities, cooking utensils, tableware, linens, and outdoor grills. All have heat and air conditioning. Cottages or cabins are a great way to camp if that's your idea of roughing it. Or just pitch a tent at either a primitive or nonprimitive campsite. On a primitive site, it's just you and the surroundings. Primitive sites usually provide either a grill or a fire pit with a cooking grate. The nonprimitive sites provide electricity and water for a little bit more money. If you intend to cook, either bring along a large container of water for cleanup or select a site that has running water.

Don't forget the hundreds of other parks of Alabama. Many parks are located on the very river you'll be paddling, making it extremely simple to do an overnighter. Some parks are located right at the put-in, and others are at the takeout.

A few rivers—such as the Styx, Escatawpa, and Perdido—allow camping on sandbars along the way, but most do not allow camping on the banks. If you intend to pitch a tent on the banks, make sure you first determine that camping is allowed.

Some of the best canoe camping can be found in the Sipsey Wilderness of the Bankhead National Forest. Here rivers like the Borden and Sipsey travel through spectacular canyons. Being in a national forest, camping is permitted anywhere along the river's route.

And always leave no trace.

For more information about camping availability and prices, see the Accommodations section located in each chapter.

Family Canoeing: "Don't Rock the Boat, Baby"

When it comes to paddling with the family—and we're talking about with kids up to their early teens—it can be a very enjoyable experience, but it requires plenty of preplanning or the trip can be a disaster for everyone.

There are five main areas that need to be considered when paddling with small children: keeping them safe, keeping them interested, keeping them fed, keeping them comfortable (weatherwise and dry), and making sure that you don't overdo the trip.

Safety is the main concern. PFDs are a must and must be worn at all times, even in shallow water. Light white water trips, like some of the Class I rapids we describe, might be suitable for older children, but don't push the younger ones. It might be fun for you, but very intimidating for them—and dangerous!

Many people love to camp out and cook on an open fire. When camping with children, it's best to cook on a camp stove. It's faster to get food to them when they're starving after a long day on the river, and it's much easier to keep them away from than a campfire (save that for the marshmallows).

Kids have an attention span of about two seconds. It's exciting to get onto a river, but after the first mile of sandbars and turtles, it's pretty routine. Don't get so self-involved with the trip that you ignore the kids. Show them and tell them about the reptiles, the flowers, and the animals you see or hope to see. Let them help with some of the chores, even with a little paddling. You will be surprised what children are willing to do if you treat them like they are part of the trip and that they aren't just along for the ride.

Camping with children is the same way. The campsite is an exciting place to explore, and there's nothing better than telling stories or playing some card games or small pocket board games around the campfire or in the tent before turning in.

So, what do kids do when you've lost their attention and they're constantly asking "What time is it?" or "Are we there yet?" They eat! Make sure to tote along plenty of snacks. Dehydrated fruits are great sweet snacks for the kids (don't tell them it's good for them). Cheese is a favorite and requires only minimal refrigeration—plus it comes in individually wrapped packages now, which makes it even easier.

Keep the main meals fun, too, and again, plan in advance. Don't make some exotic concoction that they won't try. They've had a long hard day on the river and need the nourishment as well as a little taste. Pasta is always a favorite.

And don't forget drinks! Plenty of water is important but juice boxes add a little extra treat to their day.

We grown-ups don't like to be uncomfortable on a paddle, and neither do the kids. Make sure that you have plenty of mosquito repellant and sunscreen handy. Remember to dress the kids appropriately. Two or three changes of clothes for the weekend is not pushing it. Always remember to bring hats along for them.

Do not overdo your trip. A 22-mile one-day float trip is exhausting for adults. Imagine what it will do to the children! Keep it simple with low mileage and interesting scenery and wildlife, and everyone will have a spectacular time on the river. Keep it up, and you may never have to turn on the TV again!

Be sure to check the Internet for more information and ideas. There are plenty of great sites that provide ideas for traveling the rivers with your kids.

Gulf Coast Region

The Alabama gulf coast is located in the extreme southwestern portion of the state. Geologically speaking this region is known as the coastal plain—very few hills with most of the major rivers of the state "draining" into the Mobile-Tensaw River Delta, the second largest delta in the country.

The Gulf Coast region is highlighted first by several nice float trips. These are great family outings. They are long, slow-moving waters with plenty of deep pools for swimming and beautiful white sand beaches. Three included in this book are the Escatawpa, Styx, and Perdido Rivers.

The Mobile-Tensaw River Delta ranks first in the nation in terms of number of ecosystems, with countless varieties of rare and exotic animals and plants calling the 300,000 acres home. The delta is not the place for the beginner paddler, and if you do plan a trip on your own without a guide, knowledge of orienteering (using maps and compasses) is essential!

We cover two interesting trips in the book. One is Hurricane Landing, a bayou trip where beaver and other animals frolic around your boat. The other more ambitious trip is the Rice Creek/Mound Island run. This trip takes you directly into the heart of the delta, where alligators float along the banks with your boat. This is an interesting trip historically in that it takes you to Mound Island, where eighteen Native American mounds dating back more than 1,500 years can be explored.

In the extreme southern portion of the region, you're invited to try your hand at sea kayaking along Dauphin Island and Sand Island and historic Fort Morgan, where the Battle of Mobile Bay was fought during the Civil War. More wildlife can be experienced on the Navy Cove trip, which takes you around Bon Secour National Wildlife Refuge and into the waters of Mobile Bay.

The weather in this region is considered subtropical. During summer, temperatures in the 90s and humidity that often hits 100 percent makes outdoor activity uncomfortable needless to say, but many times impossible. Keep this in mind, and bring plenty of liquids to keep hydrated.

Another weather factor is rain. The warm air and the water from the Gulf of Mexico mean that sudden and very heavy rainfall can be expected without warning. These storms do not last long, but the amount of rain they can produce is considerable. Dangerous lightening and strong winds also accompany these storms. For paddling in the gulf, Mobile Bay, or the Mobile/Tensaw River Delta, this combination can be deadly. Keep an eye on the weather, and seek safe shelter if the weather begins to look threatening.

Of course there is one more weather element to watch for in this region: hurricanes. Although the actual amount of real estate directly on the gulf is small, several strong and deadly hurricanes have hit Mobile and Baldwin Counties in the past. Keeping a watchful eye on the weather forecast will keep you safe. Hurricane season generally runs between May and November.

Escatawpa River

River Specs

County: Mobile.

Start: Ferry Road.

End: Escatawpa Hollow Campground.

Length: 12.1 miles.

Approximate float time: 5 hours.

Difficulty rating: Easy.

Rapids: None.

River type: Float. Mainly narrow river, averaging about 50 feet in width.

Current: Moderate.

Environment: Sandy beaches; a wide variety of flora and fauna.

Elevation drop: 1.7 feet per mile.

Land status: Unincorporated.

Nearest town (or city): Wilmer.

Other users: A few fishermen in small boats toward the end of the trip as the river deepens.

Getting There: Put-in and Takeout Information

To shuttle point/takeout: From Mobile take I–65 north to exit 5B. Head west on U.S. Highway 98 (Moffett Road). Stay in the center lane as you come off the interstate. Travel west exactly 22 miles. The campground and canoe rentals are to the left (there is a big obvious sign there). You are less than a mile from Mississippi. If you pass the state line, you've gone too far.

The takeout is located at the Escatawpa Hollow Campground about 300 yards past the US 98 bridge. This is the only bridge you cross under on this trip. There is a sandbar to the left as you round a bend to take out. If you pass under a railroad trestle, you've overshot the takeout. Head into the woods from the sandbar, and follow the dirt road back to your vehicle.

To put-in from takeout: There is little or no parking along the dirt road where the put-in is located. It is best to use Escatawpa Hollow Campground (see takeout section) for a shuttle. The road where the put-in is located has rather deep sand shoulders and is very narrow. Here are the directions anyway, just in case you want to give it a go: Pass the campground (mentioned in the takeout section) on US 98 heading west, and cross into Mississippi. You will pass a weigh station on the right. Make a right onto Beaver Creek Road. Continue down the narrow road, and reach a stop sign at a T intersection. Make a right turn here onto Havens Dairy Road. Continue until you come to a Y. Take the left fork. The road

Escatawpa River

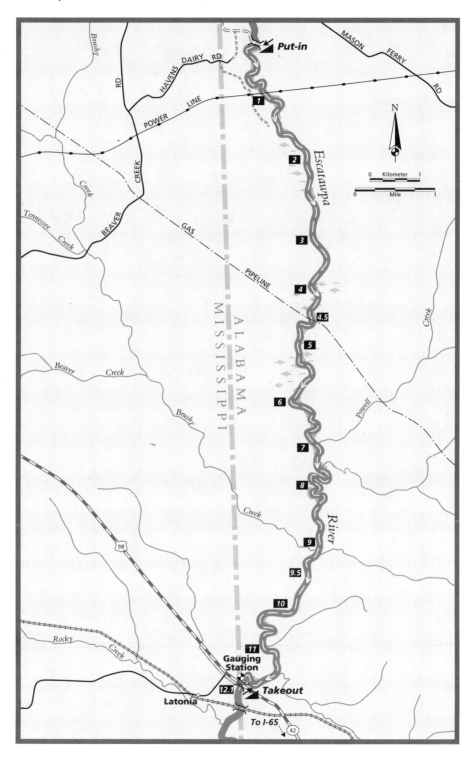

narrows, crosses over a single lane bridge, and turns into dirt. Come to another T intersection, and make a right turn at Live Oak onto Ferry Road. Cross over a one-lane bridge. The put-in is just after the bridge on the right side.

The put-in is a moderate, sandy hillside of about 50 feet to the riverbank—an easy walk.

Trip Summary

The Escatawpa is a swift-moving blackwater river with plenty of deep pools to swim in and beautiful white sandbars. The sandbars allow for overnight camping anywhere along the entire route. The river can be paddled or can be floated with an inner tube.

Trip Description

Generically they're known as blackwater rivers. These are rivers that flow fairly deep and have a dark red or black tint to them, which comes from tannic acid from the oak trees that line the riverbanks. The dark colors are accentuated by beautiful fine-grain white-sand beaches, which can be found around almost every bend. These rivers are mostly found in the lower third of the state, primarily in the Gulf Coast and southeast regions.

The Escatawpa is one such blackwater river, but what makes the river special is its location and remoteness. Other rivers of this type—such as the Styx and Perdido—pack the people in during the summer mainly because of their easy access from Escambia County, Florida, and Baldwin County, Alabama. The Escatawpa is located in a very remote section of western Mobile County. As a matter of fact, you will pass only two houses on this trip, and they are at the very beginning. Because of this isolation, if for some reason you need help, you will need to flag down passing boaters or float to the end.

Because of this remoteness and unspoiled scenery, Congress has discussed the possibility of having the river named a National Wild and Scenic River. However, there has been little success, and currently all discussions on the subject are off.

While floating the river, you will see a wide range of animals, including white-tailed deer, hawks, and wild turkey. The last quarter of the trip sees the river widen and slow down. Here, with trees lining the low, muddy banks straight to the river's edge, you will most likely see snakes—including king, marsh, and cottonmouth—sunning themselves on downed trees in the river. You will also encounter a few turtles, such as box and mud turtles. Some fish can be found in the river, primarily small minnows, but bass and bream are also there. Trees include pine, magnolia, and dogwood.

The great thing about blackwater rivers is that they make great "play" rivers. The sandbars—deemed the finest in the country—allow you plenty of places to pull ashore, eat lunch, and swim in the waters, which can be 5 plus feet deep in places. The sandbars and the remoteness also allow you to make it an overnight trip, with excellent campsites available on any sandbar. If you would like a longer overnight, you can make the river a 23-mile trip by heading farther north to County Road 96 and putting in next to the bridge.

The Escatawpa is not fed by any of the surrounding rivers, which means that it is not prone to flooding like many of the other rivers in this region. But don't get us wrong. As you paddle look for the high-water line etched into the banks from past hurricanes, such as George. The water rose about 5 feet above normal from the runoff.

For approximately 12 miles of this trip, the banks are lined with sandbars and the river has a fairly deep channel. However, the channel has a tendency to disappear at the bends in the river where the sandbars are located, making it easy to run aground on a shoal. The last 3 miles of the river become wide—approximately 100 feet. Here it runs straight and deep, with steep mud and sand embankments. There are plenty of small feeder creeks trickling in here. The river's speed also slows down, making it a prime area for mosquitoes, so bring the insect repellent.

Trip Information

Contact

Escatawpa Hollow Campground and Canoe Rental
15551 Moffett Road
Wilmer, AL 36587
(334) 649–4233
Camping and RV sites are available. Also available are air-conditioned cabins, each with a kitchen, microwave, TV, and telephone.

Season

Year-round. The water may get shallow at certain times of the year, depending on rainfall, but it is still floatable.

Fees/Permits

No permit is required for paddling the river. Escatawpa Hollow Campground rents canoes. Canoe rentals for the 7- and 15-mile trips are $30, and for the 23-mile overnight trip are $50. If you own a canoe, the campground will provide a shuttle: $18 for overnight trip ($15.00 for shuttle, $3.00 for parking).

Local Information

Mobile Convention and Visitors Commission
P.O. Box 204
Mobile, AL 36601
(800) 5–MOBILE (566–2543)
www.mobile.org

Lucedale Chamber of Commerce
P.O. Box 441
Lucedale, MS 39452
(601) 947–2755

Local Events/Attractions

Mardi Gras (two weeks before Ash Wednesday)
Mobile, Spanish Fort, and Fairhope
Mobile Convention and Visitors Bureau
P.O. Box 204
Mobile, AL 36601
(800) 5–MOBILE (566–2543)
www.mobile.org
The Mobile area is known as the "Mother of Mystics," holding the first recorded Carnival celebration in the country in 1830. Each year the revelry grows in size and popularity. Unlike the New Orleans celebration, the south Alabama variety is more family oriented.

Accommodations

Best Western Rocky Creek Inn
120 Woods Ridge Road
Lucedale, MS 39452
(601) 947–6900

Restaurants

The Country Café
13433 Moffett Road
Wilmer, AL 36587
(334) 645–5691

Rocky Creek Catfish
4196 Highway 63 N
Lucedale, MS 39452
(601) 947–6888

Organizations

Sierra Club—Mobile Chapter
P.O. Box 852102
Mobile, AL 36685
(334) 655–3090
alabama.sierraclub.org/mobile.html

Other Resources

Alabama Wildlife Federation
45 Commerce Street
Montgomery, AL 36104
800–822–WILD (9453)
www.alawild.org
E-mail: awf@mindspring.com

Exposed tree roots on the banks of the Escatawpa.

Local Outdoor Retailer

Fairhope Boat Company
702 Section Street
Fairhope, AL 36532
(334) 928–3417
Fairhope Boats is an excellent shop for canoe and kayak supplies, rentals, and general information.

Maps

USGS maps: Semmes, AL/Earlville, AL.
DeLorme: *Alabama Atlas & Gazetteer:* #62, B-5, C-5.

Hurricane Creek

River Specs

County: Baldwin.
Start: Hurricane Landing.
End: Hurricane Landing.
Length: 9.2 miles.
Approximate float time: Six hours.
Difficulty rating: Easy.
Rapids: None.
River type: Wide river. Plenty of feeders, side tributaries, and bayous to explore.
Current: Swift.
Environment: Marshy islands; a wide variety of endangered birds, black bear, and alligators.
Elevation drop: 2 feet.
Land status: National wildlife management area.
Nearest town (or city): Bay Minette.
Other users: Powerboats, anglers, hunters.

Getting There: Put-in and Takeout Information

To put-in/takeout: *Note:* For this trip the put-in and takeout are the same. From Spanish Fort take U.S. Highway 90 East 0.6 mile to U.S. Highway 225. Turn left at the light, and head north on US 225 for 12.5 miles. At the four-way stop make a left onto County Road 86 west. Travel 0.8 miles, and come to a Y in the road. Take the right fork, and continue 2 miles to the landing.

The put-in/takeout is a cement boat ramp. There is a clay landing next to the ramp that can be used.

Trip Summary

This is a nice adventure trip through the marsh islands of the delta. Customize your route through the many inlets and islands. A wide variety of wildlife will be seen on this easy float through the second largest delta in the country.

Trip Description

This course offers a placid, laid-back paddle. You can explore different branches of the area's smaller rivers and bayous, with the wide Tensaw River never far away. The Mobile-Tensaw River Delta comprises more than 300,000 acres of wetlands. We'll describe the route we took, but much of the fun in paddling this area is discovering and navigating the many short tributaries along the way. Remember: The delta is not for those who are not familiar with orienteering (using map and compass). There are many bayous that could get you off track fairly easily. If you are not experienced, use a guide (see Guided Tours).

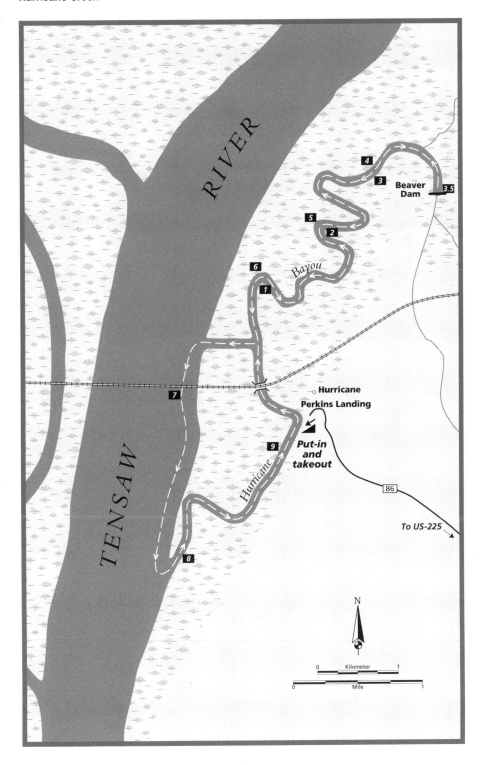

The delta itself is one of the largest wetland ecosystems in the country. Currently the federal government, in conjunction with the Alabama Wildlife Federation, is purchasing more and more acreage to ensure its pristine state for generations to come.

The course brings you back to nature. You'll see osprey, ducks, and beavers. Also, in the warm weather (about 10 months out of the year), you'll spot alligators in the water or along the banks. Don't worry too much about these guys; they're normally shy creatures unless you try to feed or taunt them. The delta is also home to the state's largest concentration of black bear. The water runs through designated hunting spots, and you'll most likely pass a few fishermen with their lines out. In the delta freshwater fish—such as bass, bream, crappie, and catfish—draw anglers from all over the world. Farther south, marine fish—such as spotted sea trout, red drum, and flounder—make their way into the lower bay where the Gulf of Mexico and the Mobile and Tensaw Rivers merge.

The swampy land is rife with diverse vegetation. You'll see lots of black walnut trees, palmettos, sawgrass, and red berry bushes, and Spanish moss and mistletoe in the trees. Interestingly because of the swamplands, there are no southern pines, which are normally commonplace in southwest Alabama.

You'll probably eat lunch in your boat, because you won't find many good picnic spots in the bayous. If you really want to stop and disembark for lunch, wait until you get onto the Tensaw River; you can pull your boat up along its sandy banks.

Hurricane Landing provides a boat ramp and a couple of different places where a canoe or kayak may easily be launched. Starting north from the launch, the river will take you within minutes underneath a railroad bridge. After the bridge you move into bayou country, where Spanish moss hangs from trees. Soon afterward you'll come to a Y in the river. A left at the Y points you west with a straight shot of about 200 yards to the Tensaw River. We'll come back to this, but for now, continue straight.

Continuing north, paddle through a pretty, winding waterway that ranges anywhere from 5 feet to 40 feet at its widest. Meandering farther up the bayou river, about 3.5 miles (or between one and two hours), the route comes to a halt where some busy beavers decided they wanted to build a dam. It is here that we turned around and retraced our route until we came back to the Y. Then, we took the short 200-yard jog west to the Tensaw River.

The Tensaw River at this point is about a quarter-mile wide and fairly swift. Depending on the wind speed and direction, the water here may get a little bit choppy. Heading south with the current and staying close to the bank, you will quickly travel about a half mile before you reach an inlet that leads in a northeasterly direction back to the landing. Here the current ceases. From this point you're just about a half an hour back to the landing. You'll pass houses on a peninsula between the canal that you're in and the Tensaw. Farther up the canal as you approach the landing, the banks of the canal get narrower.

When you reach the landing, your adventure is complete. Please remember that the bayou trip described here is only one of many such trips through the Mobile-Tensaw River Delta. The unique aspect of the delta is that it's wide open for exploration. The route is totally up to you—but again, if you do not have orienteering experience, find a guide!

Remember, too, that the current in the main river is swift with tides, so you may have to plan a shuttle to one of the landings below Hurricane Landing.

Trip Information

Contact

Perkin's Hurricane Landing
8060 Hurricane Road
Bay Minette, AL 36507
(251) 937–9133
You can contact the landing for river height and conditions.

Season

Year-round. A good flow of water no matter what the season as it heads to the gulf. Hunting is allowed within the wildlife management area to the west. It is best to contact the Alabama Wildlife Federation for dates.

Fees/Permits

No permit required for paddling the river. It is a $3.00 fee to launch from Hurricane Landing.

Local Information

North Baldwin Chamber of Commerce
301 McMeans Avenue
Bay Minette, AL 36507
(251) 937–5665
www.northbaldwinchamber.com

Eastern Shore Chamber of Commerce
327 Fairhope Avenue
Fairhope, AL 36532
(251) 621–8222
www.siteone.com/towns/chamber

Local Events/Attractions

Stapleton Bluegrass Festival (first weekend of May)
P.O. Box 310
Bay Minette, AL 36507
(251) 937–5665
www.onwire.net/users/swerdna/stapleton2.html
This is a good old-fashioned bluegrass festival with plenty of food, arts and crafts, and, of course, local bluegrass music.

Blakeley Historic State Park
33707 Highway 225
Spanish Fort, AL 36577
(251) 580–0005
www.siteone.com/tourist/blakeley
Blakeley is the site of the last major battle of the Civil War. Located directly on the Tensaw
River at about the halfway point between Hurricane Landing and Mizell's Fish Camp.

Accommodations
Star Motel
302 East 2nd Street
Bay Minette, AL 36507
(251) 937–1206

Restaurants
Street's Seafood Restaurant
251 South Highway 31
Bay Minette, AL 36507
(251) 937–2664

Blue Gill Restaurant
3775 Battleship Parkway
Spanish Fort, AL 36527
(251) 625–1998

Guided Tours
Tensaw EcoTours
3807 Battleship Parkway
Spanish Fort, AL 36527
(251) 625–0339
Tour guide: Jeff Evans
Several tours of the delta are available, including the three- to four-hour Bay Minette Basin
and Big Bateau Alligator tours, where you *will* see the 'gators from your canoe, and the all-
day Blakeley Battlefield and Mound Island Marsh tours, which take you to the Blakeley
Civil War battlefield and Indian burial mounds.

Organizations
Sierra Club–Coastal Alabama Chapter
P.O. Box 852102
Mobile, AL 36685
(251) 540–2121
alabama.sierraclub.org/coastal.html

Beavers' handiwork just east of the Tensaw River.

Other Resources

Alabama Black Bear Alliance
P.O. Box 26
Leroy, AL 36548
www.alawild.org/abba.html

Local Outdoor Retailer

Fairhope Boat Company
702 Section Street North
Fairhope, AL 36532
(251) 928–3417
Fairhope Boats is an excellent shop for canoe and kayak supplies, rentals, and general information.

Maps

USGS maps: Hurricane, AL.
DeLorme: *Alabama Atlas & Gazetteer:* #62, A-5, B-5.

Magnolia River

River Specs

County: Baldwin.

Start: County Road 49.

End: U.S. Highway 98 or loop back to CR 49.

Length: 5.9 miles point to point or 11.8 miles out and back.

Approximate float time: Three-and-one-half-hours point to point.

Difficulty rating: Easy.

Rapids: None.

River type: River float, with some open-bay paddling, depending on course.

Current: Slow on river; tidal current in bay.

Environment: Wide, flat river flowing into open bay with marsh grass bayous; various wildflowers and wildlife.

Elevation drop: None.

Land status: Private along river, Weeks Bay National Estuary along Weeks Bay.

Nearest town (or city): Foley.

Other users: Motorboats, anglers.

Getting There: Put-in and Takeout Information

To shuttle point/takeout: From the intersection of Alabama 59 and U.S. Highway 98 in Foley, take US 98 west 8.8 miles. Just before the bridge over Fish River, turn right onto Grounds Lane. Follow Grounds Lane west 0.1 mile to the parking area.

This is a nice gravel parking lot directly on the riverbank with room for fifteen to twenty cars. The put-in is 10 feet from the parking lot at the base of a T fishing pier. The bank is a low, sloping dirt bank that is easy to walk.

To put-in from takeout: Travel back up Grounds Lane to US 98. Turn left and head east 3.5 miles. Turn right onto County Road 49. Travel CR 49 south 0.4 mile. Just before crossing the bridge, a short grass strip leads off the road to the right. This is a very narrow parking area with room for about three cars.

The put-in is directly in front of the parking area under the bridge. There is a grassy path that leads 15 to 20 feet down the side of the bridge over some rocks used for the bridge foundation. The path leads directly under the bridge to a very low dirt bank.

Trip Summary

The distinguishing features on this lazy float trip down the deep, wide Magnolia are not necessarily flora and fauna; however, the area does have more than its fair share. The first part of this trip is marked by something not usually encountered on other trips in this book: houses, beautiful and ornate, lining the banks; houses that reflect old southern style and charm. The river and its surrounding beauty still shine through.

Magnolia River

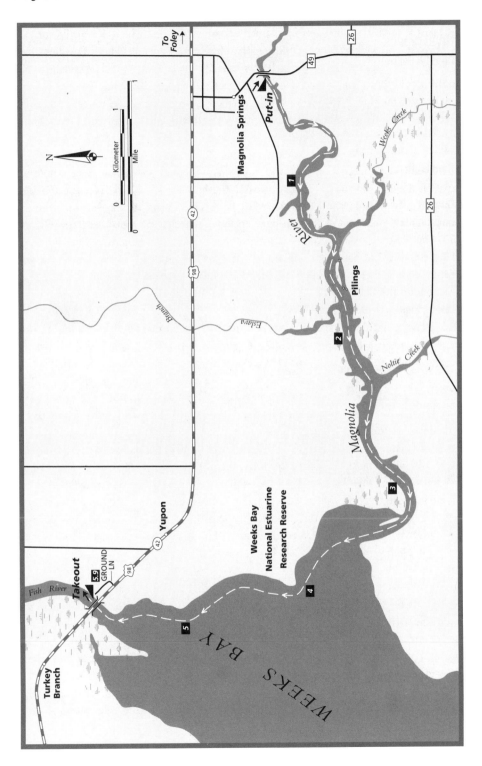

Trip Description

Alabama is a large state with diverse forms of plants and wildlife species. The Magnolia River is located in south Baldwin County, east of Weeks Bay, which is a small estuarine embayment off Mobile Bay containing approximately 3 square miles of open shallow water averaging 4.5 feet in depth. Weeks Bay is fringed with Spartina and Juncus marsh and swamp (with pine, oak, maple, and cypress trees, among others). Weeks Bay receives salt water from the Gulf of Mexico through Mobile Bay and fresh water from the Magnolia and Fish Rivers. It is a critical nursery for fish, crustaceans, and shellfish. Like the Mobile-Tensaw River Delta, the combination of salt water and fresh water makes Weeks Bay a diverse and fragile habitat for plants and wildlife.

At the put-in the river is deep and more than 100 feet wide. The current is nominal the entire length, leaving the option of an out-and-back trip. You'll head west for one-third of a mile, then bend hard toward the south. At this tight bend are some very nice houses and docks on the river. The width narrows to about 40 feet. Soon the course changes again, bending right to place you on a north-northwest bearing. Here the river widens to more than 200 feet, and houses become more sparse on the right and nonexistent on the left. You'll bend slowly left toward the west and likely begin to encounter some powerboat traffic. Stay on the right side of the river. You are just past the 1-mile mark when you travel past a small cove on the right.

Soon the river bends left again to the south, with a marshy area off to the left. You are likely to see egrets and herons around here, perched in trees and wading on the banks. At the bottom of the bend is a Y, where Weeks Creek splits to the left and the Magnolia cuts back to the west. Follow the Magnolia west. More marsh is on the right side, and off to the left is a small, flat, open area where you may stop and take a breather. The next 2 miles are generally a straight shot to the west-southwest, after which you'll enter Weeks Bay if you decide to finish up at the US 98 Fish River bridge.

Just a tenth of a mile after Weeks Creek, there is a small island on the left. There are some old pilings on both sides of the island that used to be two small piers. Many times anglers will tuck their boats in at a great fishing spot on the other side of the island. Just about another tenth of a mile past the island, you'll pass Eslava Branch off to the right, with marshy land and reeds on either side. At this point you are exactly 2 miles from the put-in. This may be a good place to turn around and head back if you don't care to finish up by paddling the open water of Weeks Bay. (It also depends on where you had left your shuttle vehicle!)

If you do choose to paddle from the put-in to the takeout, you are in for some open-water paddling for about 2 miles along the Weeks Bay shoreline on the final stretch of the trip. Anyone who has done open-water paddling knows that conditions may be quite different than a river trip. Wind is a factor when paddling on open water. It can kick up waves, and, depending on the wind's direction versus the intended course of the boat, it may greatly help or hinder forward progress.

The Weeks Bay National Estuarine Research Reserve encompasses 3,028 acres of land and water in and around Weeks Bay, Mobile Bay, and the Fish River. Acquisition of additional tracts is planned for expansion of the reserve. It presently includes an interpretive center housing four offices, a laboratory, a conference room, a small classroom, and a lobby/exhibit area as well as a 2,500-foot handicapped accessible boardwalk with observation deck overlooking the bay and a raised catwalk over a wetlands habitat. The reserve offers presentations to teachers, school groups, and the general public. Many other environmental education programs are also available.

The reserve is a productive nursery for shrimp and other commercially important fish and shellfish, as well as many marine species, such as the spotted sea trout, red drum, croaker, flounder, mullet, and menhaden. It is home to more than 180 species of fish. Fish populations in the area include freshwater and marine species. The reserve is also home to many species of mammals, reptiles, and amphibians.

Paddling the Magnolia River and Weeks Bay is a relaxing, inspiring trip. It's just one more example of Alabama's extensive natural beauty.

Trip Information

Contact
Weeks Bay National Estuarine Research Reserve
Alabama Department of Economic and Community Affairs
11300 U.S. Highway 98
Fairhope, AL 36532
(251) 928–9792

Season
Year-round. Watch for powerboat traffic in the warm months.

Fees/Permits
There is no fee for putting in, paddling, or taking out.

Local Information
South Baldwin Chamber of Commerce
104 North McKenzie Street
Foley, AL 36535
(251) 943–3291
www.southbaldwinchamber.com

Local Events/Attractions
Holmes Medical Museum
111 Laurel Avenue
Foley, AL 36535
(251) 970–1818
Open Tuesday through Saturday, 10:00 A.M.–4:00 P.M. Free admission.

One of the many beautiful sunsets as seen from the middle of the Magnolia River.

This museum is housed in Baldwin County's first hospital (1906). The museum has recreations of an actual operating room, patient rooms, an x-ray machine, and a pharmacy. Medical quackery devices are also featured.

The town of Foley is also home to several antique malls and museums.

Accommodations

Magnolia Springs Bed & Breakfast
14469 Oak Street
P.O. Box 329
Magnolia Springs, AL 36555
(800) 965–7321, (251) 965–7321
www.magnoliasprings.com

Restaurants

Lulu's Sunset Grill
U.S. Highway 98 (under the Fish River bridge on Weeks Bay)
Magnolia Springs, AL 36555
(251) 990–9907
www.lulubuffett.com
Lucy Buffett, or LuLu, opened LuLu's in March 1999 with her brother Jimmy. She lovingly calls her eclectic destination a "high-class dive," inviting you to chill out and sip a "perfect" margarita.

Lambert's Cafe
2981 South McKenzie
Foley, AL 36535
(251) 943–7655
www.throwedrolls.com
You just gotta try this place. Come hungry, and watch out for the "throwed" rolls!

Organizations
Mobile Bay Canoe and Kayak Club
boothegc@bellsouth.com
www.baykayaker.blogspot.com

Other Resources
Weeks Bay Reserve Foundation
P.O. Box 731
Fairhope, AL 36533
(251) 990–5004
www.weeksbay.org
Members provide assistance and support to the Weeks Bay Estuarine Research Reserve's goals and programs.

Mobile Bay Watch
3280 Daphin Street
Building C-124
Mobile, AL 36606
(251) 476–0328
www.mobilebaywatch.org

Local Outdoor Retailer
Camp Coleman
Riviera Centre Outlet Mall
2601 South McKenzie Street, Suite RC-1
Foley, AL 36535
(251) 970–3500

Maps
USGS maps: Magnolia Springs, AL.
DeLorme: *Alabama Atlas & Gazetteer:* #63, H-7, H-6, G-6.

Tidbits

The town of Magnolia Springs and the river are named for the abundance of magnolia trees in the area. Magnolia trees produce a beautiful white bloom in the late spring and early summer. The "Springs" part comes from the many natural springs running along both sides of the river.

Magnolia Springs has the only remaining all-water mail delivery in the United States. Mail is delivered daily by boat.

Estuaries are places where fresh water from rivers mixes with salt water. An estuary can be a bay, lagoon, or slough. These important coastal habitats are used as spawning grounds and nurseries for at least two-thirds of the nation's commercial fish and shellfish. The wetlands associated with estuaries buffer uplands from flooding. Estuaries also provide many recreational opportunities, such as swimming, boating, and bird-watching. The Weeks Bay National Estuarine Research Reserve is one of twenty-five national estuarine research reserves in the United States.

Rice Creek/Mound Island

River Specs
County: Baldwin.
Start: Rice Creek Landing.
End: Rice Creek Landing.
Length: 11.5 miles.
Approximate float time: Seven hours.
Difficulty rating: Easy.
Rapids: None.
River type: Float.
Current: Slow to moderate, depending on rainfall and tidal flows from Mobile Bay.
Environment: Marshy islands; a wide variety of endangered birds, black bear, and alligators.
Elevation drop: 0 feet.
Land status: Mixed. Much of the property has been bought by Forever Wild. The rest of the property is owned by private hunting clubs.
Nearest town (or city): Bay Minette.
Other users: Powerboats, anglers, hunters.

Getting There: Put-in and Takeout Information
To put-in/takeout: From Tensaw EcoTours in Spanish Fort, take U.S. Highway 90 east 1.8 miles until you come to a Y in the highway. Take the left fork (this is now U.S. Highway 31 north). Travel north on US 31 0.7 mile and make a left onto Alabama Highway 225 north. Travel 12.5 miles on AL 225. Come to the intersection of County Road 86 and County Road 138. Continue straight on AL 225 8.7 miles, and cross over Interstate 65. After an additional 3.7 miles, come to the end of AL 225 (a Y). Take the left fork (Stagecoach Café will be on the right). In 0.5 mile turn left onto County Road 21. Follow CR 21 1.2 miles. Make a left onto Rice Creek Road. This is a dirt road that travels through a mobile home park. In 1.4 miles you will arrive at the put-in.

The Rice Creek put-in/takeout is a beautiful bayou setting. Set deep within a cypress swamp, the low, sandy ramp into Rice Creek is very picturesque. There is plenty of parking at the launch.

Trip Summary
This trip is not for the neophyte navigator. The twisting turns and countless offshooting bayous and inlets have caused many boaters in this area to become confused and lost, prompting search-and-rescue missions. If you are not completely confident in your experience and skills, you are better off taking a guide along. Consider hiring Jeff Evans at Tensaw EcoTours, a local guide who knows the region like the back of his hand. See the Guided Tours section for more information.

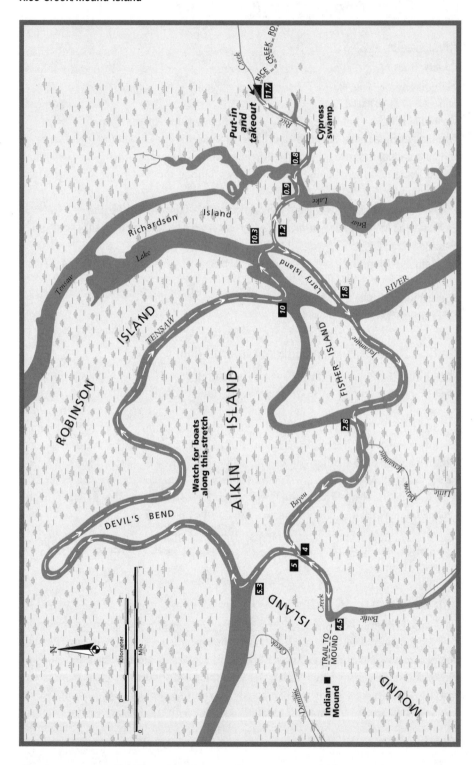

Trip Description

The variety of wildlife and vegetation are two of the features that makes this trip stand out. You'll also have the opportunity to stop at Mound Island, the site of eighteen Native American religious ceremonial mounds, the largest of which rises 45 feet. This area is designated as a National Historic Landmark, and it is a crime to remove archaeological material without permission. The area is patrolled for this reason. Archaeological surveys show that tribes lived in the delta from at least 1500 B.C. The name *Tensaw* originates from *Taensa,* an Indian tribe that once lived on the shores of the Tensaw River.

The Mobile-Tensaw River Delta is host to many special plants. Among some of the rare plants known to occur in this area are the green-fly orchid, southern rein orchid, tiny-leaved buckthorn, sarvis holly, and loblolly bay. During the float you'll see cypress trees, blue-stem (saw) palmetto, and bamboo.

As with any wildlife excursion, you may see an abundance of animals, and you may be lucky to spot a few hawks soaring high above the river. Chances are that you'll come across a fair share of animals here—perhaps an alligator or two sunning on the banks or slowly floating with only a snout and eyes visible above the water. Leave them alone and they'll do the same for you. You are also likely to see wading birds—such as herons, egrets, king-fishers, and ibises—standing in or near the water, or taking off into the air as you approach them. Ducks, bald eagles, and wild turkeys are frequently seen. And, if you look past the banks, you could spot a swamp rabbit (also called a canecutter), cottontail, or marsh rabbit. Otters, raccoons, white-tailed deer, and bobcats are common. Feral pigs run rampant and are a nuisance—even a menace—to some of the endangered plants and wildlife in the delta. Their constant eating habits reduce the number of salamanders, frogs, and snakes, and their rooting damages native plants. Hunting the pigs is encouraged, and there is no bag limit for hunters. Some black bear remain, though sightings are rare.

Of course there are countless insects, but the one that stands out because of its size and abundance is the golden orb, or banana spider. In the summer months you'll encounter these impressive spiders numerous times, waiting for prey in huge, strong, golden webs. You will know it if you get one of these webs stretched across your face. The web is so strong that small birds sometimes become entangled. The spider can bite but is not aggressive, and its bite is generally harmless to humans. The female golden orb is the more striking of the sexes and normally grows to about 3 inches, sometimes larger. The male, in contrast, reaches only one-half of an inch.

When you put in at Rice Creek Landing, you'll be awed by the classic bayou environment. It is a peaceful spot rife with lush vegetation. You'll probably encounter a few anglers in boats casting their lines for bass and bream. A half-mile from putting in, Rice Creek leads you to Briar Lake, a long, narrow lake just a few hundred yards across. Quickly crossing Briar Lake headed west, you'll enter a small stream and soon come to a Y. Go to the left. You're now passing through a narrow stream across Richardson Island for less than a third of a mile. Then you'll hit Tensaw Lake and begin a southwest jog past Larry Island for 0.8 mile, where you'll enter Bayou Jessamine, a lovely narrow river in a bayou setting. You'll be paddling by Fisher Island to your right. After a little more than 1 mile, Bayou Jessamine takes a quick turn west. Soon you'll pass Little Bayou Jessamine on your left, but continue northwest on Bayou Jessamine for 1 mile until you come to a T, which is Bottle Creek. Head to the left (southwest), and in 0.4 mile you'll come to a sharp left bend. It is here that you'll want to go straight at Mound Island and pull up on the bank for a walk around the island and perhaps a bite to eat. It's a 0.25 mile hike to get to Mound A, the largest of the eighteen mounds.

Continuing on the water, go back east, retracing your route on Bottle Creek for 0.4 mile. Pass Bayou Jessamine on your right, where you first entered Bottle Creek. Remain on Bottle Creek as it bends back north, then northwest. In less than a third of a mile, you'll be back on the wider Tensaw River. Turn right to begin a northeasterly direction. You'll begin a northerly trek to the tip of Devil's Bend, and after 5 miles of wide water, you'll be back at Tensaw Lake, then back into Bayou Jessamine. From here you're a little more than a mile from Rice Creek Landing. Continue generally east, and you'll soon arrive back at the takeout.

Trip Information

Contact

Tensaw EcoTours
3807 Battleship Parkway
Spanish Fort, AL 36527
(251) 625–0339

Season

Year-round.

Fees/Permits

No permit is required for paddling the rivers. See the Guided Tours section for more information.

Local Information

Meaher State Park
5200 Battleship Parkway East
Spanish Fort, AL 36527
(251) 626–5529
Located just off the causeway, this is a fairly small state park with limited facilities and staff. They close at 4:00 P.M. This 1,327-acre park is situated in the wetlands of Mobile Bay and is primarily a day-use park. A boat ramp and pier will appeal to anglers, and there are self-guided tours over two nature trails that include boardwalks over the Mobile Delta.

Historic Blakeley State Park
33707 State Highway 225
P.O. Box 7279
Spanish Fort, AL 36527
(251) 580–0005, (251) 626–0798

Park and trail information, (251) 937–9380
E-mail: blakeley@dibbs.net
www.siteone.com/tourist/blakeley/camping.htm
The park allows delta access from a boardwalk along the Tensaw River. Blakeley State Park is located at the site of the last major battle of the Civil War.

Guided Tours

Tensaw EcoTours
3807 Battleship Parkway
Spanish Fort, AL 36527
(251) 625–0339
Tour guide: Jeff Evans

Organizations

Forever Wild
Alabama Department of Conservation/
Alabama Division of Wildlife and Freshwater Fisheries
64 North Union Street
Montgomery, AL 36130
(334) 242–3465
www.dcnr.state.al.us/agfd/forever.html

Coastal Land Trust
P.O. Drawer 7414
Mobile, AL 36670
(334) 470–0902
This organization has bought and protected thousands of acres of delta land.

Alabama Black Bear Alliance
P.O. Box 26
Leroy, AL 36548
www.alawild.org/abba.html

Other Resources

National Weather Service
South Alabama Marine Forecast Online: www.srh.noaa.gov/mob/marine.htm
South Alabama Tidal Information Online: www.co-ops.nos.noaa.gov/tab2ec4.html#106

Shady bayou setting at the Rice Creek put-in.

Local Outdoor Retailers

Fairhope Boat Company
702 Section Street North
Fairhope, AL 36532
(251) 928–3417
Fairhope Boats is an excellent shop for canoe and kayak supplies, rentals, and general information.

Sunshine Canoe Rentals
5460 Old Shell Road
Mobile, AL 36608
(251) 344–8664

Spoke 'N Trail, Inc.
4453 Old Shell Road
Mobile, AL 36608
(251) 341–1712
Spoke 'N Trail sells canoes and kayaks, and has a great selection of river equipment.

Maps

USGS maps: Stiggins Lake, AL.
DeLorme: *Alabama Atlas & Gazetteer:* #56, G-2, G-1.

5 Navy Cove

River Specs

County: Baldwin.

Start: From Pirate Cove/State Road 180.

End: Pirate's Cove/SR 180.

Length: 7.7 miles.

Approximate float time: Varies, depending on time to explore. Short trip is four hours.

Difficulty rating: Easy.

Rapids: None.

River type: Open water/bayou canoeing.

Current: Moderate because of tides.

Environment: Wide-open bay with marsh grass bayous, white-sand beaches, and various wild-flowers and wildlife.

Elevation drop: None.

Land status: National wildlife refuge.

Nearest town (or city): Gulf Shores.

Other users: Motorboats, anglers.

Getting There: Put-in and Takeout Information

Put-in/takeout: From the intersection of State Road 59 and State Road 180 in Gulf Shores, take SR 180 west. Travel 6.3 miles; the Bon Secour Wildlife Refuge office will be on the right. Continue west on SR 180 for 12.7 miles. Turn right onto the sand road (the sand can be deep to the right side of this road, so stay to the left when you turn). The put-in is only about 100 feet down the road.

The put-in/takeout is a natural sand ramp into the bay. Parking is very limited, and you will have to share space with other vehicles and boat trailers. Park up on the obvious higher ground to make sure you don't find your car in high-tide water.

Trip Summary

The Navy Cove trip floats along the banks of Mobile Bay just on the north side of the peninsula from the Gulf of Mexico. It takes you through the salty water of the bay through the Bon Secour Wildlife Refuge, which is home to many beautiful and endangered species of wildlife and has plenty of bayous for exploring.

Trip Description

In the middle of the peninsula that forms the lower mouth of Mobile Bay, where the bay meets the Gulf of Mexico, lies the extraordinary Bon Secour National Wildlife Refuge. This is where you will find the Navy Cove run.

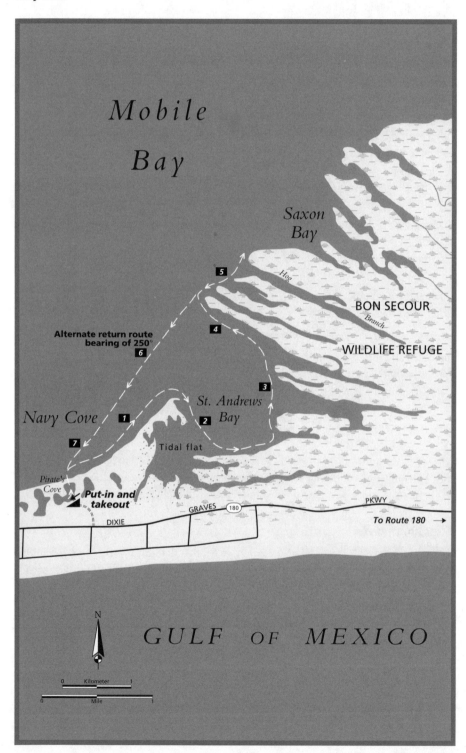

Mobile Bay

Saxon Bay

Hog

BON SECOUR

Branch

WILDLIFE REFUGE

5

4

Alternate return route
bearing of 250°

6

3

Navy Cove **1**

St. Andrews
Bay **2**

7

Tidal flat

*Pirate's
Cove*

Put-in and
takeout

GRAVES 180

PKWY

DIXIE

To Route 180 →

N

GULF OF MEXICO

0 Kilometer 1

0 Mile 1

The refuge covers 6,500 acres of land and is the home to hundreds of species of animals, including numerous endangered species. For example, along the 4-mile-long Pine Beach Trail, you can hike to the pristine white beaches of the Gulf of Mexico and visit the habitat of the endangered beach mouse or see the nesting areas of the loggerhead sea turtle and gopher tortoise.

On the opposite side of this narrow peninsula lies Mobile Bay. It is here that the salt water of the gulf mixes with the fresh water from the Mobile River to form a brackish environment for even more wildlife that is rarely found anywhere else in the world. This is where our trip begins. It will take us around the banks of Navy Cove and St. Andrew's Bay, and then to Little Point Clear, before returning to our original put-in, known as Pirate's Cove.

We call this trip Navy Cove because that's the name of the area you will first paddle through once you arrive at the put-in. The beauty of this trip is the many bayous you will pass that invite you to explore them. Feel free to do so, but you should not travel down the very narrow (3- to 5-foot-wide) bayous off to the side of the main inlets. Within the beautifully swaying marsh grass is a formerly endangered species of animal that calls the refuge home: the American alligator. The alligators that live in the refuge average 4 to 6 feet in length and can often be seen looking like a log with two eyes floating in the water. Although alligators are naturally afraid of humans, don't test the odds—stay clear of them!

There are many white sandy beaches to briefly land on to see some of the marine life that lives here. Most predominant are the large colonies of sand crabs that scurry around the beach and into their homes, which are holes in the sand.

The driftwood that has washed ashore over the years has formed beautiful and picturesque images, so you will definitely want to have a camera along. And as you paddle, keep an eye to the sky. You will see brown pelicans—which have made an astounding comeback—swooping down and catching their dinner.

While on the water, there is a good chance you will meet area fishermen checking their nets for mullet and crabs. If you like to fish, purchase a fishing license and bring along your rod. The mullet in the bayous will be jumping all around your boat.

Before you get under way, a few words of warning: First, this trip can include some open-water bay paddling. Tides can be strong at times, so be prepared for heavy paddling. Keep this in mind, and leave ample time for the return trip. Life jackets are essential on a paddle of this nature! The water can become very deep, and there are waves.

Second, keep an eye on the weather. The weather in south Alabama is unpredictable, especially in the summer, when late-afternoon thunderstorms pop up frequently with very heavy rainfall. In these situations you will face rough seas and the possibility of flooding your canoe. If you are faced with an impending storm and cannot make it back to the takeout, pull to the nearest beach, and wait it out.

This is a fun trip with plenty of exploration possibilities. The route we have outlined is only an example, and the time of the trip will vary, depending on how much you explore. One note about the paddle itself: On the return trip, from the southern finger that forms the mouth of St. Andrews Bay, you may want to shave some time off of the trip. You do not have to follow the shore back around to the put-in. With a compass, from the tip of the finger, head on a bearing of 250 degrees, and you should arrive back at Pirate's Cove (refer to the map).

As you visit the refuge, remember that this is a fragile habitat. Fires are not allowed anywhere in the refuge. Take your trash out with you, and leave the area as you found it.

Trip Information

Contact
Bon Secour National Wildlife Refuge
12295 State Highway 180
Gulf Shores, AL 35603
(251) 540–7720
bonsecour.fws.gov
The refuge office is open Monday through Friday, 7:30 A.M. to 5:00 P.M. Brochures are available in an information box outside of the office any day.

Season
Year-round.

Fees/Permits
No fee to launch or paddle this trip.

Local Information
Alabama Gulf Coast Area Chamber of Commerce
P.O. Drawer 3869
Gulf Shores, AL 36547
(251) 968–6904
www.alagulfcoastchamber.com

Local Events/Attractions
National Shrimp Festival (October)
P.O. Drawer 3869
Gulf Shores, AL 36547
(251) 968–6904
The official National Shrimp Festival held each year on the beach with plenty of entertainment and, of course, shrimp. Call for exact dates.

At the put-in, with Mobile Bay visible on the horizon.

Zooland Animal Park
1204 Gulf Shores Parkway
Gulf Shores, AL 36542–5908
(251) 968–5731
The zoo offers 250 species of animals in their natural habitat. Open 9:00 A.M. to 5:00 P.M.

Accommodations
Gulf State Park Resort Hotel
Highway 182 East
Gulf Shores, AL 36542
(800) 544–4853, (251) 948–4853
Hiking trails, beautiful pristine white public beaches, and more, plus fantastic accommodations starting at $49.

Restaurants
Original Oyster House
701 Gulf Shores Parkway
Gulf Shores, AL 36542
(251) 948–2445

Organizations
Mobile Bay Canoe and Kayak Club
www.baykayaker.blogspot.com

Other Resources
Mobile Bay Watch
3280 Dauphin Street, #124C
Mobile, AL 36606
(251) 476–0328
www.mobilebaywatch.org

Local Outdoor Retailer
Sunshine Canoes
5460 Old Shell Road
Mobile, AL 36608
(251) 344–8664

Maps
Brochures are available free at the Bon Secour National Wildlife Refuge office.
USGS maps: Bon Secour Bay, AL.
DeLorme: *Alabama Atlas & Gazetteer:* #63, B-5.

6 Perdido River

River Specs

County: Baldwin.

Start: County Road 196, Barrineau Park, Florida.

End: U.S. Highway 90, Seminole, Alabama.

Length: 18 miles.

Approximate float time: Eight hours.

Difficulty rating: Easy.

Rapids: None.

River type: Blackwater float trip.

Current: Swift for the first 15 miles, then slows considerably as it nears Perdido Bay. Anticipate a lot of paddling here.

Environment: Flat waters through pines and oaks. Plenty of bayous, feeders, and bogs.

Elevation drop: 0.4 foot per mile.

Land status: First 5 miles open; remainder has many areas posted.

Nearest town (or city): Start—Cantonment, Florida; End—Seminole, Alabama.

Other users: After Interstate 10, jet skis and motorboats.

Getting There: Put-in and Takeout Information:

To shuttle point/takeout: From the FLorida/Alabama state line take I–10 east into Florida 2 miles to exit 1. Take Alternate U.S. Highway 90 south 14.5 miles. Ruby's Fish Camp Road will be on the right (if you cross over a bridge that spans three rivers and see the Alabama state line sign, you've passed it). Turn right here. The camp and boat ramp are 0.1 mile down the road.

The takeout is a cement boat ramp. Watch for it as you round the final bend of the trip. The river becomes wide, with a few houses on the left at the final bend. If you come to the US 90 bridge, the third bridge on the trip, you've overshot the takeout.

Put-in from the takeout: Travel 0.1 mile from the takeout ramp down Ruby's Fish Camp Road to Alternate US 90. Turn left, and take US 90 north 18 miles to the intersection of U.S. Highway 29. Turn left, and head north on US 29 for 10 miles. Make a left turn onto County Road 196. Continue on CR 196 for 3 miles, and it will merge with CR 97. Travel an additional 2.8 miles, and County Road 99 will make a sharp right turn off of CR 196. Continue straight on CR 196. It becomes a dirt road. After traveling 1.4 miles, cross railroad tracks. At 0.1 mile, you'll come to a wooden bridge over the river. Park before the bridge on the right side of the road. The put-in is also on the right.

There are several excellent places to put in here, all with a short 10 to 15-foot sand bank to the river's edge. The landing is a hangout after hours for partiers, so leaving your car overnight here is possible, but not recommended.

Perdido River

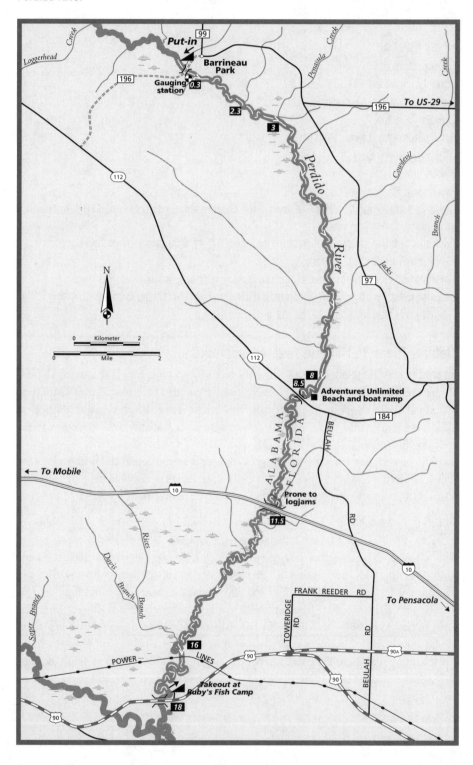

Trip Summary

The Perdido River demarcates the state line between Alabama and Florida. At the Barrineau Park put-in, the Perdido begins semiswiftly and continues this way for about 10 miles, where the flow begins to slow slightly. For the final 4 or 5 miles, you must actually use your paddle to propel your boat, for the current is minimal. During the first half of the trip, you'll have plenty of pebbly white beaches where you can set up camp or romp in the water. The second half brings you through wider and deeper water that is serene and well suited for both paddleboats and anglers in motorboats.

Trip Description

The trip begins at Barrineau Park at an old wooden bridge. There is a wide beach here, where parents like to take their kids during the day. After dark the place sometimes becomes more of an adult playground, where people congregate around campfires for fun. Unfortunately, the beauty of the river is somewhat spoiled by careless visitors who use it as their beverage-can trash bin.

The miles of wooded areas along the banks of the Perdido are a sportsman's paradise. Along the route you'll see lots of NO TRESPASSING signs and signs for hunting camps. Much of the land along the river is private hunting camps. You'll see a few trailers set up on the larger beaches where hunters spend the night. The final section of the river is popular with anglers, who reel in bass and bream.

You'll see lots of small bayous and feeder streams that can be navigated for short distances. If you paddle into a bayou or stream, many times you'll get a glimpse of an environment that's quite different from that of the river itself. There are a few bayous along the way covered in lily pads that provide the nesting ground for tiny frogs no bigger than your little fingernail. If you exit your boat, watch where you step; you're likely to get some of the creatures underfoot.

At about the halfway point—or 8 miles from the put-in—there is a wide, sandy area of the river where Adventures Unlimited has a canoe and tube rental outpost. This is one of just a couple popular spots along your way where you'll see quite a few people floating around and living the good life. Aside from this you won't see much as far as civilization; most areas are relatively remote. Just after the outpost the river takes a Y. You'll probably want to take the path to the left, but check out the water to the right if you feel inclined.

This is the vicinity of Jack's Branch, a tributary feeding the Perdido from the Florida side. From 1979 through 1981, an oil recovery facility operated close by. The plant discharged waste materials, including waste oils, petroleum refining waste, wood-treatment process waste, spent solvents, and various paint wastes. In 1984 and 1985, the Florida Department of Environmental Regulation excavated 40,000 cubic yards of contaminated soil and placed it in a lined vault on site to prevent further contamination of the groundwater. Quarterly monitoring of the site will be performed until 2003.

In about five minutes you'll pass an old ruined bridge, which has lots of posts invisible just underwater. There is a swift current for a short span. It's easy to get caught up here if you don't choose the correct path. Stay left, and you should be all right. This area opens up, and there's a large sandy beach just before you pass over a gas pipeline and under Highway 112. At Highway 112 there is a nice boat ramp and put-in. There is supposedly a put-in fee, but when we passed by in the early afternoon, there was nobody at the ramp to collect.

Another half an hour down, there is a small lagoon on the Alabama side to your right. The view changes briefly as you pass by, as there are trees with large trunks growing out of the water. The banks at this point become rather dark and grassy, some even muddy.

Shortly and suddenly as you round a bend left, there is a large impassable logjam, about 30 yards in length and stretching the river's width. You'll have no alternative but to pick up your boat and carry it around. The best bet is on the left—up a bank and around the jam. This turned out to be a fairly simple portage with two men; probably a little tougher with just one. Just a few minutes after the logjam, you'll cross under the I-10 bridge.

A little more than an hour before the end of the trip, there is a tricky spot where you could end up following a dead-end river trail if you're not careful. The river appears to go both straight and left. Logically, the straight path would appear to be the main river, but it will lead you to nowhere. Watch for a wide, nearly hairpin bend to the left; that's where you want to go. If you look at a compass while in this area, don't be surprised; you'll be traveling north for a short stretch, as the river nearly bends back upon itself.

After an hour or so, you'll get to put another notch in your canoe. If your rear end's not a little bit sore after this one, you used too much padding.

Trip Information

Contacts

West Florida Canoe Club
P.O. Box 17203
Pensacola, FL 32522
(850) 492–7174
www.pcola.gulf.net/~jimgoff/index.html

Florida Department of Environmental Protection
3900 Commonwealth Boulevard MS49
Tallahassee, FL 32399
(877) 822–5208
www.dep.state.fl.us/gwt

Season

Year-round.

Fees/Permits

No fees or permits required for the put-in. $3.00 to take out at Ruby's Fish Camp. Freshwater fishing license is required for fishing.

Gorgeous May greenery (black and white really doesn't cut it here).

Local Information
South Baldwin County Chamber of Commerce
104 South McKenzie Street
Foley, AL 36535
(251) 943–3291
www.southbaldwinchamber.com

Local Events/Attractions

Elberta Sausage Festival (Last Saturday of March and October)
Elberta, AL 36530
(251) 986–5805
This semiannual event features homemade sausage cooked in a variety of ways, plus plenty of music, activities for the kids, and arts and crafts. Started in 1977, all proceeds benefit the Elberta Volunteer Fire Department.

Flora-Bama Lounge
17401 Perdido Key Drive
Perdido Key, FL 32507
(251) 980–5118
florabama.com
The Flora-Bama straddles the Florida/Alabama state lines. Not only is there great food and drink here, but also the world-famous World Championship Mullet Tossing Competition held the end of each April. Contestants see who can throw a dead mullet the farthest over the state line. Football star Kenny Stabler throws out the first mullet each year.

Organizations

Friends of Perdido Bay
2233 Club House Drive
Lillian, AL 26549
(334) 962–2360

Other Resources

Alabama Wildlife Federation
46 Commerce Street
Montgomery, AL 36104
(334) 832–9453

Maps

River map available at Ruby's Fish Camp for $3.00.
USGS maps: Barrineau Park, FL/Seminole, AL.
DeLorme: *Alabama Atlas & Gazetteer:* #63, D-10, E-10, F-10.

⊞ 7 Sand Island

River Specs

County: Mobile.
Start: Dauphin Island beach, near Isle Dauphine Golf Club on Dauphin Island.
End: Dauphin Island beach, near Isle Dauphine Golf Club on Dauphin Island.
Length: Varies.
Approximate float time: Varies.
Difficulty rating: Easy to difficult, depending on experience and weather conditions.
Rapids: None.
River type: Open ocean (Gulf of Mexico).
Current: Sometimes strong.
Environment: Beach.
Elevation drop: None.
Land status: Island.
Nearest town (or city): Dauphin Island.
Other users: Anglers, sailboats, jet skis.

Getting There: Put-in and Takeout Information

To put-in/takeout: From I–10 in Tillman's Corner, take Alabama Highway 193 south (Rangeline Road). Go 7.3 miles until the road comes to a T. Turn left, continuing on AL 193 south. After 0.7 mile turn right, staying on AL 193 south. Travel 18.4 miles until you are on Dauphin Island, then turn right at the stop sign onto Bienville Road. Drive for 0.5 mile. Just over a small bridge, turn left onto Orleans Drive. Follow Orleans Drive for 0.8 mile until it dead-ends into the Isle Dauphine parking lot. There is plenty of parking space here. Carry your boat for about 50 yards down a concrete trail next to the golf pro shop. There is a wooden boardwalk that you may use, it has a fairly sharp turn, which may require you to lift your boat over. It's also possible to walk on the beach just to the right of the boardwalk. The put-in is on the beach just about 100 yards from where the boardwalk begins.

Trip Summary

The Sand Island trip is a welcome break from the typical river trip and has converted many canoe enthusiasts to the world of sea kayaking. Marine wildlife abounds on this trip, and navigating the waves in the salt air is exhilarating. The trip is close enough to the mainland to provide even the beginner with a wonderful first-time sea-kayaking experience.

Trip Description

Paddling the waters of the Gulf of Mexico offers a real change of scenery from the typical river trip. The view and the wildlife is striking to say the least, and the options for sea kayaking are unlimited. One of our favorites is the Sand Island trip.

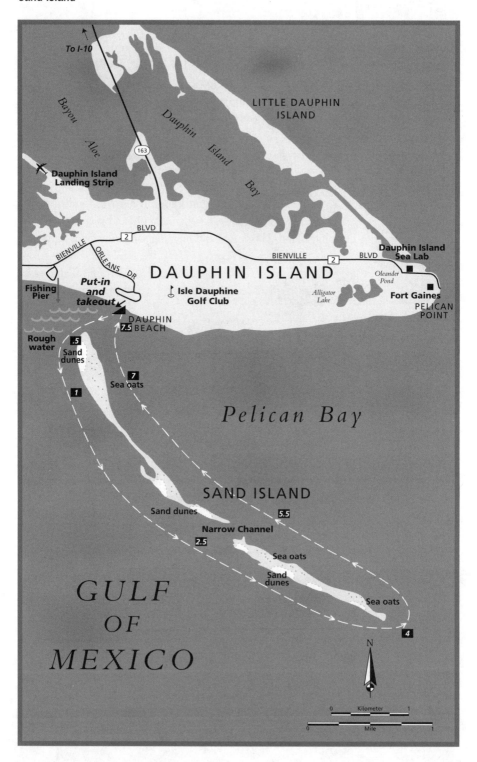

To I-10

Bayou Aloe

Dauphin Island Landing Strip

DAUPHIN ISLAND

163

LITTLE DAUPHIN ISLAND

Dauphin Island Bay

BIENVILLE   BLVD   2

BIENVILLE   BLVD   2

ORLEANS DR

Fishing Pier

Put-in and takeout

Isle Dauphine Golf Club

Alligator Lake

Oleander Pond

Dauphin Island Sea Lab

Fort Gaines

PELICAN POINT

DAUPHIN BEACH

7.5

Rough water

.5   Sand dunes

7   Sea oats

1

Pelican Bay

SAND ISLAND

Sand dunes   5.5

Narrow Channel   2.5

Sea oats

Sand dunes

Sea oats

4

GULF OF MEXICO

N

0   Kilometer   1

0   Mile   1

The distant view consists mainly of open-water expanse meeting the sky. Along the horizon oil rigs, with their tower lights blinking on and off, can be seen. You will see pelicans, including the formerly endangered brown pelican, flying in formation and diving for fish. Hundreds upon hundreds of pelicans and seagulls hang out on the island and watch as you pass by. Marine fish of every type jump around your boat. And offshore you will most likely see dolphins traveling in groups breaching the water's surface.

On the island itself, the dunes are beautiful with the pristine white sand for which the Alabama Gulf Coast has become world renown. On top of the dunes, green and gold sea oats sway in the breeze.

Depending on your time constraints and endurance, you can choose to paddle around the entire island or simply paddle partially up one side and back. Sand Island has a long crescent shape that extends about 3 miles southward from Dauphin Island. Today you can reach the northern tip of Sand Island from Dauphin Island in just one-third of a mile. Interestingly, as recently as twenty years ago, the northern tip of Sand Island was located about 4 miles from Dauphin Island. Hurricanes and ongoing southerly winds have gradually shifted the island northward. Another nearby island, Pelican Island, shows up on many maps but has since disappeared entirely. The proximity to Dauphin Island makes this an ideal trip not only for experienced sea kayakers, but also for beginners who want to try it out.

Sea kayaking has become quite popular in recent years. The industry offers many types of kayaks, many designed to be very steady for the beginner. If it's your first time in a kayak, it's best to rent a sea kayak first and try it out (see Outdoor Retailers below). If you just have to buy one, choose a design that's built for stability, not for pure speed.

One of the really great aspects of sea kayaking on Alabama's Gulf Coast is that for the most part, you're not dependent on a seasonal schedule as long as you're able to endure the heat of the summer. Stay off the water in the wintertime, of course, as the average temperature in the Gulf of Mexico around Dauphin Island normally reaches the mid-50s Fahrenheit, and the gulf waters themselves become dangerously cold.

During the extremely hot, humid summer weather typical in south Alabama, make sure that you keep fully hydrated and wear protection from the sun. It's always a good idea to take these precautions on any canoe or kayak trip, but when paddling in the open waters of the gulf on a clear day, nature offers no protection from the sunlight, as trees often do when paddling a river. Wear sunscreen, a hat, light loose clothing, and keep fully hydrated. The combination of high heat and high humidity decrease the ability of the human body to get rid of excess heat. Make sure to drink plenty of liquids before, during, and after the trip. Many times on open water, your body will get a better workout (thus sweat more) than it would on a river because of the increased natural elements of wind and waves encountered.

Another precaution to take before planning a paddle on open water is to get the weather report. Use common sense. Thunderstorms may sometimes—even after a clear weather prediction—crop up and move toward you in a matter of minutes. It is both scary and dangerous to get caught on open water while lightning flashes and thunder rolls nearby. If you are on the water and you see a storm approaching, do the safe thing: Get off the water immediately.

Many of today's kayaks are very stable, so even if you lean way over, the boat will not tip over. Be especially careful of waves, though, during your paddle to and around Sand Island. As you paddle parallel to the island's shoreline, your kayak will be subjected to waves from the sides. If you get too close to the island, the waves may begin to break over the side of your kayak, and the possibility of capsizing increases. Remember to ride into the waves instead of paddling parallel, and use those skirts to keep the water out. Also keep in mind that you will probably be sharing the water with quite a few fishing and recreational craft, some of which are large and can produce hefty trailing wakes.

All in all, you'll thoroughly enjoy a visit to Dauphin Island, and you'll probably want to stay a while. Besides kayaking, you can deep-sea fish, pier fish, boat, swim on sugary sand beaches, camp, golf, and more. History buffs will surely want to visit Fort Gaines, which, along with Fort Morgan to the east, was the site of the Battle of Mobile Bay. Fort Gaines also has a rich history from before the Civil War.

The Dauphin Island Sea Lab provides an estuarium, including the beautiful Living Marsh boardwalk, a 10,000-square-foot exhibit hall, and the weather station. You'll enjoy exciting visual displays and engaging interactive exhibits.

A visit to Dauphin Island is time well spent.

Trip Information

Contact
Sunshine Canoe Rentals
5460 Old Shell Road
Mobile, AL 36608
(251) 344–8664

Season
Year-round. It is not recommended to paddle the Gulf of Mexico around Dauphin Island and Sand Island during the winter months, when the water temperature dips into 50 degrees Fahrenheit.

Fees/Permits
There are no fees or permits required to paddle in the gulf.

Local Information
Dauphin Island Chamber of Commerce
1011 Bienville Boulevard
Dauphin Island, AL 36528
(877) 532–8744, (251) 861–5524
dauphinisland.cc

Local Events/Attractions

Fort Gaines Historic Site
P.O. Box 97
Dauphin Island, AL 36528
(251) 861–6992

Fort Gaines is located at the eastern end of Dauphin Island, looking out over Mobile Bay and the Gulf of Mexico. Fort Gaines was a key stronghold guarding Mobile Bay before and during the Battle of Mobile Bay. On 5 August 1864, Rear Admiral David G. Farragut famously said "Damn the torpedoes," which were early versions of naval mines, and passed Fort Gaines and Fort Morgan. In the southern part of Mobile Bay, Farragut engaged and defeated the ironclad *Tennessee* and a small Confederate fleet. Although the port of Mobile was closed, the city itself didn't surrender until 13 April 1865. Visitors can explore the battlements, living quarters, tunnels, and bastions of Fort Gaines. It is open daily from 9:00 A.M. to 5:00 P.M. A small admission fee is charged. Civil War reenactments and special events are scheduled occasionally.

For more information on events and attractions on Dauphin Island, including fishing and boating, camping, bird-watching, and golf, go to gulfinfo.com and dauphinisland.cc.

Dauphin Island Sea Lab
101 Bienville Boulevard
Dauphin Island, AL 36528
(251) 861–2141
www.disl.org
The Dauphin Island Sea Lab is Alabama's marine education and research center.

Accommodations

Gulf Breeze Motel/Harbor Lights Inn
1512 Cadillac Avenue
P.O. Box 107
Dauphin Island, AL 36528
(800) 286–0296

Restaurants

Top of the Palms (located at the Island Club)
100 Orleans Drive
Dauphin Island, AL 36528
(251) 861–5255

Dine in a tiki-hut setting of bright tropical colors, artwork, and Caribbean music as you look out over the top of the palms at the breathtaking sunsets on the Gulf of Mexico. With a 360-degree view of the gulf and the island, there isn't a bad seat in the house.

With the sea kayak's bow pointed west, a storm cloud quickly approaches.

Seafood Galley
1510 Bienville Boulevard
Dauphin Island, AL 36528
(251) 861–8000

Faux Pas Cafe
1102 DeSoto Avenue
Dauphin Island, AL 36528
(251) 861–4002

Other Resources
National Weather Service
South Alabama Marine Forecast Online: www.srh.noaa.gov/mob/marine.htm
South Alabama Tidal Information Online: www.co-ops.nos.noaa.gov/tab2ec4.html#106

Local Outdoor Retailer
Sunshine Canoe Rentals
5460 Old Shell Road
Mobile, AL 36608
(251) 344–8664
Sunshine Canoe Rentals rents both canoes and kayaks.

Maps

USGS maps: Fort Morgan, AL.

DeLorme *Alabama Atlas & Gazetteer:* #64, B-3.

Note: Notice that the Delorme *Atlas & Gazetteer* shows the location of Sand Island in grid coordinate B-4. From the time the map was created in 1981, hurricanes and ongoing southerly winds have shifted Sand Island to its current location in B-3.

Tidbits

The name *Mobile* comes from a French adaptation of the name of a local Native American tribe, the Maubilian, which means "canoe paddler."

The Battle of Mobile Bay and Other Sea-Kayaking Adventures

Sand Island is only one of many sea-kayaking trips that can be taken in south Alabama. One of the more interesting trips includes the north side of Dauphin Island, where a series of small islands and Indian Mound Park can be paddled.

In Baldwin County, across from Dauphin Island at the mouth of Mobile Bay, is Fort Morgan. This is the site of the Battle of Mobile Bay, which took place in August 1864 during the Civil War. A paddle around the fort will take you past a marker buoy, which marks the resting site of the USS *Tecumseh.* This was a monitor-class ironclad that was supposed to strengthen Admiral David Farragut's forces blockading the bay. On 5 August 1864 Farragut's ships and the *Tecumseh* began firing on the fort. The ship veered to the left to take on a Confederate ram, but instead ran into an underwater mine and sank. As the ship started sinking, the fort opened fire on it and completed the kill, killing its captain and crew of ninety-two. With that, Farragut uttered those now-famous words, "Damn the torpedoes, full speed ahead!" and the rest is history.

In 1967 the Smithsonian Institution discovered the wreckage of the *Tecumseh* and turned over custody of the ship to the General Services Administration, which marked the site and is now considering what can be done to preserve the wreck.

8 Styx River

River Specs

County: Baldwin.
Start: County Road 64.
End: River Landing Road.
Length: 15.4 miles.
Approximate float time: Seven and one-half hours.
Difficulty rating: Easy.
Rapids: None.
River type: Mainly narrow river, averaging about 50 feet in width.
Current: Swift to moderate. Expect considerable paddling after Interstate 10.
Environment: Sandy beaches, a wide variety of flora and fauna.
Elevation drop: 1.7 feet per mile.
Land status: Varied. Generally unincorporated to the north, private below I–10.
Nearest town (or city): Robertsdale, Loxley.
Other users: A few anglers in small boats halfway down the river. As the river gets deeper and wider as it meets the Perdido, large pleasure boats and jet skis.

Getting There: Put-in and Takeout Information

To shuttle point/takeout: From Robertsdale take U.S. Highway 90 east from County Road 59. Head east on US 90 for 16.4 miles. Veer right onto Brown's Landing Road, and travel 0.7 mile. Follow the road as it turns to the right ninety degrees (don't go straight on Brown's Landing Extension). After just 0.2 mile, turn left onto Lost River Road. Travel 0.9 mile, following the road as it curves to the right. Turn left onto River Landing Road, and in 0.1 mile come to the public boat ramp. Parking signs will tell you where you may park your car on the side of the road. In front of you, directly across the Perdido River, is Florida.

As you get close to the end of the paddle, the Styx River merges into and actually becomes the Perdido River. At this point the boat ramp will be a short distance (less than 0.5 mile) away on the right side of the river, hidden away between two bulkheads. Stay to the right, and you'll see the back of the signs at the boat ramp.

To put-in from takeout: Travel back to US 90, and head back east (left from Brown's Landing Road) for 12.8 miles. Turn right, and head north on County Road 83. After 3.5 miles, CR 83 becomes County Road 64. Continue north another 3.7 miles, and cross over I–10. After crossing I–10, continue north for 1 mile. When you come to the bridge over the Styx, cross over it, make an immediate left turn down a short strip of paved road (which becomes dirt), and follow it back under the bridge. There is plenty of parking space here.

The put-in is down a low, moderate, sandy hillside to the riverbank.

Styx River

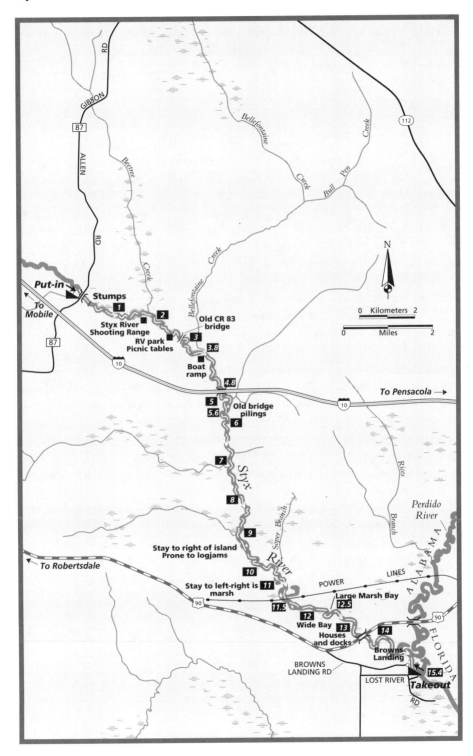

Trip Summary

Of all the float trips in the Gulf Coast region, the Styx has some of the most diverse fish and wildlife to be seen. It is a fairly deep river and should be floatable, except for some bottoming out up to I–10, even in late summer. Numerous islands make the river prone to massive logjams, which require portaging.

Trip Description

The River Styx has been synonymous with religious beliefs since the dawn of man. It is believed the Styx was the link between the world of the living and the world of the dead. An old "pilot" would ferry humans down the river into what is known as purgatory. How the Styx in Baldwin County received its name is anybody's guess, but it is far from the river of the dead!

The Styx is another example of the dark-water rivers that flow through the Gulf Coast region as they head to the Gulf of Mexico. The Styx, however, shows more signs of wildlife than we've seen on other trips. The catfish in the upper portion of this trip are huge. Keep your eyes on the river near your boat to see a wide variety of turtles running on the bottom or plunging into the river from the banks. And hawks and giant heron are not afraid of the passing paddler if you are quiet and patient.

For the most part, the banks of the Styx are steep, 15-foot muddy banks. Thick covers of magnolia, honeysuckle, and scrub pines make climbing the banks nearly impossible. In the first half of the trip, each bend is lined with a pebbly grain sandbar, which is perfect for getting out, having lunch, and taking a swim in the cool water (there's usually a good swimming hole near every beach). Just behind some of the sandbars, maybe 15 to 20 feet or so up the banks, the property is marked as being private, but the signs indicate that the owners don't mind you stopping on the beach. There are just as many sandbars, however, that are not posted and could offer nice overnight camping spots.

In many areas, the river is surrounded by marshland, which provides many interesting inlets and bayous that you can paddle up and explore. The river also has several islands. Although interesting in themselves, these pose a problem for the paddler in that they create several areas that are prone to severe logjams. In our trip, we passed through four jams: two that we could navigate through or around, and two that gave us some serious portaging to do.

And now for the bad news. Of all of the float rivers in the Gulf Coast region, the Styx had to be the worst for trash. Beer cans and uncollected trash dot the beaches. In the water along one stretch, the beer cans looked like pavers lining the walkway to a house. The upper portion of the Styx from the put-in to I–10 is nestled between two county roads, giving easy access to anyone who feels like having an outing along the river, and needless to say, when they're done, they leave the rest of us a reminder of their visit.

As for the trip itself, it begins with a fairly swift flow. You'll pass several areas of stumps within the first mile that you will have to navigate around, but after that, it is fairly clear sailing. You will come across an occasional remnant of an old bridge with pilings peeking through the water, but these are easily passable.

In just less than 3 miles, you will pass by—and hear—the Styx River Shooting Range, which is located just off of I–10. Shortly after you will float by the Styx River Bend RV Park and Campground, a family-oriented camping area with access to the river. You will also pass by the put-in and takeout for a canoe renting facility called Kicks on the Styx. The put-in has a sign asking floaters not to drag their canoes and tubes over the cement boat ramp. Later, just before I–10 and just before passing under the Old County Road 87 bridge, you will see their takeout with a large sign marking the landing.

Once you pass I–10, the flow of the river slows considerably as it begins to head toward Perdido Bay. Here anglers in motorboats will become more prevalent. More inlets and marsh areas will be seen, inviting exploration off the main river. The river will begin to widen until it becomes a good 100 to 200 feet in width and very deep.

As you head toward the US 90 bridge, elegant houses, docks, and boats line the shore to the right. Along the bends here, it is advisable to keep to the shore as close as you can to avoid meeting motorboats speeding around the curves not expecting a canoe.

Just after passing the US 90 bridge, the Perdido River and the Styx join together. There are several large inlets along this stretch that could cause you to head off the main river. Follow the map and you'll make it to the boat ramp with no trouble.

Trip Information

Contact
Kicks on the Styx
26175 U.S. Highway 90
Robertsdale, AL 36567
(251) 942–1807

Season
Year-round.

Fees/Permits
No permit is required to launch from CR 64 or takeout at the public boat ramp.

Local Information
Central Baldwin Chamber of Commerce
22193 Highway 59, #A
Robertsdale, AL 36567
(251) 947–5932
www.cbchamber.org

Scrub pine growing from sandy banks.

Local Events/Attractions

Baldwin County Fair (last week of October)
22193 Highway 59, #A
Robertsdale, AL 36567
(251) 960–1379
A good old-fashioned county fair with plenty of rides, agriculture competitions, entertainment, and, of course, food!

Styx River Water World
24875 Water World Road
Loxley, AL 36551
(251) 960–1118
The first water park in the region, Water World offers giant waterslides and a variety of other water-related fun.

Accommodations

Wind Chase Inn
13156 North Hickory Street
Loxley, AL 36551
(251) 964–4444

Restaurants

Ivey's
18427 Pennsylvania Street
Robertsdale, AL 36567
(251) 947–4000

Mama Lou's Restaurant
22288 Pine Street
Robertsdale, AL 36567
(251) 947–1988

Organizations

Mobile Bay Canoe and Kayak Club
boothegc@bellsouth.com
www.baykayaker.blogspot.com

Other Resources

USGS River Gauge Online:
wwwdalmtg.er.usgs.gov/rt-cgi/gen_stn_pg?station=02377570

Local Outdoor Retailer

Fairhope Boats
702 Section Street
Fairhope, AL 36532
(251) 928–3417
Fairhope Boats is an excellent shop for canoe and kayak supplies, rentals, and general information.

Maps

USGS maps: Elsanor, AL/Seminole, AL.
DeLorme: *Alabama Atlas & Gazetteer:* #63, D-8, D-9, E-9, F-10.

Southeast Region

Located above the Florida panhandle and bordered by the states of Georgia and Florida, the southeast region is a bit more hilly than the Gulf Coast region but is still considered to be coastal plain.

However, with these hills comes our first glimpse of white water in the state. The rivers here are a great combination of the flat-water float trips we have seen in the Gulf Coast region, but also some nice Class I rapids.

A prime example of this is the Sepulga, a wide and swift river that has some nice deep pools and beautiful scenery. It culminates in a wonderful set of Class I rapids with a series of drops (from 6 inches to 2 feet) and, in times of higher water, some nice standing waves.

Another outstanding trip in this region is the West Fork of the Choctawhatchee. Again, the river has some of the characteristics of the float trips of the Gulf Coast region with beautiful white sand beaches, but also some nice Class I rapids and even alligators.

Weather is a key element when traveling this region. Like the Gulf Coast region, the climate is subtropical. Late-summer heat combined with high humidity can make outdoor activity impossible at times. Carry plenty of water and, of course, insect repellant because many of the rivers travel through and near thick marshes and swamps.

And don't forget those surprise thunderstorms. They can pop up without notice and are short-lived, but can be severe with heavy rain, dangerous lightening, and strong winds. And even though the region is not located directly on the gulf, it still can experience the full force of a hurricane or tropical storms. A watchful eye on the weather is required during hurricane season (May through November). A hurricane that pushes on shore from the gulf can mean dangerous tornadoes and flash flooding to these inland areas.

With that said there is great weather the rest of the time, with temperatures in the fall and winter ranging from the mid-60s to low-70s Fahrenheit. It gets a bit colder in this region than in the gulf, with temperatures averaging in the 40s in January and with more frequent cold snaps of below 30 degrees.

Big Escambia Creek

River Specs
County: Escambia.
Start: County Road 27/Sardine Bridge.
End: U.S. Highway 31.
Length: 13.3 miles (or 6 with an alternate takeout).
Approximate float time: Four hours.
Difficulty rating: Easy.
Rapids: Fast shoals bordering on Class I, depending on level.
River type: Float/easy white water.
Current: Fast first three-quarters, slow last quarter.
Minimum level: 2.0 foot stage.
Environment: Mixed forest of longleaf pines, magnolias, and wildflowers. Intriguing rock formations, and gravel and sand beaches through quarries.
Elevation drop: 3.7 feet per mile.
Land status: Escambia Wildlife Management Area first 6 miles; private last half.
Nearest town (or city): Atmore/Flomaton.
Other users: None.

Getting There: Put-in and Takeout Information
To shuttle point/takeout: From the intersection of State Road 21 and U.S. Highway 31 in Atmore, take US 31 north 14.4 miles to the bridge over the river in Flomaton. Just before crossing the bridge, there is a very small picnic area (two picnic tables and a sign). The "park" is a bit overgrown, but there is parking there.

When we ran this trip, the US 31 bridge was under reconstruction. Normally there is a dirt road that leads about 200 feet down to the muddy riverbank. However, with heavy equipment in the way, the portage could be a bit longer. You may want to scope out the takeout before leaving your car there. From the river the takeout is on the right on the upstream side of the bridge.

There is an alternate takeout, however, that has easier access but cuts the trip down to 6 miles in length. To get there travel 8.8 miles from Atmore on US 31 north, and make a left turn onto Sardis Church Road. Travel up Sardis Church Road and in 2.4 miles, turn right onto the dirt Murray Branch Road. In 0.6 mile turn right onto a smaller dirt road, and travel less than 0.1 mile to the parking area. The river is just over a very large gravel/sand dune that shouldn't be driven over (maybe with an SUV), so a portage of 50 yards will be required (see the text for a description of recognizing this takeout from the river).

Big Escambia Creek

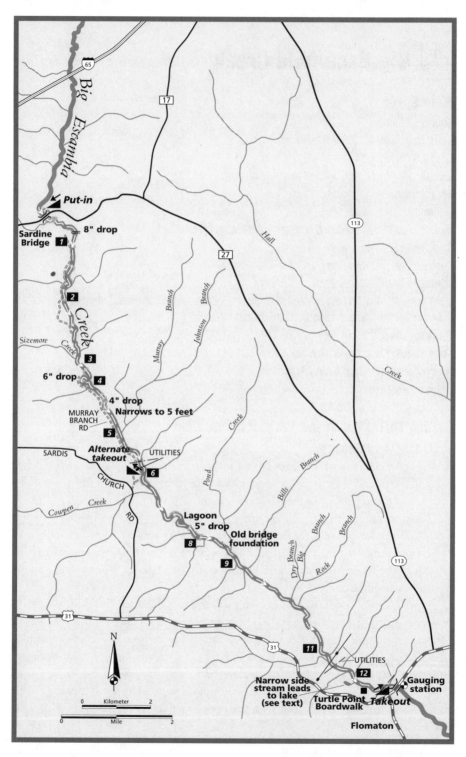

To put-in from takeout: Take US 31 south 5.6 miles. Make a right turn onto Sardis Church Road. Travel 6.3 miles, and turn right onto Cowpen Creek Road. Follow Cowpen 1.1 miles and come to a T intersection with Hobbs Circle. Make a right turn, and travel 0.5 mile to the intersection with County Road 27. Turn right, and travel 3.5 miles to the Sardine Bridge (it isn't marked). Cross the bridge and turn left onto a dirt road with WILDLIFE MANAGEMENT signs lining the entrance. The put-in is just past 0.1 mile down the road, which is moderately rutted but passable. There is plenty of parking.

From the alternate takeout to the put-in, head back up the dirt road and turn left onto Murray Branch Road. Travel 0.6 mile and turn right onto Sardis Church Road. From here, travel 3.9 miles and turn right onto Cowpen Creek Road. Continue from here with the directions above.

The put-in is a nice sloping sandy bank into the river on the upstream side of the bridge. The sand is extremely loose here, so expect to carry your canoe a good 50 feet to the river.

Trip Summary

This is a gem of a trip with frequent shoals—one borders on a Class I rapid (and an 18 inch drop) in the first 6 miles. The river travels through several quarries. These provide long stretches of sand and gravel beaches. The rocks, which are actually hardened clay, give a moonlike landscape and *very* deep channels. The second half of the river becomes a float trip with deep pools.

Trip Description

The Big Escambia, with its clear waters, is an interesting river with a split personality. The first half has plenty of shoals that border on Class I rapids (depending on the river flow). Those are fun for the whole family. The second half is a nice float trip to Flomaton. Generally the river is floatable all year, but watch the gauges, because it could get quite low in late summer and early fall.

The first 6 miles of the Big Escambia are located within the Escambia Wildlife Management Area. Here a wide variety of birds and wildlife can be found, including woodpeckers, such as the red-cockaded, red-bellied, and pileated. The area is also rich in amphibious life, including dusky gopher frogs, Pine Barrens tree frogs, and assorted snakes.

Remember that this is a wildlife management area. That means that hunting is allowed, generally between November and February. If you plan on paddling the river during this time of year, it is best that you contact the Alabama Division of Wildlife and Freshwater Fisheries or visit their Web site for dates and restrictions (see Organizations section).

Beautiful wildflowers and trees bloom along the banks of this area, including dogwood trees, cloudberry flowers (which smell like apples), and one-flower hawthorn, which is a member of the rose family.

Through this section during times of low water, the riverbanks look more like the surface of the moon. The rocks are covered in a coating of thick, hard clay. Traveling through a series of old quarries, the riverbanks also have several areas with wide and deep gravel banks, which make nice places to stop and have lunch.

For the most part, the shoals are pick your own way, with none being very difficult. At 0.75 mile you will encounter a nice 18-inch drop, with the best path through the chute in the center. At levels of 3 feet or so, this borders on being a Class I rapid.

Another 6-inch drop comes at around mile 4. Finally a fast set of shoals stretching about 150 yards in length is reached at mile 4.5. You won't notice this during higher water levels, but in lower water, you will see in this stretch that the channel sometimes narrows to only 5 feet wide (but it is *very* deep).

At mile 6, the river makes a bend to the right and crosses under a set of power lines. Immediately following the crossing, a gravel beach will be encountered on the right. This steep and wide stretch of beach is the intermediate takeout for this trip.

From this point to the end of the ride in Flomaton, the trip turns into a nice float trip. The banks become thick in brush and mud. There are still a few more shoals—one with a small but noticeable drop at mile 8.

As you reach the 12-mile mark, keep an eye out to the right for what looks like a small feeder stream entering the river through thick grass. The stream is only about 2 feet wide. It's worth your while to paddle up the stream because after 30 to 50 feet, the stream comes out of the grass and into a very pretty lake where you may be able to see herons, cuckoos, and carnivorous pitcher plants.

At mile 12.4 the boardwalk for the Turtle Point Environmental Center will be passed on the right. *Do not get out here or use this as a takeout!* The US 31 bridge soon will be upon you, and the takeout is to your right.

It's a nice little trip for the entire family that won't take the entire day but is full of nature and fun.

Trip Information

Season

Although the river can be run year-round because of several large feeders, you should still keep an eye on the gauge during the summer months. A stage of less than 2 feet would be too low to run, and you could end up dragging your boat in some areas. Also, watch the gauges for flooding in the spring.

Fees/Permits

There is no fee to launch or float the river.

Local Information

Atmore Area Chamber of Commerce
501 South Pensacola Avenue
Atmore, AL 36502
(251) 368–3305
www.frontiernet.net/~atmoreal

Hard, weathered clay along the banks gives an extraterrestrial appearance.

Flomaton Area Chamber of Commerce
307 Ringold Street
Flomaton, AL 36441
(251) 296–2431

Local Events/Attractions

Poarch Creek Indian Pow-Wow (Thanksgiving weekend)
5811 Jack Springs Road
Atmore, AL 36502
(251) 368–9136, ext. 2205
Tribal members gather on the original Creek land to celebrate their heritage, and everyone is invited. The pow-wow features Native American arts and crafts, dancing, and food.

Turtle Point Environmental Science Center
20959 Highway 31
Flomaton, AL 36441
(251) 296–3401
dgonza365.tripod.com/turtlepointSC
The goal of the TPESC is to provide opportunities for students and citizens to develop an understanding of the Ecology of Big Escambia Creek, the Conecuh River Basin, and sur-

rounding wetlands. There are a variety of programs and exhibits at the center, located approximately 0.5 mile before the takeout on US 31 in Flomaton.

Accommodations
Royal Oaks Bed and Breakfast
5145 Highway 21 North
Atmore, AL 36502
(251) 368–8722

Restaurants
Mama's
Highway 31 North
Flomaton, AL 36441
(251) 296–9103

Creek Family Restaurant
6141 Highway 21
Atmore, AL 36502
(251) 368–4422

Organizations
Alabama Water Watch
203 Swingle Hall
Department of Fisheries
Auburn University, AL 36849
(251) 844–4785
www.auburn.edu/aww
Alabama Water Watch is a group of volunteers who monitor the streams and lakes in Alabama and shared waterways of neighboring states to help improve the quality of water.

Alabama Division Wildlife and Freshwater Fisheries
64 North Union Street
Montgomery, AL 36130
(334) 242–3623
www.dcnr.state.al.us/agfd/wildsec.html

Other Resources
USGS River Gauge Online for Big Escambia Creek:
waterdata.usgs.gov/al/nwis/uv?02374950

Maps

USGS maps: Flomaton, AL.

DeLorme: *Alabama Atlas & Gazetteer:* #57, F-7, G-7, G-8.

Tidbit

Baseball is big in Alabama, and many of the game's biggest stars came from the state, including Hank Aaron, Ozzie Smith, and Satchel Paige. Cleon Jones and Tommy Agee of the "Miracle Mets" of 1969 are from Mobile. And plenty of future major league stars have passed through, including Mark McGwire, who played for the Huntsville Stars minor league team. NBA Hall of Famer Michael Jordan played with the Birmingham Barons for a season.

Choctawhatchee River

River Specs

County: Dale.

Start: U.S. Highway 231.

End: US 84.

Length: 4.1 miles (12.2 miles with an alternate takeout).

Approximate float time: Two and one-half hours (longer trip: five to six hours).

Difficulty rating: Easy.

Rapids: None.

River type: Float.

Current: Moderate.

Environment: Water cascades down limestone bluffs with banks lined with cypress, sweet gum, beech, and longleaf and slash pines.

Elevation drop: 2.7 feet per mile.

Land status: Unincorporated county land, private property.

Nearest town (or city): Enterprise.

Other users: Motorboats, anglers, and hunters.

Getting There: Put-in and Takeout Information

To shuttle point/takeout: From Enterprise, at the intersection of Alabama Highway 192 and U.S. Highway 84, take US 84 east 6.8 miles. Turn left onto Alabama Highway 85. Travel 0.9 mile. Turn right onto Alabama Highway 134. Travel 6.9 miles, and turn right onto Alabama Highway 123. Travel 0.3 mile, and turn right onto a paved road that will become dirt. Follow the road to the picnic area of the Newton Recreational Area.

To find this takeout from the river, float under the AL 134 bridge, and look for the tall remains of another old cement bridge to the right. The takeout is on the right downstream side of this column. The actual takeout starts as a steep 20 foot climb up a dirt-and-brush-covered bank. It levels out and continues another 50 feet to the recreation area. You can maneuver your car closer to this point over a grassy picnic area.

To get to the alternate takeout from the intersection of Alabama Highway 167 and US 84, take US 84 east 9.8 miles. Turn right onto the small paved/dirt road to the right. Travel 0.2 mile to the river. This takeout is a nice, low sand bank, about 50 feet from the road to the river.

To put-in from takeout: Take AL 123/AL 134 north 1.7 miles. Turn right onto County Road 18. Travel 2.6 miles, and turn right onto U.S. Highway 231 south. Travel 1.5 miles. Cross over the US 231 bridge, to the right will be a dirt road. Turn right onto this road, and follow it 0.2 mile under the bridge.

From the alternate takeout take US 84 south 0.6 mile. Turn left onto County Road 31. Travel 6.8 miles to the intersection of CR 31 and AL 123. Take a left onto AL 123, and almost immediately County Road 14 will be on the right. Turn right onto CR 14, and travel 3.4 miles. Turn left onto US 231 north. Travel 1.2 miles. On the left will be a dirt

Choctawhatchee River

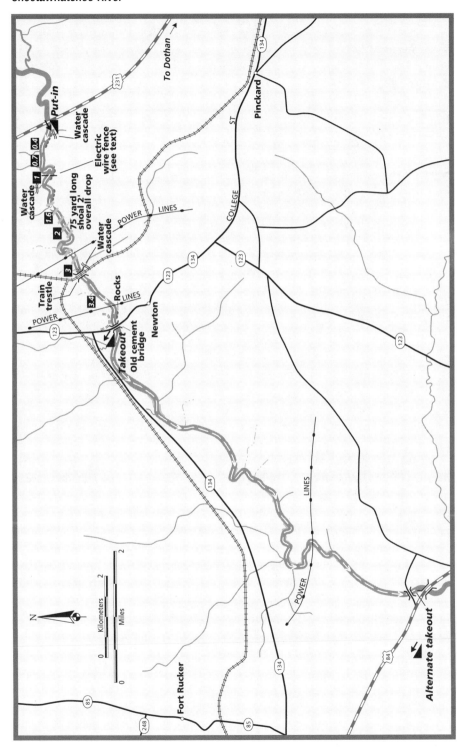

road just before the bridge. Turn onto this road, and follow it approximately 0.2 mile to a point under the bridge.

The put-in here is *very* steep. When you pull your car under the bridge and as you look toward the river, the best carry will be to your left next to the bridge. It is at least a 50- to 75-foot descent down large rocks used for erosion at the base of the bridge. A wide strip of shoulder is available for parking just a few feet farther up this road.

Trip Summary

The Choctawhatchee River features several streams that cascade down rock bluffs and channels, which make the trip very picturesque. The river flows through short 15-foot limestone bluffs that are beautifully accentuated with green ferns. There are several deep pools that make excellent swimming holes in the summer.

Trip Description

The Choctawhatchee River is another excellent example of the long flowing rivers of the southeast region of Alabama. The river actually begins at the confluence of the West and East Forks of the Choctawhatchee River (please refer to the West Fork of the Choctawhatchee River trip). In all, the river flows more than 170 miles southward. In the town of Geneva, the Pea River joins the river as it flows into Choctawhatchee Bay and eventually into the Gulf of Mexico. As it crosses into the Florida panhandle, it becomes part of the Florida Canoe Trails.

The river is naturally yellow in color from silt that it picks up along its route from the many tributaries that feed it.

When canoeing the river, keep in mind that it is one of the few free-flowing (undammed) rivers left in the state. This means that heavy rainfall can cause dangerous flash flooding.

Unlike the West Fork trip, this section of the river is more of a float trip, with the river widening from 50 feet to 80 feet. The banks are moderately steep slopes with few places to take out and relax. They are lined with oak, cypress, beech, and sweet gum trees, as well as a variety of pines, such as longleaf and slash. Early in the trip there are several nice rock outcroppings lined with thick ferns that add to the scenery. Large gar will be seen swimming just below the surface. Keep your eyes to the skies for egrets, hawks, and osprey.

This section of the Choctawhatchee River is not only a float trip. There is a fast shoal at about 1.6 miles into the trip. It is a long stretch—about 75 feet—with a 2-foot overall drop.

One of the highlights of this trip is the water cascades. There are three in all: just after the put-in to the left, another just after 1 mile, and a third at the railroad trestle at 3 miles. The cascades are soothing and beautiful to watch.

One strange sight on the river comes just as you round the bend and head to the northwest at 0.8 mile. There is a steel T-post in the middle of the river with red paint on the top. The flow is fairly swift here, and as we quickly came up on the post, we noticed that there were three more posts heading toward the right bank. They were all connected by a hotwire, used with electric chargers to keep livestock in their place. Now, it's hard to believe that it was electrified, but hitting it at a considerable speed could hurt. Head to the far left, and you'll have plenty of clearance.

The section we describe here is only 4.1 miles in length, but there are several options available to lengthen the trip. You can lengthen it to 12.2 miles by using the U.S. Highway 80 takeout (see the directions to the alternate takeout, above). This provides a full day trip, and more sandbars are available for relaxing, grabbing lunch, swimming, or possibly camping (just watch for those beaches that are posted).

You can also lengthen this trip 5.7 miles by putting in at the West Fork of the Choctawhatchee River trip. This adds a few more shoals to the run.

Trip Information

Contact

Choctawhachee, Pea, and Yellow Rivers Watershed Management Authority (CPYRWMA)
400 Pell Avenue
Collegeview Building
Troy, AL 36082
(800) 652–2019, (334) 670–3780

Season

Year-round.

Fees/Permits

There is no fee to launch or float the river.

Local Information

Enterprise Chamber of Commerce
553 Glover Street
Enterprise, AL 36330
(800) 235–4730
www.enterprisealabama.com

Local Events/Attractions

Boll Weevil Festival (last weekend of October)
P.O. Box 310577
Enterprise, AL 36331
(800) 235–4730, (334) 347–0581
Why such a fuss over a bug that killed off the main staple of commerce in the south? Because it didn't! The boll weevil actually forced farmers to diversify their crops and helped preserve agriculture in the south. In honor of this, the town of Enterprise had a boll weevil monument constructed. Each year this festival takes place with your usual fare of arts and crafts, music, and food.

Little Red Schoolhouse
US 84 Bypass (Boll Weevil Circle)
Enterprise, AL 36331
(334) 393–3977
An exact replica of how school used to be in days gone by. The museum is highly detailed, right down to the pot-bellied stove. Open Monday through Friday 10:00 A.M. to 3:00 P.M., Saturday 10:00 A.M. to 12:00 P.M. Admission is free.

Accommodations
The Rawls
116 South Main Street
Enterprise, AL 36331
(334) 347–2582
Originally built in 1903, the Rawls was the center of activity in Enterprise until it finally closed in the early 1970s. In the 1990s the building was renovated and made into a bed and breakfast, complete with a restaurant, Hayden's Tavern, and a coffee and pastry shop. It has been listed on the National Register of Historic Places.

Restaurants
Carlisle's on Main
401 South Main Street
Enterprise, AL 36331
(334) 347–8108

Coffee Kettle
906 Rucker Boulevard
Enterprise, AL 36331
(334) 347–8156

Organizations
Alabama River Alliance
2027 2nd Avenue North, Suite A
Birmingham, AL 35203
(205) 322–6395
www.alabamarivers.org

Other Resources
USGS River Gauge online for Choctawhatchee River near Newton, AL:
waterdata.usgs.gov/al/nwis/uv?02361000

A stream cuts through high banks.

Maps

USGS maps: Pinckard/Daleville, AL.
DeLorme: *Alabama Atlas & Gazetteer:* #60, B-5, C-4, D-4.

Tidbit

Alabama Trivial Trivia:

- The Vulcan statue in Birmingham honoring the steel industry is the world's largest cast-metal statue.
- The world's largest chair, a 33-foot-tall office chair, can be found in Anniston.
- Benedictine Monk Joseph Zoettel constructed 125 exact replicas of famous buildings, all in miniature, which can be seen in Ava Maria Grotto near Cullman.
- The "bass fishing capital of the world" is Lake Eufaula in Eufaula. Here you can visit Tom Mann's Fish World. Tom is a world-famous fisherman and ESPN reporter. The museum features a 33,000-gallon aquarium and all sorts of artifacts dealing with the "lure" of fishing.
- Adolf Hitler's typewriter is on display at the Burritt Museum in Huntsville.

11 | Conecuh River

River Specs

County: Covington.

Start: County Road 107 public boat ramp.

End: County Road 58/Prestwood Bridge Road.

Length: 4 miles.

Approximate float time: Two and one-half to three hours.

Difficulty rating: Easy.

Rapids: None.

River type: Float.

Current: Slow to moderate.

Environment: Towering longleaf and slash pines line the river, as do flowering magnolias. A very interesting rock formation is found at the waterfall at Prestwood Creek.

Elevation drop: 1.5 feet per mile.

Land status: Unincorporated land.

Nearest town (or city): Andalusia.

Other users: Small fishing boats in the spring when the river is high.

Getting There: Put-in and Takeout Information

To shuttle point/takeout: From the intersection of U.S. Highway 29 and U.S. Highway 84 in Andalusia, take US 29 south 0.8 mile. Turn left onto County Road 58 (Prestwood Bridge Road). Travel down CR 58 for 1.9 miles. The pavement ends, and it becomes a dirt road. Continue straight an additional 0.2 mile. Just before the bridge, turn left onto a dirt road that circles underneath the bridge.

The road actually loops under the bridge and comes out on the other side. It is a gravel road with enough parking for maybe four to five cars at one time.

The takeout is directly under the bridge on the left side of the river. You have to scramble over some rocks used in the bridge construction; then it's a steep 75-foot climb up a sandy hill to the parking area.

To put-in from takeout: Turn left, and head back up CR 58 (Prestwood Bridge Road) 2.1 miles. Turn left onto US 29 north. Travel north on US 29 for 0.8 mile, and turn left onto US 84 west. Travel up US 84 west 3.1 miles. Turn right onto County Road 107. Almost immediately you will see a BOAT RAMP sign. Turn right here, and follow the dirt/gravel road straight 0.2 mile to the put-in.

The put-in is very nice. It is in a public boat ramp area and has an excellent 100-foot cement boat ramp on the upstream side of the bridge. You can drive your car right to the river, and there is plenty of parking in a grass field at the top of the hill next to the bridge.

Conecuh River

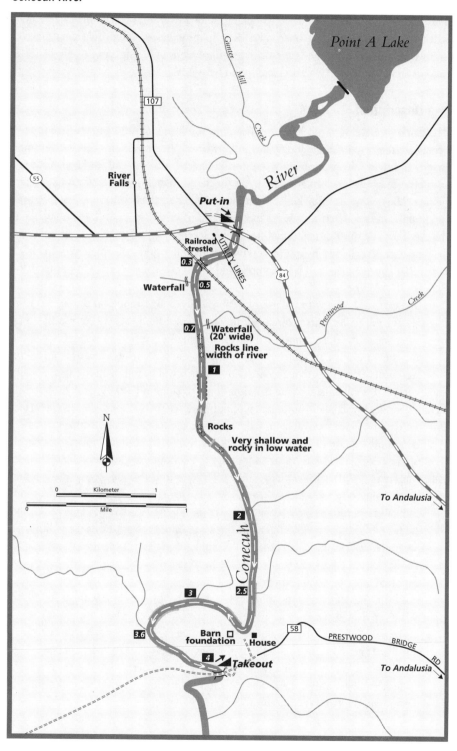

Trip Summary

This is a great little float trip if you're looking to hit a river for a quick one. Only 4 miles in length, this section of the Conecuh is a lazy trip through some beautiful scenery, including two waterfalls and some interesting rock formations. The trip can be lengthened to make it an 8.6-mile trip (see Trip Description below).

Trip Description

The Conecuh River is a wonderful trip from just south of Point "A" Lake (where this trip begins) all the way to the Florida panhandle (where it becomes known as the Escambia River), and then into Escambia Bay, eventually flowing into the Gulf of Mexico. Longer trips provide excellent overnight adventures for the paddler as the river heads 68 miles to Florida. The trip we describe here is a simple 4-miler, but it's good for just grabbing your canoe and paddle at short notice. It's especially nice if you have small children because of the easy flow, the short distance, and the sights to see.

The river actually begins in Pike County, many miles north of where we start. It is a rather low, narrow river until it is dammed and forms Gantt Lake and, a few miles below that, Point "A" Lake.

The Conecuh, along with the nearby Sepulga, have long histories in the state as commerce rivers. For many years before levels became too low and the Civil War came, these rivers were key routes of transportation for the thriving lumber industry.

From the start of the trip, the geology of the river and the many streams that feed the Conecuh paint a very picturesque scene. Two waterfalls will be found on this trip. The first comes at the 0.5 mile mark of the trip, just after crossing under the Louisville-Nashville Railroad trestle. It will be to your right and tumbles down the soft rock wall a good 50 feet. It's a pretty sight, and it's possible to walk under the fall under a small overhang.

The second fall comes at 0.7 mile, where Prestwood Creek flows into the Conecuh. This fall may not be seen if the water is too high. The mouth of Prestwood Creek and the fall spans about 100 feet in width. The fall is about 3 to 4 feet tall and spans the entire width of the intersection of the two rivers.

Wildflowers and flowering trees add color to the trip no matter what time of year you float the river. In the spring beautiful white dogwoods bloom along the banks. A little later in the year, the fragrant blooms of magnolias will be seen. And come the fall you can see plenty of black-eyed Susan and bristly locust, which was the first recorded American shrub to be exported and planted in Europe.

Another plus to this trip is the wildlife. The entire region is blessed with an abundance of it. While we floated the river, we twice saw white-tailed deer swimming across.

This area is a bird-watcher's paradise. Among some of the species that may be seen are osprey, mallard and wood ducks, northern pintail, wild turkey, and a variety of heron. And although they are a rare sight, bald eagles have been spotted here.

Finally, if you like to fish, then bring your rod (and fishing license) to catch wild river bass, bream, and the famous Conecuh River cats.

By the way, just to the north of the put-in is Point "A" Lake. This is an excellent lake for fishing, general boating, canoeing, swimming, and the like. There are also picnic areas and campgrounds.

For the truly adventurous, you could actually make the Conecuh a week-long adventure, paddling another 70 miles to just past the Florida state line and taking out at Florida State Road 4. But if you aren't *that* ambitious, a nice day-long trip would be to continue past the takeout we mention in this text and travel an additional 4.8 miles to a takeout at State Road 42. The lazy rolling waters of the Conecuh continue through swampland, but some additional nice falls will be seen as Bullpen Creek and Fall Creek flow into the river.

Trip Information

Season
Normally floatable all year. As with all Alabama rivers, the level can be quite low in late summer.

Fees/Permits
No fees to launch or float the river.

Local Information
Andalusia Chamber of Commerce
1208 West Bypass
Andalusia, AL 36420
(334) 222–2030
www.alaweb.com/~chamber/city.html

Local Events/Attractions
Three Notch Museum
Historic Central Street
Andalusia, AL 36420
(334) 222–0674
This museum is located in the historic Central of Georgia Railroad depot, which was built in 1899. The museum traces the agricultural and railroad history of the region. They are open Saturdays and Sundays and other days by appointment only. Admission is free.

Conecuh National Forest/Conecuh Trail
Conecuh National Forest Ranger Office
Andalusia, AL 36420
(334) 222–2555
A great weekend hiking experience awaits you on this 20-mile point-to-point trail. The walking is easy over rolling hillsides, through pastureland and pine forests, and past cypress swamps. Contact the ranger office for more information on the trail and restrictions during winter because of hunting.

Water falls into the Conecuh from Prestwood Creek.

Accommodations

Town Line Inn
1106 West Bypass (US 29)
Andalusia, AL 36420
(334) 222–3191

Restaurants

Crow's Nest
614 West Bypass (US 29)
Andalusia, AL 36420
(334) 222–4614

Organizations

Alabama River Alliance
700 28th Street Suite 202G
Birmingham, AL 35233
(205) 322–6395

South Alabama Birding Association
1040 Fort Dale Road
Greenville, AL 36037
(800) 382–2696
www.alaweb.com/~kenwood/saba/index.html

Other Resources

USGS Online River Gauge: waterdata.usgs.gov/al/nwis/uv?02372422

Wildflowers of Escambia County
c/o Darryl Searcy
HC–60, Box 36 E
Range, AL 36473
206.202.10.48/wildflowers
This site provides excellent slide shows of the flowers of the region.

Maps

USGS maps: River Falls, AL.
DeLorme: *Alabama Atlas & Gazetteer:* #58, C-5.

Tidbit

Alabama–The Facts:

- Became a state on 14 December 1819
- State bird: Yellowhammer
- State flower: Camellia
- State reptile: Red-hill salamander
- Highest point: Cheaha Mountain (2,407 feet)
- Lowest point: Sea level (Gulf of Mexico)
- Climate range: To the north in Birmingham: January—46 degrees F, July—80 degrees
  To the south in Mobile: January—52 degrees, July—85 degrees

▦ **12** Pea River

River Specs

County: Geneva.
Start: County Road 17.
End: Alabama Highway 87.
Length: 11.6 miles.
Approximate float time: Six hours.
Difficulty rating: Easy.
Rapids: None
River type: Float.
Current: Moderate to swift.
Minimum level: 6.2-foot stage.
Environment: Mix of longleaf and slash pines, magnolias, dogwoods, and wildflowers.
Elevation drop: 2.7 feet per mile.
Land status: Private property and unincorporated land.
Nearest town (or city): Geneva.
Other users: Anglers, small motorboats in higher water.

Getting There: Put-in and Takeout Information

To shuttle point/takeout: From the intersection of Alabama Highway 196 and Alabama Highway 27 in Geneva, take AL 27 south 4.8 miles to the Florida state line, where it becomes Florida Highway 185. Continue on FL 185 south 6.5 miles, and turn right onto Florida Highway 2A. Travel west on FL 2A for 8.8 miles, and turn right onto FL 2. Head north on Florida Highway 2 for 10 miles, where the road becomes Alabama Highway 87 at the Alabama state line. Continue north on AL 87 for 0.3 mile to the bridge over the Pea River. Cross the bridge, and make a right turn onto a gravel and pavement road that parallels the bridge on the east side. Follow the road 0.2 mile to a boat ramp at the end of the road. There is plenty of parking in the grassy area under the bridge and to the left of the ramp.

From the river, cross under the bridge. The boat ramp will be on the left.

To put-in from takeout: Follow the road to the boat ramp back to AL 87. Turn right, and head north 2.8 miles. Turn left onto River Road (this is a dirt road). Travel on River Road 5.7 miles until you come to the intersection with County Road 17 (a paved road). Cross CR 17, and follow the paved road on the opposite side. The road turns left and parallels CR 17 on the right side of the road as it makes its way 0.2 mile to the river and the boat ramp put-in.

The put-in is excellent, being located in a sport fish restoration site created by the state. There is parking for at least thirty vehicles in the paved lot. The put-in itself is a cement boat ramp to the river's edge.

Pea River

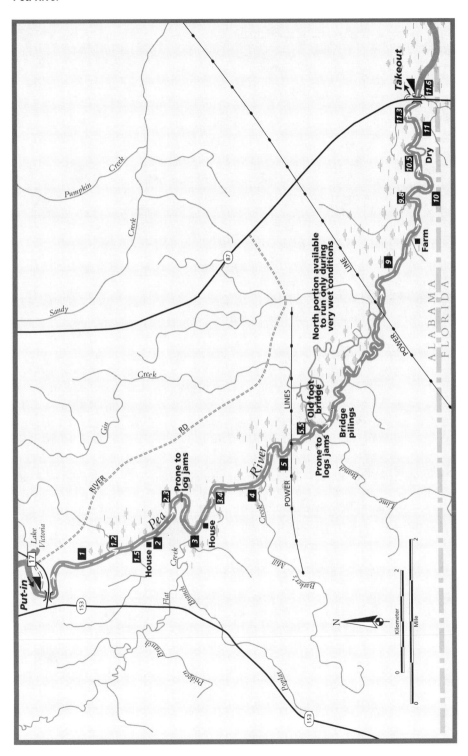

Trip Summary

The Pea River is a beautiful and historic river float trip. Along this stretch of the river, you will float through beautiful stands of pine and hardwood trees, and by dozens of nice sand beaches perfect for spending an afternoon. The banks are lined with beautiful cypress, beech, and sweet gum trees, plus a wide variety of wildflowers that bloom throughout the year.

Trip Description

The Pea River is aptly named. For the most part, its color is a deep pea green, caused mostly by the thick moss and algae growth beneath the surface.

The Pea begins far north of here in Bullock County near Union Springs, Alabama. From here, it widens as it flows freely to the town of Geneva (just east of this trip), where it joins with the Choctawhatchee River and eventually flows into the Gulf of Mexico.

Overall this is a moderate-flowing river that requires only a minimum amount of paddling to get to where you're going. You'll find yourself easily averaging 2 miles an hour.

There are plenty of opportunities to stop and relax, catch lunch, or maybe take a swim from one of the many sandbars along the way. Remember, however, that some of the land is private property. Respect the signs!

Along this stretch of the Pea, there are two areas that are prone to logjams. One comes at mile 2.4, the other at mile 5.6. We found it easier to pull our boat over the logs than to portage it around the jams through the thick vegetation-covered banks.

There are also two areas of note marked on topographic maps and indicated on our maps. At mile 5.5 the river appears to Y. The right fork is the main river channel. The left fork has been dry for *many* years, and who knows if it will ever fill with water enough to float again? You can get out of your boat here and take a look around. The sand in the split forms what looks almost like an alluvial fan. The beach is deep and white as you walk inland, and 0.1 mile up this fork you will see an old footbridge spanning the dry riverbed. Continue floating the river down the right fork, and eventually, after paddling almost 3 miles, you will float past the area where the two forks would remerge.

The other area is at approximately mile 10.5. The river appears on maps to form an island here. It may be possible to float the southern half of the loop around this island during higher water; however in low water the split in the river can't even be seen. The best bet is to float the north side. In 0.2 mile you will come to the end of the island, and at this junction, even in low water, you'll be able to see the junction with a huge sandbar dividing the two splits, and a decent flow of water coming in from the west.

Your usual fare of birds—osprey, hawks, heron, etc.—will be seen, as well as wood ducks. There are plenty of turtles sunning on downed trees and along the riverbank. The Pea and its surrounding drainage basin are also known for freshwater mussels. Unfortunately, out of the twenty-six species found here, twelve are on the endangered species list.

What on Earth Is "Worm Fiddling"?

When we researched and floated the Pea River, we came across a term we had never heard before: worm fiddling. What the . . . ? This called for more investigation!

Worm fiddling, also known in different regions as worm snoring and worm doodling, is the art of bringing worms out of the earth to be used for fishing. There are various methods for doing this. One is to plunge a pitchfork into the ground and "twang" the handle protruding from the ground. The vibrations drive the worms to the surface.

Another method is to cut a sapling down to about 2 feet tall. The fiddler then takes a handsaw and cuts through the stalk sticking up from the ground. Again, the vibrations drive the worms to the surface.

If you would like to see worm fiddling at its finest, visit the town of Geneva's Festival of the Rivers (see Local Events/Attractions), during which a worm-fiddling contest is held.

Trip Information

Contact

Choctawhachee, Pea, and Yellow Rivers Watershed Management Authority (CPYRWMA)
400 Pell Avenue
Collegeview Building
Troy, AL 36082
(800) 652–2019, (334) 670–3780

Season

Floatable most of the year, but again, late-summer droughts can cause some bottom dragging.

Fees/Permits

There is no fee to launch or float the river.

Local Information

Greater Geneva Chamber of Commerce
517 South Commerce Street
Geneva, AL 36340
(334) 684–6582
www.genevaalabama.com

The placid Pea River protected from wind by tall trees on a November day.

Local Events/Attractions

Festival on the Rivers (last weekend in April)
517 South Commerce Street
Geneva, AL 36340
(334) 684–6582
www.genevaalabama.com/riverfestival.html
A packed weekend is in store, dedicated to celebrating the rivers—the Pea and Choctawhatchee. Contests include the world championship sculling contest, canoe race, and worm fiddling (see sidebar). The festival includes food, arts and crafts, and entertainment, including some big names in country music.

Accommodations

Live Oaks Bed and Breakfast
307 South Academy Street
Geneva, AL 36340
(334) 684–2489

Restaurants
Two Rivers Restaurant
105 Washington Avenue
Geneva, AL 36340
(334) 684–8188

Organizations
Pea River Historical Society
108 South Main Street
Enterprise, AL 36330
(334) 393–2901
www.rootsweb.com/~alprhgs

Other Resources
USGS River Gauge online for Pea River at Elba, AL:
www.dalmtg.er.usgs.gov/rt-cgi/gen_stn_pg?station=02364000

Maps
USGS maps: Hobbs Crossroads, Samson, Darlington, AL.
DeLorme: *Alabama Atlas & Gazetteer:* #59, F-10, G-10.

13 Sepulga River

River Specs

County: Conecuh.
Start: U.S. Highway 31.
End: U.S. Highway 84.
Length: 6.8 miles.
Approximate float time: Four hours.
Difficulty rating: Easy.
Rapids: Class I.
River type: Float/white water.
Current: Swift.
Environment: Lush forest of weeping willow, catalpa, scrub pine, and oaks.
Elevation drop: 2.9 feet per mile.
Land status: Unincorporated.
Nearest town (or city): Evergreen.
Other users: None.

Getting There: Put-in and Takeout Information

To shuttle point/takeout: Take exit 93 from I–65 at Evergreen. Follow U.S. Highway 84 east 0.7 mile to the junction of U.S. Highway 31 north. Travel on US 31 north/US 84 east 9.2 miles. The highway comes to a Y. Take the right fork (this is where US 84 and US 31 separate). Continue on US 84 east 8 miles. The takeout is a small, barely noticeable dirt road just before the bridge on the right. This is a narrow, sandy, 0.2-mile, one-lane road that ends at a moderate-sized grassy parking area beneath the US 84 bridge.

Locating the takeout from the river is easy enough. You must pass under the US 84 bridge (the only one on this trip) and start making a right bend. A narrow sand beach will be seen to the right. The takeout here is a steep 20- to 30-foot climb up a sandy hillside. The parking area is directly at the top of the climb.

To put-in from takeout: Travel up the dirt road from the takeout 0.2 mile to US 84. Make a left, and head north on US 84 for 4 miles. Make a right turn onto County Road 63, and travel 3.5 miles to the intersection of US 31. Make a right turn, and travel 0.1 mile on US 31 north. You will pass over the Travis Bridge. The road to the put-in is a dirt road on the left immediately after you cross the bridge. It can have large gullies after a good rain, so keep that in mind. Travel 0.1 mile down the road to a large grass parking area under the US 31 bridge.

The put-in here is a short, moderate 20-foot descent down a sandy hill to the riverbank. The launch area is narrow but relatively level and provides a nice put-in.

Sepulga River

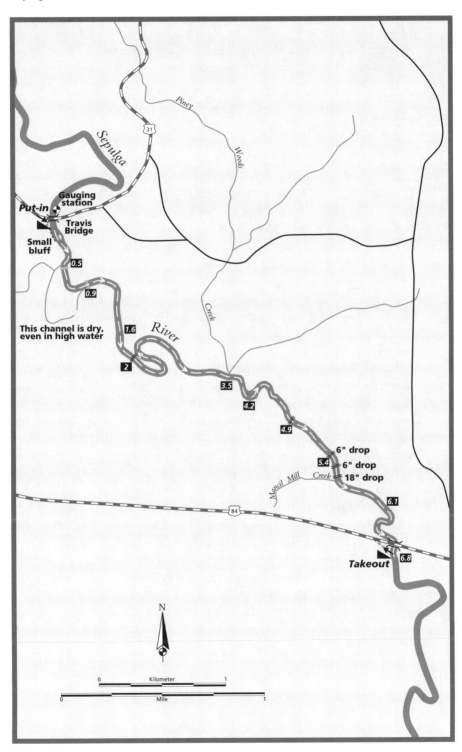

Trip Summary

The Sepulga is an interesting river in that it is generally a nice float trip through lush forest of magnolia, weeping willows, oak, and scrub pine. But unlike many rivers south of Montgomery, it has a few fast shoals to maneuver through, as well as a great Class I section with a series of drops that can be easily handled by beginners and intermediate paddlers.

Trip Description

Before researching this book, we had only *heard* of the Sepulga. Most of our paddling friends had never heard of it or didn't know anyone who had paddled it. We had heard tales of people growing up along the river and swimming in its muddy waters, or stories about their grandparents who worked on paddleboats that would move cargo and people up and down its length to the gulf in days long gone, but that was the extent of it.

So there we were, sitting around one rainy Sunday thinking about a river that we could do that was fairly close by, and we said, what the heck, let's give it a try. It proved to be a great decision. We found a river with lots of surprises.

The Sepulga begins its flow near Midway. The entire river flows more than 40 miles before it joins with the Conecuh River and eventually flows into Florida and then into the Gulf of Mexico. Throughout the trip the river runs between 30 and 40 feet in width with a very swift current.

As with most rivers in the region, the banks are low—about 5 to 10 feet high—and moderately steep. There are few places to put ashore, with the occasional sand bank or trail to pull up to. The banks are lined with thick brush and forest, including hickory, dogwood, magnolia, and longleaf pine trees. Catalpa trees, with fruit that resembles very long green beans dangling from the branches, will be seen frequently. In the spring and summer, black-eyed Susans add color to the banks and reflect brilliantly off the muddy brown water.

Watch the skies as you paddle this river for interesting birds, including blue herons and a wide variety of woodpeckers, such as the red-cockaded woodpecker, which is making a dramatic comeback in the area after being placed on the endangered species list.

What makes the river interesting is that besides the long, peaceful stretches of float time, there are numerous shoals and, yes, a couple of nice Class I rapids. Some of the small shoals turn into rapids during high water, including those at mile 2.

There is also a Class I rapid at about the 5-mile mark. The best set on the river is a group of three at mile 5.4. As this trip nears its end, two creeks, including Mancil Mill Creek, add to the flow. The first two rapids have 6-inch drops, whereas the third has a 2 foot drop. During times of high water, the last rapid has some great standing waves.

And there's one more important fact about the Sepulga: The water level is usually high enough to float most any time of the year.

Trip Information

Season
Year-round.

Fees/Permits
No fee or permit required to paddle the river or put in and take out.

Local Information
Evergreen/Conecuh County Chamber of Commerce
100 Depot Square
Evergreen, AL 36401
(251) 578–1707
www.evergreenal.com

Local Events/Attractions
Lucky 3 Ranch
Route 1
Evergreen, AL 36401
(251) 578–5000
The kids will love this ranch-style stable with zebras, donkeys, plenty of horses, and more.
Admission is free. Open during daylight hours.

Booker's Mill
CR 21, Route 2
Evergreen, AL 36401
(251) 578–1681
This is a beautiful 1887 log cabin homestead demonstrating life during the period. There
are nature trails, a gristmill, a cotton gin, and a waterfall. Admission is free.

Accommodations
Evergreen Inn
Highway 83
Evergreen, AL 36401
(251) 578–5500

Raindrops appear on the water's surface during a light sprinkle.

Restaurants

Zack's Restaurant
US Highway 31
Evergreen, AL 36401
(251) 578–2005

Organizations

Conecuh/Sepulga Watershed Alliance
PO Box 2792
Brooklyn, AL 36429
(251) 867–2445
www.ag.auburn.edu/grassroots/cswa

Maps

USGS maps: Old Town, AL/Brooks, AL.
DeLorme: *Alabama Atlas & Gazetteer:* #58, A-3, B-3.

West Fork of the Choctawhatchee River

River Specs

County: Dale.

Start: Alabama Highway 27.

End: U.S. Highway 231.

Length: 5.7 miles.

Approximate float time: Two and one-half hours.

Difficulty rating: Easy.

Rapids: None.

River type: Float. A few quick white water shoals add excitement.

Current: Moderate.

Environment: Low limestone bluffs with banks lined with cypress, sweet gum, beech, and long leaf and slash pines.

Elevation drop: 2.3 feet per mile.

Land status: Unincorporated county land, private property.

Nearest town (or city): Dothan.

Other users: Motorboats, anglers, and hunters.

Getting There: Put-in and Takeout Information

To shuttle point/takeout: From the intersection of U.S. Highway 84 (not Business 84) and U.S. Highway 231 in Dothan, take US 231 north for 11.1 miles. Turn left off of US 231 just before the bridge. There is a nice gravel road that you can follow for about 0.1 mile to get close to the river. The best spot to take out is on this side (downstream) of the dual bridge spans (beneath the southbound span). You can drop your boat off here, but the only decent parking spot is to cross underneath the spans and park in one of just two or three spots as the gravel road turns right back toward the south. Any way you slice it, this is a pretty tricky takeout, but definitely doable. Taking out, there are large rocks (averaging about 1 foot in diameter) to scale from the river for about 40 feet at a 45-degree grade. You will then need to carry your boat across another 40 feet or so of the same rocks over level ground.

To put-in from takeout: Take US 231 north 1.1 miles, and turn right onto County Road 18. Travel 3.3 miles, and turn right onto AL 27. Travel 0.1 mile, and turn right onto a dirt road that runs parallel to the highway and leads to the downstream side of the river next to the bridge. There is good parking, and the put-in is a flat beach.

Trip Summary

One of the best things about the West Fork of the Choctawhatchee River for paddlers is that there are multiple easy bridge-access spots. The West Fork of the Choctawhatchee runs through formations of a soft chalklike rock called soapstone. Erosion has formed minia-ture caves in the soapstone bluffs. Beautiful fern glades grow out from the soft rock. The

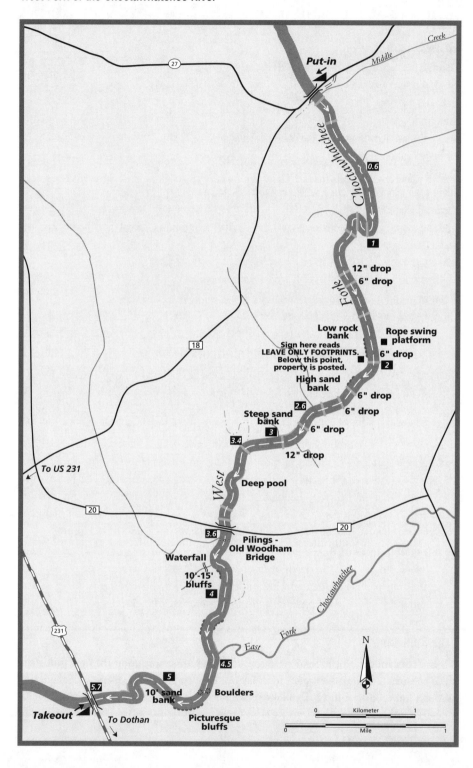

current, even at relatively high water levels, is slow, but there are a few white water shoals—uncommon in this region—along the way to keep you from getting too relaxed.

Trip Description

The West Fork of the Choctawhatchee River begins in Barbour County at the confluence of Jackson Creek and Pauls Creek, then flows south until it meets the East Fork in Dale County, where those forks meet to become the Choctawhatchee. The total length of the West Fork from top to bottom is about 35 miles. The southernmost section described here is 5.7 miles.

The rich soils on the bluffs surrounding the river are covered with hardwood stands known as beech-magnolia forests. These forests have an abundance of the evergreen southern magnolia and American beech. They also contain a great diversity of trees, both deciduous and evergreen, such as laurel oak, basswood, Florida maple, and American holly. These stands of trees contain more species of trees than any other forest type in temperate North America, including a southern relative of the white pine called spruce pine. Two of Alabama's palm species are found here: the dwarf palmetto and the needle palm. At some places they form a thick understory—a thick vegetative layer between the forest canopy and the ground cover—giving the forest a tropical jungle atmosphere.

Right off the bat as you begin the southeasterly trip, Middle Creek, a small tributary, flows in on the left just about 500 feet from the put-in. Immediately after that is a shoal about 75 yards long. We floated at low water, and the floatable path was on the right, but at average water levels the entire width would be achievable. You'll then encounter two more smaller shoals.

Mile 0.6 brings you to a nice unnamed stream on the left. Then, just before mile 1, approaching a hard right bend, there is another rocky shoal leading into the bend, with lots of rocks in the middle. The river turns toward the northwest, then turns back with a hard left bend toward the south. During the S formed at these turns, you'll see two more streams entering the main river; on the left, then on the right. The second stream is a pretty sight, with water cascading down rock a few feet high, then spreading and spilling into the West Fork. Just 20 feet past the stream is a small wide shoal stretching across river. Soon after there are two more shoals with about a 1-foot drop and a 6-inch drop, respectively.

During a south-southeasterly straightaway before mile 2, there is a picnic area with a pavilion and a couple of picnic tables off to the right up a high clear bank. There is a sign here reminding people to keep the place clean by leaving only footprints. This may be private property where paddlers are welcome to take a break as long as they are quiet and play by the rules. Directly across, however, on the other side of the river, are PRIVATE PROPERTY and NO TRESPASSING signs. Continuing on this straight shot, you'll flow down three more small shoals.

Just after mile 2, you'll bend right toward the southwest. During the next mile there are three streams, all on the right. You may not even be able to see some of these during dry conditions. After mile 3, you'll bend left to head due south. At the end of this bend is a small pool. Soon you will approach many pilings and the County Road 20 bridge.

Directly under the bridge is a shoal. After crossing under the bridge, there are some striated formations of rocks on the banks, a rare sight on this river. Soon after, on the right, a wonderful unmarked stream gushes down rocks 4 feet high.

You may find a few downed trees during the next stretch. There was easy passage around the trees at the time we ran the river. After mile 4, there are some flat beaches on the inside of the bends. At mile 4.5, the East Fork of the Choctawhatchee merges with the West Fork to become the Choctawhatchee. You'll find that when you continue, the current slows, the river widens to about 50 feet, and the bottom and banks become more sandy. There are some large boulders forming parts of the bluffs.

The final section before the takeout is marked with two streams cutting in sand ridges about 30 feet high on the left side. The streams themselves are only a couple feet in width, but the Spanish moss–filled trees on the steep banks that they have sliced are a fine-looking sight.

The takeout is on the left at the US 231 bridge. The easiest climb up is beneath the southbound span. Overall, the West Fork makes a good river for those who enjoy a normally slow float, with a little added excitement from the easy shoals.

Trip Information

Contact
Choctawhachee, Pea, and Yellow Rivers Watershed Management Authority (CPYRWMA)
400 Pell Avenue
Collegeview Building
Troy, AL 36082
(800) 652–2019, (334) 670–3780

Season
Year-round.

Fees/Permits
There is no fee to launch or float the river.

Local Information
Dothan Area Chamber of Commerce
440 Honeysuckle Road
P.O. Box 638
Dothan, AL 36305
(334) 792–5138, (800) 221–1027
www.dothan.com

A small waterfall.

Dothan Area Convention and Visitors Bureau
3311 Ross Clark Circle, NW
P.O. Box 8765
Dothan, AL 36304
(334) 794–6622, (888) 449–0212
www.dothanalcvb.com

Local Events/Attractions
The Wiregrass Festival of Murals
3311 Ross Circle NW
Dothan, AL 36304
(888) 449–0212, (334) 793–3097
The historic downtown district of Dothan has been transformed into an ecomuseum of history and local culture. Walk among these giant works of art, and you'll see how people, places, and events shaped this area.

Accommodations

Comfort Inn
3593 Ross Clark Circle
Dothan, AL 36303
(800) 474–7298, (334) 793–9090
Recipient of the Gold Award for Hospitality for the past ten consecutive years and one of the Top Five Comfort Inns in the United States in 1999.

Adams Inn
3145 Montgomery Highway
Dothan, AL 36303
(334) 793–4557

Restaurants

Basketcase Café
228 South Oates Street
Dothan, AL 36301
(334) 671–1117

Organizations

Alabama River Alliance
2027 2nd Avenue North, Suite A
Birmingham, AL 35203
(205) 322–6395
www.alabamarivers.org

Other Resources

USGS River Gauge Online for Choctawhatchee River near Newton, AL:
waterdata.usgs.gov/al/nwis/uv?02361000

Maps

USGS maps: Pinckard/Ewell, AL.
DeLorme: *Alabama Atlas & Gazetteer:* #60, B-5.

Tidbit

Approximately half the peanuts grown in the United States are grown within a 100-mile radius of Dothan, Alabama. The National Peanut Festival, the nation's largest peanut festival, is held in Dothan every year to honor peanut growers and celebrate the harvest season. The event brings more than 120,000 guests to the area.

⊞ 15 Yellow River

River Specs

County: Covington.
Start: Alabama Highway 55.
End: County Road 4.
Length: 12.7 miles.
Approximate float time: Five to seven hours.
Difficulty rating: Easy.
Rapids: None.
River type: Blackwater.
Current: Slow to moderate.
Environment: Evergreen and mixed forest.
Elevation drop: 2.3 feet per mile.
Land status: National Forest, Wildlife Management Area.
Nearest town (or city): Florala.
Other users: Hunters, anglers.

Getting There: Put-in and Takeout Information

To shuttle point/takeout: From the intersection of U.S. Highway 331 and Alabama Highway 55 in Florala, take AL 55 north 2 miles. Turn left onto County Road 4. Head west on CR 4 for 11.2 miles. Turn left before the bridge onto a dirt road that leads to a public boat ramp. Plenty of good parking is available.

To put-in from takeout: Go back to CR 4 and turn left, heading east 4 miles. Turn left onto CR 20. Travel 6.1 miles, and turn left onto Yellow River Ranch Road. Follow Yellow River Ranch Road 1.4 miles to AL 55. Turn left, and head north on AL 55, 0.3 mile to the bridge. Cross the bridge, and turn left, making your way back toward the river for about 0.2 mile. The regular path becomes somewhat rutted, but you may be able to navigate even a compact car close to the water's edge by rolling over hard-packed sand covered with grass. The put-in itself is a nearly flat beach.

Trip Summary

The Yellow River is another example of a blackwater run typical in the southeast region. The run is slow for the most part, with one quick stretch just past the halfway point. Wildlife enthusiasts will love the vast array of fauna evident here; the huge variety of birds is an ornithologist's delight. In the forest along the river are white-tailed deer, Eastern wild turkeys, bobcats, fox, river otters, alligators, and many species of snakes.

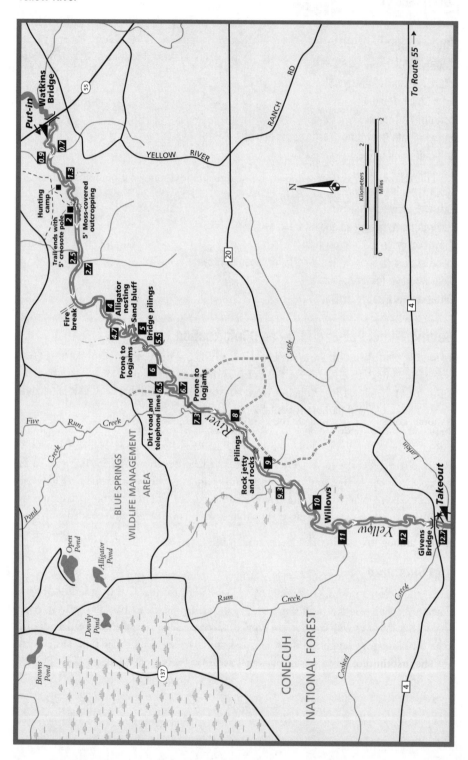

Trip Description

The Yellow River is another river in the southeast region of Alabama that is highly subject to water levels. Recently a rainfall and river stage gauging station was set up at the put-in bridge on AL 55. The gauge has become a part of a basinwide flood warning system operated and maintained by the Choctawhatchee, Pea, and Yellow Rivers Watershed Management Authority. In addition to providing paddlers with needed information, this gauge provides two main functions: first, to keep a history of the levels there; and second, to prepare local officials with advance notice so they can warn citizens in that area and those who are using that route as an evacuation route. Previously the Yellow River was the largest river in Alabama without monitoring gauges.

The Yellow River is widely known as one in its natural state—an outdoors enthusiast's paradise. Anglers love the abundance of fish found here, which include largemouth bass, catfish, and bream. At several places along the river, you'll paddle by pools and see lures caught on brush along the banks, telltale evidence of good fishing spots. Covington County is the home of numerous outdoor recreational facilities, including Point "A" Lake, Open Pond, Gantt Lake, and Blue Lake. The Yellow River itself runs through the Conecuh National Forest and the Blue Springs Wildlife Management Area. It begins near Rose Hill, in the very northern section of Covington County, about 5 miles east of Gantt Lake; makes its way south and southwest; and finally flows into Blackwater Bay, about 20 miles northeast of Pensacola, Florida.

The Conecuh National Forest, one of four national forests in Alabama, has a distinct southern flavor of hardwood swamps, pitcher-plant bogs, and southern coastal plain pine forest. These coastal plains are also home to longleaf pine, upland scrub oak, and dogwood, as well as to an aquatic labyrinth of winding creeks and cypress ponds. The Conecuh National Forest was clear-cut in the 1930s, then later reforested with slash pine, which reduced the number of nesting trees for the endangered red-cockaded woodpecker. The forest is currently undergoing a reforestation from slash pine to the native longleaf. As the trees mature over time, this should increase the number of red-cockaded woodpeckers. Yellow River actually forms the eastern boundary of the forest for several miles. The forest provides opportunities for camping, fishing, boating, swimming, picnicking, hiking, backpacking, mountain biking, and hunting. The well-known 20-mile Conecuh Trail, a favorite among hikers, also meanders through this forest.

The put-in at AL 55 is a flat beach and a very easy start to the trip. The width here is about 40 feet. The entire stretch of this 12.7-mile section ranges from about 30 to 80 feet wide. The overall current flow is fairly slow, with one exception: right before Five Runs Creek enters just past mile 7. The first part of this swift water is filled with small trees, then opens up for a clear, quick, 100-yard run, ending where Five Runs Creek flows in on the right. Five Runs Creek runs through the middle of Blue Springs Wildlife Management Area.

The first third of this trip is open, with low banks and beaches on the inside of bends. The middle third is a little more rocky on the bottom, with the banks and trees reaching higher. The final third is similar to the first.

Most likely, you will have to portage around or over a few logjams. The close proximity of pine trees to the water makes the river prone to jams. At the time we ran this section,

A close-up of some interesting rock formations.

we had to get around three. The good news is that the jams are periodically cleared with chainsaws, so there is rarely a large buildup of trees and debris.

There are also several spots where you'll notice vehicle access to the river's edge. These spots are where anglers reach the water to throw in a line. There is also a popular place just after mile 8 where there is a deep pool with a wooden diving platform. This area is rather special, highlighted by a few small streams, with one stream flowing into the Yellow through a small cave set in the clay bank.

After this middle third of the river, you'll notice that the environment begins to appear more like the first third. The banks and bottom become sandy again, and there are low beaches around the bends. There is nothing very exciting left for the remainder of the trip, but you probably will see more wildlife . . . maybe a group of turkey vultures perched high in tree limbs.

From a hard-core paddler's perspective, the Yellow River is not real exciting. But if it's nature you love and want to take a quiet trip, easy access both on and off make this river a good choice.

Trip Information

Contact

Choctawhachee, Pea, and Yellow Rivers Watershed Management Authority (CPYRWMA)
400 Pell Avenue
Collegeview Building
Troy, AL 36082
(800) 652–2019, (334) 670–3780

Season

Year-round.

Fees/Permits

There is no fee to put in or paddle the river.

Local Information

Florala Chamber of Commerce
405 South 5th Street, Suite 100
Florala, AL 36442
(334) 858–6252

Accommodations

The Lake House Bed and Breakfast
1109 East 5th Avenue
Florala, AL 36442
(334) 858–2070

Florala State Park
P.O. Box 322
Florala, AL 36442
(334) 858–6425
Located along beautiful Lake Jackson, this 40-acre park offers swimming, fishing, a community building, campground, and picnic area along the shore.

Restaurants

Westside Café
1638 West 5th Avenue
Florala, AL 36442
(334) 858–7827

Organizations

Choctawhatchee, Pea, and Yellow Rivers Watershed Management Authority
  (CPYRWMA)
400 Fell Avenue
Troy, AL 36082
(800) 652–2019, (334) 670–3780

Maps

USGS maps: Watkins Bridge, AL/Givens Bridge, AL.
DeLorme: *Alabama Atlas & Gazetteer:* #59, F-6, G-5.

Tidbit

Lake Jackson, in Florala, was named for President Andrew Jackson and his 1,200 soldiers who spent three weeks on the shores of its pristine waters. It is Alabama's largest natural lake.

Central Region

The white water begins to froth in the central region. It is here that we begin to see some substance to the white water adventures. The rivers are narrow and have cut through the rocky terrain over the centuries, creating some great shoals, falls, and rapids up to Class III.

Among the highlight trips in this region is the Coosa River near Jordan Dam. There is a classic kayak training run here—Moccasin Gap, where the river funnels down narrow chutes and creates an outstanding Class III run that is actually navigable by beginners. This river has recreational flows released by Alabama Power through Jordan Dam, giving us a rare white water ride through late summer.

Another pair of fun runs in the region is the Hatchet North and Weogufka. These rivers are overloaded with fast shoals and plenty of wild Class I rapids.

Nearby is the Little Cahaba River. Not only does this river have a great swimming hole—McGuire's Ford, which is nestled in the midst of huge rock cliffs—but also a Class III rapid that includes a 3-foot fall. Again, this is runnable by beginners and is a rush for paddlers of any ability.

With the Tallapoosa River run, we've added a little bit of history to our trips in this region. This trip takes us to Horseshoe Bend National Park, the site of the famous battle between Native Americans and General Andrew Jackson in 1814. Following an uprising by a renegade band of Native Americans, which resulted in the massacre of a settlement near the town of Bay Minette, General Jackson retaliated with an attack at this location. The victory for Jackson resulted in the turning over of what amounted to thousands of acres of Native American land to the federal government and the removal of the tribes from the region in what became known as the Trail of Tears.

The weather plays an important factor when planning a trip to the central region. The best times to run these rivers is during the winter and spring, when runoff from the winter snows and spring rains give us high water and wild rides. The heat of summer, however, causes most of the rivers in the region to run to a trickle. Keep an eye on the river gauges (we provide Web sites where you can see them online). Those sudden and heavy thunderstorms the south is known for provide spikes in the flows. Suddenly an unrunnable river gives you a unique summer white water run.

16 Coosa River

River Specs

County: Elmore.

Start: Jordan Dam.

End: Company Road/Coosa River Adventures.

Length: 6.8 miles.

Approximate float time: Three to four hours.

Difficulty rating: Moderate.

Rapids: Class I to Class III.

River type: White water.

Current: Fast.

Environment: A combination of wide, flat-water floating and Class I to Class III rapids set in thick forests with scenic rock outcroppings and islands.

Elevation drop: 3.2 feet per mile except at Moccasin Gap where the river drops 30 feet in 0.7 mile.

Land status: A mix of private and Alabama Power land to the left, and private and public land to the right.

Nearest town (or city): Wetumpka.

Other users: Motor boats, anglers.

Getting There: Put-in and Takeout Information

To shuttle point/takeout: Take I–65 north 9 miles to exit 181 (Wetumpka/County Road 14) north of Montgomery. Travel on CR 14 east 2.3 miles. Make a right turn (still on CR 14). Continue 4.3 miles, and make a left at the intersection, continuing on CR 14 east. Travel 1 mile, and come to a stoplight. Continue straight on CR 14. In 1.3 miles, make a right turn at the light. Stay in the right lane (turning lane). This now becomes Company Street. Continue 1.3 miles. Coosa River Adventures is on the right in a small white building with a sign next to the road.

The takeout is located just after the last set of islands. You will see the historic Bibb Graves bridge with its five arches farther down. A small set of rapids will be encountered as you pass the right side of the islands. Make an immediate left turn after passing the islands, and you will see the white COOSA RIVER ADVENTURE sign on the left shore. There is a wooden dock here perfect for landing.

To put-in from takeout: From Coosa River Adventures, turn left onto Company Street, and head 1.3 miles to U.S. Highway 231. At the light, make a left turn onto US 231 north. Travel 3.5 miles, and turn left onto County Road 667 (a sign on the right side of US 231 points to the left and says JORDAN DAM at the turn). Travel 2.5 miles to a Y in the road.

Coosa River

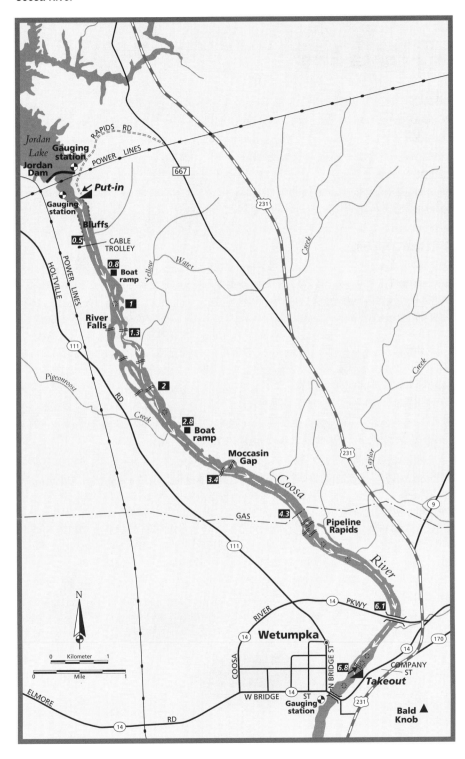

Jordan Lake

Gauging station

Jordan Dam

Gauging station

Put-in

RAPIDS RD

POWER LINES

667

231

Creek

Yellow

Water

Bluffs

0.5

CABLE TROLLEY

0.8 ■ Boat ramp

1

HOLTVILLE

POWER LINES

River Falls

1.3

111

Pigeonroost

RD

Creek

2

2.8 ■ Boat ramp

3.4

Moccasin Gap

Coosa

GAS

4.3

Pipeline Rapids

Taylor

Creek

9

River

111

N

Kilometer

0   1

Mile

0   1

RIVER

14

Wetumpka

14

COOSA

N BRIDGE ST

6.1

PKWY

14

6.8

Takeout

COMPANY ST

14

170

ELMORE

RD

14

W BRIDGE

14 ST

Gauging station

231

Bald Knob ▲

Take the left fork. Continue 0.75 mile, and make a left turn onto the dirt road called RAPIDS ROAD. Follow the dirt road as it winds down to the bank of the river. Jordan Dam will be to the right of the put-in.

The put-in is a very nice, gentle slope with plenty of parking. The landing is clay/dirt with excellent footing.

Trip Summary

A fun white water trip if ever there was one. The water from Jordan Dam is regulated for recreational use during the summer months, providing deep water, but there's plenty of white water, including the challenging Class III Moccasin Gap. Although intimidating to look at, most of the rapids are manageable for novice to intermediate paddlers at up to 8,000 cfs flow. The banks are lined with oaks, magnolia, dogwood, azaleas, and interesting rock formations, including dozens of islands for stopping and relaxing in the middle of the river.

Trip Description

The town of Wetumpka is best known for the Coosa River, which is just plain and simply a fun river. For the most part the river is wide—300 feet in some areas—with rock bluffs and outcroppings. The banks are generally steep and thick in brush (and harbor a variety of snakes), but there are plenty of rock islands along the way to stop and have lunch.

Through the hard work and effort of the Coosa River Paddling Club, an agreement was reached with the Alabama Power Company to open Jordan Dam to provide recreational flows seasonally as follows: 8,000 cfs from 6:00 A.M. to 12:00 P.M. every day in April and May; 4,000 to 8,000 cfs on weekends from June through October; and special releases of 10,000 cfs on Memorial Day, Fourth of July, Labor Day, and for the annual white water Festival. Normal flows are at 2,000 to 4,000 cfs. This is obviously a favorite training ground for kayakers.

Despite the Class III rapids at Moccasin Gap, plenty of families come out to try their hand at the river. Generally the water is deep during recreational flows, so a mishap at one of the rapids results in no more than a red face. But, as always, follow the safety tips we outlined earlier in the book.

The running of the river is a nice mixture of wide, flat water with three distinct sets of rapids ranging from Class I to Class III. When you first put in, paddle to midstream for a great view of Jordan Dam. From here you will pass through some very scenic rock bluffs with one particularly impressive rock to your immediate left. You will also pass your first set of rock islands.

After 0.5 mile you will pass under an old cable and trolley that spans the width of the river, which is more than 300 feet at this point. At 1.3 miles you will come to your first set of rapids, known as River Falls. This is a series of small islands with trees and rocks. The river narrows here and provides three sets of Class I and Class II rapids on either side of the islands. The main thing to remember is to avoid the extreme left and right banks. The water becomes shallow here, with stumps and jagged rocks under the surface. This is a prime area to meet a snake in the low-hanging tree branches.

The river widens following the islands and once again becomes a float trip for 1.4 miles. You will pass a boat ramp on your left and start to hear the roar of Moccasin Gap. The gap comes at the midway point of the trip, about 3.4 miles into it. Two large rock islands form the gap. To the left side are Class II rapids; to the right, Class III. If you feel the rapids on either side may be too much for you, paddle hard straight down the center to the island where you can take out and portage to the other side.

Otherwise either side provides a wild ride. Most everybody tries his or her hand at the Class III side. The water rushes to the right of the island. Paddle hard and straight to the right of the island, and you'll be through. Two rocks form a chute to the right of the main route. Again, if you find yourself veering to the right through this chute, paddle hard straight through and you will make it; otherwise you will be broadsided by the wave.

After surviving Moccasin Gap (there are shirts available that say this), the river turns once again into a float trip for the next mile. (If you do turn over in the gap, unless you have someone to help you out, you'll have to float a little way down the river for a place to take out and flip your boat over.)

At 4.3 miles you will pass over an underriver gas pipeline and in 0.1 mile reach the third set of rapids known as the Pipeline. Again, these rapids are formed by several rock islands and provide excellent Class I and Class II rapids, depending on the flow of the river. There is no right or wrong way through, but you will have to do a bit more maneuvering through this set than at Rapid Falls.

Finally, at 6.1 miles, you will cross under the towering Alabama 14 bridge. Another 0.5 mile later a series of small islands will be on your left. Don't try to paddle the extreme left side or through the islands. The water gets shallow through here. Continue to the end of the islands, where a small set of Class I rapids stretches across the river before you. Make a left turn here, and you will see the takeout with a white COOSA RIVER ADVENTURE sign and a wooden landing dock.

Trip Information

Contact

Coosa River Adventures
415 Company Street
Wetumpka, AL 36092
(334) 514–0279
www.coosariveradventures.com
Be sure to sit and talk with the owner Jerry about the river and the colorful locals after your trip (see Fees/Permit information below).

Season

River runs year-round, with higher recreational flows (8,000 cfs +) beginning mid-May; otherwise minimum water release is 2,000 cfs.

Fees/Permits
No fees to put in or take out unless using Coosa River Adventures. They charge $8.00 to shuttle to the put-in, $30.00 to rent a canoe, and $20.00 to rent a kayak. They do not charge for parking.

Local Information
Wetumpka Chamber of Commerce
110 East Bridge Street
Wetumpka, AL 36092
(334) 567–4811
www.wetumpkachamber.com

Local Events/Attractions
Jasmine Hill Garden
3001 Jasmine Hill Road
Wetumpka, AL 36903
(334) 567–6483
www.jasminehill.org
Year-round floral beauty in what has been called "Alabama's little Greece" is in store at this garden. Twenty acres of flowers and reproduction Greek statues keep visitors coming back time and time again.

Coosa River Whitewater Festival (May and October)
c/o Southern Trails Inc.
5143 Atlanta Highway
Montgomery, AL 36109
(334) 272–0952
This is a semiannual event for kayakers. Jordan Dam is opened to 10,000 cfs and the best kayakers around test their skills on the Coosa. Call for the exact dates.

Accommodations
Fort Toulouse Historic and Jackson State Park
2521 West Fort Toulouse Road
Wetumpka, AL 36093
(334) 567–3002
www.alabamafrontierdays.com/index2.html
This is an excellent facility with nonprimitive camping (water and electricity). Overnight camping is only $11. This is an active archeological site of an authentic colonial French fort. The fort has been reconstructed for visitors.

A view of Jordan Dam looking upstream from the put-in.

Key West Inn
4225 U.S. Highway 231
Wetumpka, AL 36093
(334) 567–2227

Restaurants

The Landing
203 Orline Street
Wetumpka, AL 36093
(334) 514–6044

Catfish Country
5311 U.S. Highway 31
Wetumpka, AL 36092
(334) 514–1300

Organizations

Coosa River Paddling Club
c/o Southern Trails Inc.
5143 Atlanta Highway
Montgomery, AL 36109
(334) 272–0952

Other Resources
Coosa River Society
816 Chestnut Street
Gadsden, AL 35999
(205) 546–4429

Local Outdoor Retailer
Southern Trails, Inc.
5143 Atlanta Highway
Montgomery, AL 36109
(334) 272–0952

Maps
Brochures: Free from the Wetumpka Chamber of Commerce.
USGS maps: Elmore/Wetumpka, AL.
DeLorme: *Alabama Atlas & Gazetteer:* #45, A-8, B-8, B-9.

The Coosa and the Sailorman

The Coosa River begins its journey in Rome, Georgia, and flows through Alabama until it meets the Alabama River near Montgomery. As with many rivers of the south, the Coosa had its share of steamboat traffic, the first being the USM *Coosa,* which first took to the river in 1845 under the command of Captain James Lafferty. Until the Civil War these steamboats earned quite a handsome profit, hauling goods such as cotton north through these rivers.

The legends of the steamboats along the Coosa led to the birth of a famous sailor. In 1913 a lock and dam was completed by the U.S. Army Corps of Engineers at Mayo's Bar to help with navigation on the river. To keep the channel clear, the Corps purchased a ship called the *Leota,* piloted by a Captain Sims. His son, Tom Sims, began doodling cartoons and tucking away stories of life on the river and eventually landed a job drawing for a comic strip called "Thimble Theater."

Until this time the strip had a relatively unknown sailor as a character who worked for a shipping company owned by the Oyl family. His name was Popeye. By using his family's experiences on the Coosa and changing the river into the open sea, Sims brought the character to the forefront and created a national comic hero.

17 Elkahatchee Creek

River Specs

County: Tallapoosa.

Start: Elkahatchee Road at Russell Pond Spillway.

End: County Road 63.

Length: 1.2 miles.

Approximate float time: One and one-half to two hours.

Difficulty rating: Difficult.

Rapids: Class I to Class III.

River type: White water.

Current: Moderate to fast.

Minimum level: On the Hatchet gauge, 400 cfs for a low ride, 700–800 cfs for optimal ride.

Environment: Mixed forest of pines and hardwoods through a gauntlet of granite ledges and boulders.

Elevation drop: 37.3 feet per mile.

Land status: Private and unincorporated.

Nearest town (or city): Alexander City.

Other users: None.

Getting There: Put-in and Takeout Information

To shuttle point/takeout: From the intersection of Alabama Highway 22 and U.S. Highway 280 in Alexander City, take US 280 east 1.6 miles, and turn right onto County Road 63. Travel 2.1 miles, and turn left onto a dirt road. Follow the dirt road 0.2 mile. It will come to a Y, with the right fork going over the river on the triple-arch bridge, looping back to the highway. The left fork leads down a short hill to the river. There is plenty of parking at the top of this hill in a grassy area.

The takeout will be on the left downriver side after you cross under the triple-arch bridge. There is an excellent set of Class III rapids here that extends about 0.1 mile past the takeout, so you may want to linger. The takeout is a nice sloping natural dirt boat ramp with low granite rock at the bottom.

To put-in from takeout: Head back up the dirt road to CR 63 and return the way you came. In 0.8 mile, turn left onto Lambert Road. Travel 1.1 miles, and turn left onto Elkahatchee Road. In 0.8 mile you'll come to a ROAD CLOSED sign. At the time of this writing, the bridge over the river was under construction, and it looked like it would be awhile before it was completed. Travel around the sign to the end of the road. The Russell Pond dam/spillway will be to your right.

The put-in is about a 100-foot walk from the road down soft clay and sand to the river. A dirt road of sorts (unsuitable for driving, probably just for workers to walk on) was built across the river where the bridge used to be. This road has been cut in half by the flow of

Elkahatchee Creek

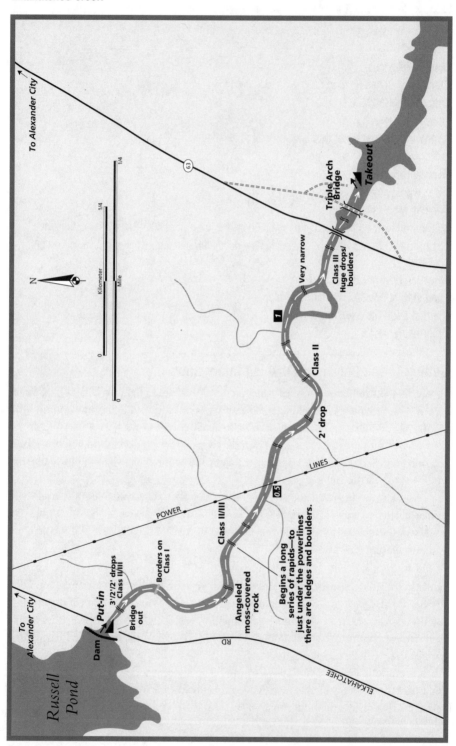

the river. Because of this "road," the put-in is a rather murky, swampy-looking area. As you walk down be careful of rebar that was left behind. Basically you'll have to find a good way down to the river. This will vary with water levels.

Trip Summary

This is a rocking little river at the right levels. The granite boulder-lined Elkahatchee features beautiful Class III rapids with some huge 4- and 5-foot drops and plenty of Class IIs that give you a chance to practice your maneuvering through the maze of boulders, down ledges, and waves.

Trip Description

Many rivers of the state that feature white water paddling flow through limestone and sandstone formations, but the Elkahatchee is one of the few that travels through a bed of granite and granite boulders. Because of this and the 40-foot-per-mile gradient, this short stretch of creek provides some excellent white water paddling, with two distinct Class III rapids and a good smattering of Class IIs. All along the rocky trip, catalpa trees line the banks. You can occasionally spot ducks, great herons, turtles, and deer here.

Located in Alexander City, the creek is bounded by Russell Pond to the north and Lake Martin to the south. Lake Martin is a 1,445-acre lake that is a favorite of sports enthusiasts and recreationists. Russell Pond is formed by a spillway-dam at its southern terminus, which presents a picturesque scene at the put-in.

Before getting to the good stuff, a word about the put-in: As of this writing—and it looks like it will be this way for a while—the bridge over the creek on Elkahatchee Road was demolished and was being completely rebuilt. The road to the creek ends abruptly. It is a bit of a carry to a decent launching site from this point, and it varies with the water level. Be careful of rebar that is haphazardly sticking up through the sand and clay.

A word of caution is in order: This river can be rather difficult, challenging, and potentially dangerous, so beginners should only attempt it with experienced supervision. This is also one of those tricky runs in the state in that you have to catch it when the level is just right. In summer and fall you can run the creek immediately after a decent rainfall, but soon after it will dry, and you will be dragging your boat down many of the drops.

After getting into the river, you will immediately be met with your first Class III. This set consists of three drops: one 3-foot drop and two 2-foot drops. One of these is apparently created from an old cement bridge that once spanned the creek (some of it can still be seen along the banks).

The biggest and best of the Class III rapids are encountered as you near the end and actually go a bit past the takeout. In all this set drops 24 feet in 0.2 mile. Large boulders create a variety of chutes, waves, and eddies that are sure to get your blood pumping. A nice path to the left with sweeping water pushes you around the CR 63 bridge.

There are a bunch of Class II rapids on this river. Most of these consist of granite ledges that form nice drops of up to 3 feet and are generally pick your way. The set at 0.5 mile is a long one, stretching at least 100 yards as you cross under the power lines. The last set of these occurs at the 1-mile mark. The creek splits and forms a small island. Take the left path for the fast water. The river narrows to 20 feet along this stretch through a "rock garden." This is about the only section where you will run into a few trees in the creek.

We would be remiss if we didn't mention a bit of Elkahatchee history. Just north of here is the Tallapoosa River and the infamous Horseshoe Bend where General Andrew Jackson and the Tennessee Volunteers virtually ended the Creek Indian War of 1813. Chief Menawa, who led the Red Stick tribe during the battle, was severely wounded and left for dead on the battlefield. The story goes that he managed to make his way to the Tallapoosa, found a canoe, and floated to Elkahatchee Creek, where Creek women and children were kept in seclusion from the battle. Here Menawa recovered, joined with the survivors of the battle in mourning for the dead, and formulated a plan on making peace with the United States.

There you have it. Take a couple of hours on your way through the area and get ready for some great white water action.

Trip Information

Contact
Alexander City Chamber of Commerce
120 Tallapoosa Street
Alexander City, AL 35010
(256) 234–3461
www.alexandercity.org

Season
Runnable at various times of the year but a fickle river. During the summer and fall, watch for decent rain to run this river—but it has to be almost immediately after the rain because the level drops off rapidly.

Fees/Permits
No fee or permit is required to launch or paddle the river.

Local Information
Alexander City Chamber of Commerce
120 Tallapoosa Street
Alexander City, AL 35010
(256) 234–3461
www.alexandercity.org

Local Events/Attractions
Wind Creek State Park
4325 Alabama Highway 128
Alexander City, AL 35010
(256) 329–0845

Nearing the takeout, County Road 63 spans the Elkahatchee, and the old triple-arch bridge appears behind it.

Known as the largest state-operated campground in the country, Wind Creek State Park is located just south of Alexander City near the Elkahatchee. The park is located on the 1,445-acre Lake Martin, which, along with the park, provides excellent fishing, swimming, boating, and hiking. The park has 642 campsites, many located right on the shores of the lake. Camping is $16.00 per day for improved sites, and $3.00 to $10.00 for primitive sites, depending on the location near bathhouses.

Accommodations

Alex City Motel
2595 Dadeville Road
Alexander City, AL 35010
(256) 329–8441

Mistletoe Bough Bed & Breakfast
497 Hillabee Street
Alexander City, AL 35010
(877) 330–3707
Listed in the National Register of Historic Places, the Mistletoe is known as the "Grand Old Lady of Herzfeld Hill." Built in 1890 by the Reuben Herzfeld family, it was owned by the family until 1993, when it was restored to its Queen Anne elegance.

Restaurants

Fillin' Station
11093 Highway 22 East
Alexander City, AL 35010
(256) 215–4000

Other Resources

USGS River Gauge Online for Hatchet Creek at Rockford:
wwwdalmtg.er.usgs.gov/rt-cgi/gen_stn_pg?station=02408540

Maps

USGS maps: Alexander City, AL.
DeLorme: *Alabama Atlas & Gazetteer:* #39, F-6.

18 Hatchet River North

River Specs

County: Coosa.

Start: U.S. Highway 280 bridge.

End: U.S. Highway 231 bridge.

Length: 12.75 miles.

Approximate float time: Seven hours.

Difficulty rating: Moderate.

Rapids: Class I to Class II.

River type: White water.

Current: Moderate to fast.

Minimum level: 500–600 cfs.

Environment: 30- to 40-foot-wide river with lots of shoals and drops. Mostly steep and rocky or thick and brushy banks.

Elevation drop: 12.5 feet per mile.

Land status: Mostly open, some private property.

Nearest town (or city): Sylacauga.

Other users: None.

Getting There: Put-in and Takeout Information

To shuttle point/takeout: From Clanton take I–65 south to exit 205. Take U.S. Highway 31 south 4.1 miles. Turn left onto State Road 22 east. Travel 21.5 miles to US 231. Make a left turn onto US 231 north, and travel 4.0 miles.

The takeout is next to the US 231 bridge. There is a rather large gravel parking area on the right side of the highway just before the bridge. You can park here, or there is a rutted dirt road that heads down the bank to another dirt parking area (SUVs might make it— small cars are doubtful). If you park here, it's about 20 yards to the lower parking area, and then another 10-yard steep drop to the river itself. When paddling the river you will find the takeout trail just feet away from the US 231 bridge upriver and to the left. The trail could be overgrown at times, so look carefully. Also, be careful when carrying your boat and belongings back up the hill after your trip is complete; the hillside is pretty steep and grassy, and most likely will be somewhat slippery with mud in some places.

To put-in from takeout: Take US 231 north and cross the river. Travel 4.0 miles, and make a right turn onto County Road 49. Travel 5.2 miles to the intersection of U.S. Highway 280. Make a right turn onto US 280 south. Travel 2.0 miles, crossing the bridge over the river. There is a gravel parking area on the left. At the far end is a gravel and dirt road that leads to an area under the bridge for parking.

The put-in is just downriver from the bridge and is a short and moderately steep walk down a 10- to 20-foot grassy slope. There is evidence that this parking area is used as a

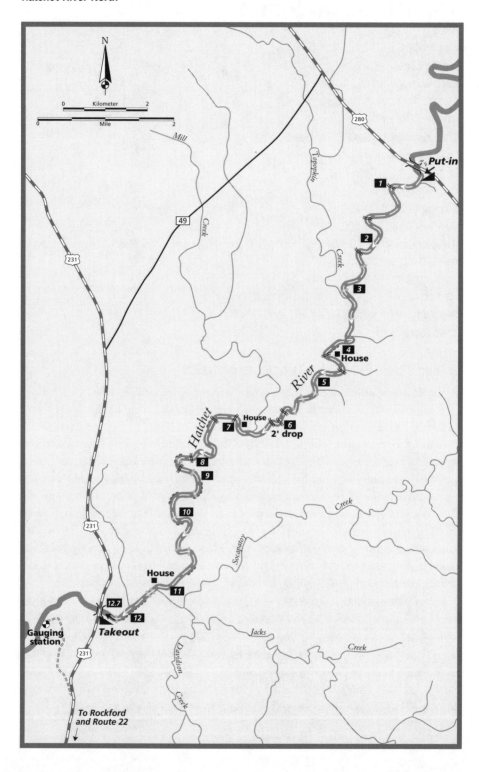

party place. You may want to consider dropping your boat off, driving back to the upper parking area to leave your car, and then walking back to the river.

Trip Summary

This section of Hatchet Creek is probably the best for canoeing. The optimum flow is between 500 and 600 cfs. At 300 we had to carry the canoe over rocks just a few times. Aside from that you can count on at least one long shoal around every bend. A lot of the fun comes from choosing a path heading into each shoal, then picking your way around the rocks.

Trip Description

Being a seasonal creek the speed and depth of the Hatchet will vary, depending on the time of year you choose to run it. The greatest flow occurs in February, during which it averages 800 cfs. The lowest flow occurs in the autumn months, with an average of just 200 cfs. We recommend a flow of at least 500–600 cfs for the best ride, but as low as 300 will work.

From the put-in to the takeout, you'll encounter a shoal around every bend. As you enter each shoal, you're exhilarated by the acceleration and the smell of the river's mist in the air. One of the special things we noticed on this river is the diversity of fragrance experienced along the way. There are a few cabins and houses built high up on the banks. You'll see that the placement of these houses normally provides the owners with spectacular views of wide, flowing falls.

The water is very clear, giving the paddler a great look at many large and varied rock formations just beneath the surface. The rocks are not sharp, making it easier when you get stuck and have to exit your canoe (as always, however, be cautious—the large, smooth-faced rocks may be slippery). Several intermittent streams and a few larger streams flow into the Hatchet. If it's fishing you like, bass are usually plentiful and may be had by casting your lure close to the banks. You'll also see many species of birds, including wild turkeys.

The banks of the creek are normally sheer rocky bluffs, providing visual stimulus. Finding a stopping place is not hard, though if you intend to set up camp, you'll have to look a little harder. There are a few sandbars along the way, usually hidden behind tangles of vines and briers.

Just after mile 3 you'll see Topopkin Creek coming in from the right. This creek merges as not much more than a trickle and follows a shoal (of course!), so it's not hard to miss if you happen to be on the left part of the Hatchet and you're not looking for it.

As you approach the halfway point and after you come around a hard right bend in the river, you'll encounter a 2-foot fall, probably the biggest drop of the run. High up on the left bank is a house looking down on the lovely rocky falls. Here you can choose to paddle through either the far right or far left. The right path will accelerate you through a short, quick chute. The chute was a little too much for us, and we capsized in a flash. After collecting our belongings, and curious about the left-side run, we paddled back upstream a few feet and came back down the left side. Hugging the extreme left, we shot down 50 feet or so of fast water. This one was fun.

At mile 11.75, you'll begin to hear the rushing water of Socapatoy Creek as it merges and falls into the Hatchet. Socapatoy explodes into view on your left as you paddle past thick forest (which, until this point, has blocked the creek from your vision). High up on your right is a house strategically placed for a marvelous view of the converging creeks. You'll want to stop and look around here (you may be forced to stop anyway because of the relatively shallow depth and rocky bottom) to take in the splendor. Here the Hatchet widens for a brief way as the two rivers merge. Now you're just 1 mile from the takeout at the US 231 bridge. After passing Socapatoy you'll navigate a long set of shoals for the next quarter-mile or so. In about twenty minutes, you'll come to the US 231 bridge and the end of the run. The takeout is a fairly steep slope of about 40 feet or so.

Trip Information

Contact

Coalition for the Preservation of Hatchet Creek
P.O. Box 583
Sylacauga, AL 35150
(256) 245–5635
www.alabamarivers.org/dirabc.htm

Season

Best run in winter and spring. Other times the creek can be very low. A minimum of 500 to 600 cfs is required for a decent run, but 300 gets you by.

Fees/Permits

No fee to put in or take out.

Local Information

Sylacauga Chamber of Commerce
17 Fort Williams
Sylacauga, AL 35150
(256) 249–0308
www.sylacauga.net

Local Events/Attractions

Festival of Trees
P.O. Box 185
Sylacauga, AL 35150
(256) 249–0308
www.sylacauga.net
Held annually beginning the end of November through Christmas.

Typical Hatchet scenery: beautifully clear water flowing over and around rocks.

Isabel Anderson Comer Museum and Arts Center
711 North Broadway
Sylacauga, AL 35150
(256) 245–4016

Accommodations

Jackson's Trace Motel
411 West Fort William Street
Sylacauga, AL 35150
(256) 245–7411

The Jameson Inn
89 Gene Stewart Boulevard
Sylacauga, AL 35151
(800) 541–3268, (256) 245–4141

Towne Inn
U.S. Highway 280
Sylacauga, AL 35150
(256) 249–3821

Coalition for the Preservation of Hatchet Creek
P.O. Box 583
Sylacauga, AL 35150
(256) 245–5635
www.alabamarivers.org/dirabc.htm
The purpose of the Coalition for the Preservation of Hatchet Creek is to promote the environmental integrity of Hatchet Creek and its watershed; to advocate the wise use and preservation of natural resources in the watershed to the aesthetic, recreational, and economic benefit of the citizens of the state; and to educate the general public in regard to the interrelationship of our waters, soils, plants, animals, and people in the earth's ecosystem, and the effects of human actions on that relationship.

Other Resources

USGS River Gauge Online:
wwwdalmtg.er.usgs.gov/rt-cgi/gen_stn_pg?station=02408540

Maps

USGS maps: Holling, AL/Rockford, AL.
DeLorme: *Alabama Atlas & Gazetteer:* #38, C-4, D-4, E-4, E-3.

Tidbit

Jimmy Buffett sang a song written by Mitchell Parish and Frank Perkins called "Stars Fell on Alabama." The title was inspired by the story of Isabel Anderson Comer who, in 1954, had the misfortune of a meteorite landing in her living room! The meteorite can be seen at the Alabama Museum of Natural History in Tuscaloosa.

19 Little Cahaba River

River Specs

County: Bibb.

Start: Carlton Pass Road/Cahaba Valley Baptist Church.

End: Bulldog Bend Canoe Park.

Length: 6.4 miles.

Approximate float time: Four hours.

Difficulty rating: Moderate.

Rapids: Class I to Class II.

River type: White water.

Current: Fast most of trip.

Environment: 30- to 40-foot-wide river with plenty of shoals, drops, and a 3-foot fall that beginners and intermediates love. There are pools for swimming and long stretches through lush oak, magnolia, dogwood, and, of course, pine forest.

Elevation drop: 8.1 feet per mile.

Land status: Coosa Wildlife Management Area.

Nearest town (or city): Montevallo.

Other users: None

Getting There: Put-in and Takeout Information

To shuttle point/takeout: From Clanton take I–65 north to exit 228, and take State Road 25 south. Travel 0.9 mile, and turn left onto U.S. Highway 31 south. Continue another 0.1 mile, and make a right onto SR 25 south. In 6.8 miles you will pass through the intersection of SR 25 and State Road 119. Continue on SR 25 south another 8.6 miles, and turn right onto County Road 65. Travel 3.6 miles, and Bulldog Bend Canoe Park will be on the right just before the bridge over the Little Cahaba.

The takeout is easy to find—it's at the only bridge you will come to on the river. The river will bend to the left, and a nice dirt landing will be seen to the left. There is a small boat ramp here. Bring your car down to load up or climb the 20 yards up a steep but grassy hillside to the parking area.

To put-in from takeout: Leave Bulldog Bend, and turn left onto CR 65. Travel 3.6 miles, and make a left onto SR 25 north. Travel 2.5 miles, and make a left onto Carlton Pass Road (a sign that reads CAHABA VALLEY BAPTIST CHURCH will be on the right). In 0.4 mile come to a stop sign at a T intersection. Make a right turn. Travel 1.25 miles. The parking area is to the left across from the Cahaba Valley Baptist Church. This is a small gravel area with cement picnic tables. Do not block the picnic area. Park off to the right of the parking area near the road.

The put-in is a slippery slope to say the least. It is a steep and muddy 20 to 30 feet to the riverbank. The bank itself is only a small strip of shoreline. You can continue up the

Little Cahaba River

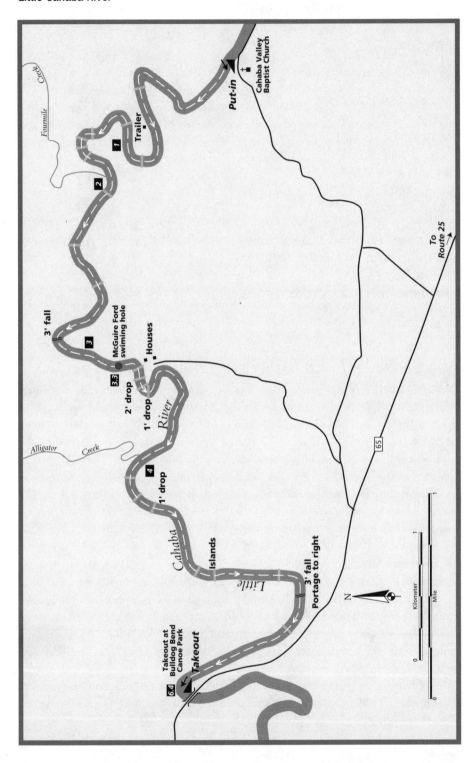

road about 0.1 mile to another area off to the left, but parking is *very* limited here, and you could end up blocking the shuttle trucks.

Trip Summary

Beginners and intermediate paddlers love this river. The scenery is beautiful, with plenty of interesting rock formations lining many of the banks. In the spring a variety of wild-flowers, including the Cahaba lily, add color to the dense forest lining the banks. Approximately midway through the trip, a favorite swimming hole—McGuire's Ford—gives you a chance to relax and enjoy the cool water. As for the ride itself, there are plenty of shoals and drops, and a fantastic 3-foot fall.

Trip Description

It is unusual for a state to have two rivers with the same name, but Alabama does in the Little Cahaba River. The first is located east of Birmingham near Leeds and is floatable only seasonally. The second, and the one we describe here, is located southwest of Birmingham and is floatable most times of the year. This Little Cahaba is packed with fast shoals, deep pools, a couple of nice rapids, and a 3-foot fall that can be run even by beginners.

The charm of this trip begins at the put-in, which is located across from the old Cahaba Valley Baptist Church. Here local families have been congregating every weekend since the early 1900s for fellowship and to catch up on the week's news and reminisce about the past. There are cement picnic tables here next to the riverbank that they use to picnic on, and they love to include you in the conversation. Just remember when parking here to be considerate, and park closer to the road than the picnic tables.

Until midday the put-in can be crowded with throngs of canoeists arriving and launching their boats through one of the local canoe outfitters—either Limestone Park or Bulldog Bend (see Local Information). Usually the traffic thins out along long stretches of river, but through the shoals it can become congested.

Once on the river the scenery is very picturesque. Immediately large rock formations and outcroppings line the riverbanks. Most of the large rocks along the shoreline are low enough that you can land and have lunch or take in a little sun. Otherwise there are few decent beaches to land on because the banks are generally steep, 5-foot, mud-and-vegetation-covered slopes.

The water clarity is on the muddy side, which makes maneuvering through shoals a bit tricky but not impossible. Overall the river runs between 30 and 50 feet wide.

There are plenty of fast shoals to tackle. Overall these are pick-your-own-way shoals. We ran the river during July with fairly low water but found that each shoal had a swift flow, and we were able to get through with relatively no problem. Several included drops ranging from 1 to 2 feet. In higher water these drops would make nice Class I and II rapids, with a wide range of passage possibilities.

There are several highlights to the Little Cahaba run, the biggest being a 3-foot fall approximately halfway through the trip. You will hear the roar well before you get to it, even in low water. Upon reaching the fall you will see a rock wall spanning the width of the river, which at this point is about 50 feet wide.

Many beginners can navigate the fall, but if you feel like you don't want to, or you don't want to go for a swim, you can portage your canoe on a trail to the extreme right side of the fall.

To run the fall there is a chute of water that rushes through the rocks to the very right side of the fall (it is right next to the bank). Paddle hard and head straight down the chute, and you should make it through. Many canoes torpedo their nose straight into the pool at the bottom of the drop, but keep your weight back as much as you can, and again, you should make it through just fine. As we said, there is a deep pool at the bottom, but there is also a good place to take out right next to it if you dump while going over. After going over you may want to head to the beach to the far left and join others watching other canoes try their hand at the drop.

Another favorite spot follows the fall: McGuire's Ford. Here the river gets *very* deep. To the left is a sand beach that used to be an old water park. To the right is a beautiful, sheer 50-foot rock cliff. Someone had long ago built a steel ladder onto the cliff, and to this day people climb the ladder and take the plunge into the deep ford.

Immediately following the ford there are a series of shoals and rapids with a 1- and 2-foot drop. The first as you come around a bend is the 2-foot drop. The 1-foot drop comes immediately after the 2-foot drop. There is no right or wrong way through it, just pick your own way. To the far right is a simple shoal. The extreme left is where you'll find the drop. During low and moderate water flows, this provides a fun ride. In higher water be cautious of a curl at the bottom of it.

There is one feeder of note along the river: Alligator Creek. You can paddle a few hundred yards up this narrow, 5-foot-wide feeder to see turtles and small fish, but we didn't see any alligators.

The final fall on the trip is a 3-foot drop over some jagged boulders and sharp rocks. The current is extremely fast here. It is runnable by more experienced paddlers, but many—especially beginners—portage around it. Stop about 10 to 15 yards before the fall on the right side for a trail around the fall.

Trip Information

Contact
River information is available from one of the local outdoor retailers/outfitters listed below.

Season
Year-round.

Fees/Permits
No fee to put in or take out. There is a $4.00 parking fee at Bulldog Bend Canoe Park. They will shuttle your canoe/kayak for $12.00. Canoes are also available to rent here.

Local Information

Bulldog Bend Canoe Park
3224 Bulldog Bend Road
Brierfield, AL 35035–3759
(205) 926–7382
See Local Outdoor Retailers below for more information.

Limestone Park Canoes
Rural Route 1
Centreville, AL 35042
(205) 926–9672
See Local Outdoor Retailers below for more information.

Local Events/Attractions

Heart of Dixie Railroad Museum
1919 9th Street
Calera, AL 35040
(800) 943–4490, (205) 668–3435
www.heartofdixierrmuseum.org
This is a museum "dedicated to preservation, restoration and operation of historically significant railway equipment." The museum is housed in a 100-year-old railway station. Call for schedule and admission.

Brierfield Ironworks Historic Park
240 Furnace Parkway
Brierfield, AL 35035
(205) 665–1856
www.brierfieldironworks.com
The twin brother of Tannehill Ironworks, Brierfield was used during the Civil War to create munitions for the Confederate Army. The foundry was destroyed by Union troops toward the end of the war. Although not rebuilt like the Tannehill site, Brierfield and its surrounding buildings of the period give a unique look at an interesting piece of American history.

Accommodations

Brierfield Ironworks Historic State Park
240 Furnace Parkway
Brierfield, AL 35035
(205) 665–1856
www.brierfieldironworks.com
Primitive camping is available for $7.50 per night for as many as four people. There is a bathhouse with showers and a swimming pool with lifeguard.

Looking back at a rocky fall.

Restaurants

Barnstormer Pizza
980 Main Street
Montevallo, AL 35115
(205) 665–1166

Organizations

Fellows and Advocates of the Little Cahaba
P.O. Box 1000
Brierfield, AL 35035
(205) 665–5650

Other Resources

Bama Environmental News (BEN)
2617 11th Avenue South
Birmingham, AL 35205
(205) 226–7739
www.bamanews.com

Local Outdoor Retailers

Bulldog Bend Canoe Park
3224 Bulldog Bend Road
Brierfield, AL 35035
(205) 926–7382
Located at the takeout of the trip described. A variety of trips are available, including an overnight.

Limestone Park Canoe Rentals
RR 1
Centerville, AL 35042
(205) 926–9672
A variety of canoe trips are available for everyone ages six and older on the Little Cahaba.

Maps

USGS maps: Aldrich, AL/West Blocton East, AL.
DeLorme: *Alabama Atlas & Gazetteer:* #37, C-6; #36, C-5.

20 Tallapoosa River

River Specs

County: Tallapoosa.

Start: Buttston Road.

End: Alabama Highway 49.

Length: 9.6 miles.

Approximate float time: Five hours.

Difficulty rating: Moderate.

Rapids: None.

River type: Float/shoals.

Current: Slow to moderate.

Minimum level: 700 cfs.

Environment: Thick brush-lined banks of catalpa, magnolia, and oak trees and areas of pasture-land. Clear water with green tint over granite rock and ledges.

Elevation drop: 4 feet per mile. Largest drop is 24 feet over 0.5 mile of Griffin Shoals.

Land status: First 6.5 miles unincorporated private property; last 3.1 miles within Horseshoe Bend National Military Park.

Nearest town (or city): Dadeville.

Other users: Motorboats.

Getting There: Put-in and Takeout Information

To shuttle point/takeout: From the intersection of Alabama Highway 49 and U.S. Highway 280 in Dadeville, head west on US 280 1.2 miles. Make a right onto AL 49 north. Travel 11.3 miles. Just before crossing the bridge, make a left turn down a paved road. It is a short drive to the river.

The takeout is a beautiful cement boat ramp provided by the park. There is a picnic area here with plenty of parking.

From the river you will pass a large island on its right side. At the end, just before the AL 49 bridge, paddle to the far left bank. Cross under the bridge but don't pass the now mostly dismantled Miller Ferry Bridge.

To put-in from takeout: Head south on AL 49 for 3.3 miles, and turn left onto Elder Road. Travel 4 miles, and turn left onto Buttston Road. This road starts paved and quickly becomes dirt. Travel 3 miles, and make another left onto Germany's Ferry Road. Travel 0.7 mile, crossing the bridge over the river. Just after crossing make a left turn onto a short paved road that leads to the river.

This is another beautiful cement boat ramp right to the river with plenty of parking available.

Tallapoosa River

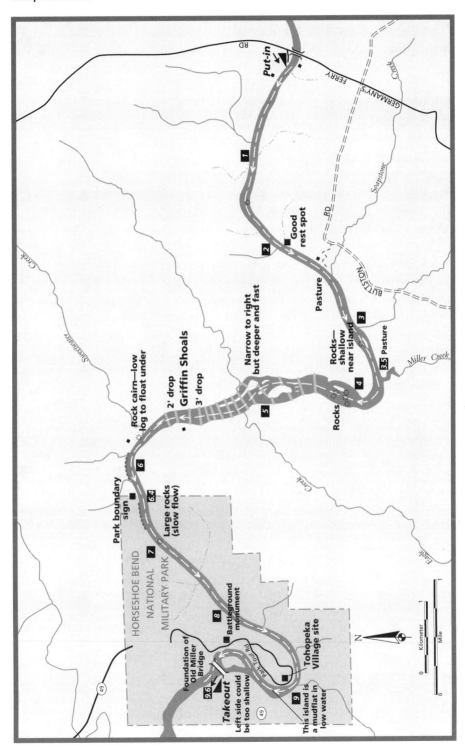

Trip Summary

A grand float trip if there ever was one, the Tallapoosa is a wide, deep river for the most part, but then comes Griffin Shoals: 1.5 miles of swift water through granite rocks and down 2- to 4-foot drops and ledges. The trip culminates through the peaceful and historic Horseshoe Bend National Military Park. This trip can be made into a nice overnight.

Trip Description

The Tallapoosa River is a major player in the Mobile River Basin, beginning in Georgia and flowing some 270 miles to join the Alabama River near Montgomery. Although the river has been dammed in a few places (Thurlow the most notable, with a great 1.5-mile Class IV white water run), the river still supports more than 40 species of fish, 33 types of mussels, and 110 species of snails, many only found here and nowhere else in the world. The residents along the river are currently waging a battle with the state of Georgia in what has been called The Water War. The state wants to build a dam in Haralson County, Georgia, which would threaten several species of fish, crayfish, and snails that are currently on the endangered species list.

This section of the Tallapoosa is famous for being the site of the Battle of Horseshoe Bend (see sidebar). The river itself averages between 150 and 300 feet in width, most of it flowing through deep pools of clear but green-tinted water. In several areas you will see large granite boulders sticking up through the surface. Because of the width a stiff breeze is the norm, and you may find yourself paddling hard against it, especially in late fall and winter. The banks average between 5 and 10 feet in height, with some higher in the area of the shoals. These are mostly thick, brush-covered, muddy banks; however, you will pass through some grass-covered pastures.

As you float the 9.6 miles, you will notice that there are not many places to pull over and take a break. The brush is thick and the banks steep (and mostly private property). Along the way, you will pass several islands. These make for nice break landings or even camping (a particularly nice island is just to the right at the end of Griffin Shoals). There is also a dirt road at mile 2 that leads up from the river into the woods. This is apparently part of a hunting club's property, but we were able to stop for a couple of minutes and take a break. Just remember to use the old outdoor etiquette—leave it better than when you arrived!

For paddlers the main attraction to the Tallapoosa is the shoals. Generally large granite boulders and long ledges form outstanding swift flows and some great drops and chutes. A few people we talked to said the first shoal would come up on us at about mile 1.5. However, even in low water, this area is just a ripple in the water and easily passable.

The first real shoal comes at 4.2 miles and, like all of the shoals on the river, is pick your own way. If you hit this during times of low water (600 cfs or lower), you may want to hug the right bank and paddle to the right of the island. Here the river narrows to about 20 to 30 feet, the flow is very fast, and there are plenty of shoals to shoot through. Just watch toward the end for the tree blocking the river. If you are at low levels, you will be able to float under it, but the current is very fast, and you could hit your head pretty hard.

Also here to the right you will see an old stone cairn. The use and age of the structure is unknown.

The largest of the shoals is named Griffin Shoals. It begins at mile 4.4 and stretches 1.5 miles in length. Through the shoals the river widens to almost 300 feet in places. The fun is the 2-, 3-, and 4-foot drops you'll encounter through this run.

After the shoals it is a leisurely float trip toward the takeout. At 6.4 miles, you will pass a sign on the right bank that reads BOUNDARY–HORSESHOE BEND NATIONAL MILITARY PARK. Beautiful rock formations jut out from the banks in some areas, looking like they were man-made with pavers. Watch along the banks, especially near trees with exposed roots in the water, for beavers busy at work. And turtles can be seen in abundance floating and sunning.

As you float around the horseshoe, you will pass directly next to the road used by visitors to the park to explore the battlefield. Many times friendly tourists will wave and want you to stop and chat. This is also the area that was known as the Tohopeka Village. Read the sidebar we've included about the history of this battle, and as you float through, the solitude and stillness makes it hard not to sit and reflect on what occurred here almost 190 years ago.

Trip Information

Contact
Horseshoe Bend National Military Park (see Local Events/Attractions).

Season
Floatable all year. Watch the gauge in late summer for below-minimum flows.

Fees/Permits
No fee or permit is required to launch or float the river.

Local Information
Dadeville Chamber of Commerce
185 South Tallassee Street, #103
Dadeville, AL 36853
(256) 825–4019
www.dadeville.com

Local Events/Attractions
Alexander City Jazz Festival (first weekend of June)
120 Tallapoosa Street
Alexander City, AL 35010
(256) 234–3461
Great southern jazz and blues is the fare, with a good helping of food.

The sun peeks over clouds, reflecting off the river's rippled surface.

Horseshoe Bend National Military Park
11288 Horseshoe Bend Road
Daviston, AL 36256
(256) 234–7111
www.nps.gov/hobe

Accommodations
Heart of Dixie Motel
1775 East South Street
Dadeville, AL 36853
(256) 825–4236

Restaurants
Circle A Catfish
1637 Agricola Road
Dadeville, AL 36853
(256) 825–5677

Oskar's Café
6684 Highway 49 South
Dadeville, AL 36853
(256) 825–4827

Organizations

Lake Watch of Lake Martin
P.O. Box 72
Alexander City, AL 35011
(256) 825–9353
www.Lakewatch.org

Other Resources

USGS River Gauge Online for Tallapoosa near New Site (Horseshoe Bend):
waterdata.usgs.gov/al/nwis/uv?02414715

Local Outdoor Retailer

Southern Trails, Inc.
5413 Atlanta Highway
Montgomery, AL 36109
(334) 272–0452

Maps

Brochures: Horseshoe Bend National Military Park (see Local Events/Attractions).
USGS maps: Buttston, AL.
DeLorme: *Alabama Atlas & Gazetteer:* #39, D-9, D-8.

The Battle of Horseshoe Bend

Horseshoe Bend National Military Park sits along the banks of the Tallapoosa River, where the decisive blow came during the Creek Indian Wars of the early 1800s.

Before this time the U.S. government and the Creek Indian Nation had been attempting in various ways to trade and maintain and acquire land, sometimes by negotiations, other times by force. The method in which the Creeks dealt with the Americans led to a civil war between the Lower and Upper Creeks. The Upper Creek, led by Shawnee Chief Tecumseh, called for armed resistance. The Lower Creek thought that diplomacy was the only way. In 1813 a splinter group of the Upper Creek known as Red Sticks attacked and killed seven American settlers in Tennessee. To prevent an all-out war with the United States, the Lower Creek ordered the hunting down of the murderers.

A militia from Mississippi fought the Red Sticks at the Battle of Burnt Corn. It was an indecisive fight and only served to fuel the rage of the Red Sticks, who discovered that Lower Creeks were fighting along with the militia.

In retaliation the Red Sticks attacked Fort Mims near present-day Bay Minette, killing 250 people, including some women and children. This was the attack that caused the United States to declare war on the Red Sticks.

After a series of battles, the Red Sticks moved their women and children to Horseshoe Bend with the hopes that their religious leaders' magic and a log barricade would protect them, and that they would eventually defeat the United States.

The decisive battle came on 27 March 1814. More than 1,000 warriors, led by Chief Menawa, assembled behind the barricade. Five hundred women and children were moved to the "toe" of the horseshoe, which was known as Tohopeka Village. The Americans, led by Andrew Jackson, began the assault, with 500 Cherokee, 100 Lower Creek, and 2,600 American soldiers.

During the battle several of Jackson's men swam across the river at the "toe," stole the tribes' canoes so they couldn't escape, burned Tohopeka Village, and took the women and children prisoner.

By the time the battle was over, more than 300 warriors were wounded and 557 either died on the battlefield or drowned while trying to escape by swimming across the river.

Following the battle Jackson, going against orders, negotiated his own treaty with the tribes, calling for the ceding of twenty million acres of land, almost half of their territory, to the United States. This eventually led to what was known as the Trail of Tears, which forced the relocation of many tribes west when Jackson became president.

21 | Weogufka Creek

River Specs

County: Coosa.
Start: County Road 29.
End: County Road 16 low-water bridge.
Length: 7.2 miles.
Approximate float time: Four hours in low water.
Difficulty rating: Easy to moderate.
Rapids: Class I to Class II.
River type: Mainly narrow white water river, averaging about 40 feet in width.
Current: Swift.
Environment: Rocky muddy banks and beautiful rocky ridges.
Elevation drop: 14.9 feet per mile.
Land status: Coosa County Wildlife Management Area.
Nearest town (or city): Clanton.
Other users: None.

Getting There: Put-in and Takeout Information

To shuttle point/takeout: From Montgomery take I–65 north travel 27 miles to exit 200. Turn right onto County Road 59 north, and go 3.3 miles. Turn left onto U.S. Highway 31 north and continue 1.3 miles. Turn right, and head east on Alabama Highway 22 for 13.4 miles until you come to Kelly's Crossroads (there is a small country store at the intersection of AL 22 and County Road 29). Make a left onto CR 29 north, and travel 9 miles. Turn left onto County Road 16. In just a few hundred feet, you'll pass over a low-water bridge (this is the takeout). Travel past the bridge about 100 feet to the bend in the road. There is a narrow strip of shoulder to the right to park on next to a cornfield.

The takeout is the only bridge you will encounter during the trip, and it is too low to pass under. The takeout itself is on the upriver side of the bridge to the left, next to a house. It is a 30-foot clay/dirt bank with a moderate slope to the roadway. It is a good idea to leave a note in the window of your car letting the local people know who you are, that you are canoeing the river, and what time you expect to be back.

To put-in from takeout: From CR 16 head back to CR 29 and turn left (north). Travel 3.2 miles. On the right, and just before you cross a small bridge over the Weogufka, you'll find the home of Coosa County Constable Chris Culver. Stop by the house, and Mr. Culver or his family will take you to a good spot to put-in 0.25 mile downstream to avoid massive logjams.

The put-in is behind Mr. Culver's aunt's house. Don't drive back there alone! Several springs feed through the pasture behind the house, and your car could sink. There's a fairly steep, 30-foot muddy hillside to the riverbank.

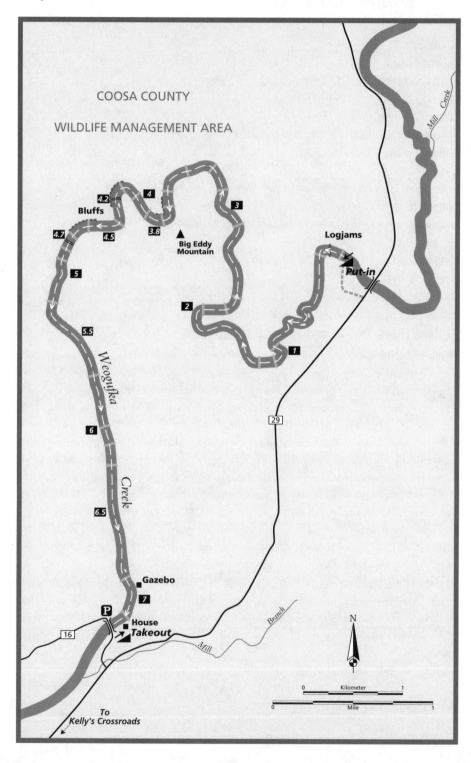

COOSA COUNTY

WILDLIFE MANAGEMENT AREA

Mill Creek

4.2
4
3
Bluffs
4.7
4.5
3.8
Big Eddy Mountain
Logjams
5
Put-in
2
1
Weogufka
5.5
6
Creek
29
6.5
Gazebo
7
P
House
Takeout
16
Branch
Mill
N
To Kelly's Crossroads

| 0 | Kilometer | 1 |
| 0 | Mile | 1 |

Trip Summary

The Weogufka is a swift-running rocky river. The banks are muddy and dense with trees, and there are few places to dock. You'll be impressed by the vertically escalating rocky ridges halfway into the trip. In higher water the shoals and rapids are excellent.

Trip Description

The Weogufka is a river that people have heard of but don't know much about. Located just east of the Coosa Wildlife Management Area, the Weogufka rushes over rocky shoals as it heads toward Mitchell Lake.

During low water prepare to carry your boat and do lots of pushing. The best time to paddle the Weogufka is in the early spring (March, April, and early May) when the water is highest. You'll float past breathtaking tree-lined ridges with rocky faces rising hundreds of feet skyward. The locals refer to one of these ridges as Big Eddy Mountain, which rises 969 feet above sea level. Big Eddy Mountain is so named because the creek below the mountain at one time formed a large eddy, about 300 yards wide and 12 to 14 feet deep.

The entire trip is far removed from civilization, with a single visible gazebo encountered along the way. Green moss growing on the rocks under the shallow water gives it a beautiful green hue. Many times the river flows over green grass growing out from the edges of the bank.

You'll see huge alligator gar that hang out on the mossy rocks in the slower water. These fish are not particularly good for eating, and they are actually a menace to other, more popular fish, because the alligator gar feeds on their eggs. Game fish caught in the creek include bass, bream, catfish, crappie, drum, and some pike. Crawfish and mussels may also be seen.

Farther south, close to Lake Mitchell where the Weogufka and Hatchet Creeks flow into the lake, walleye can be caught. The walleye is the largest member of the perch family and is a favorite of anglers because of its sweet taste. Also expect to see snakes, beavers, and otters. Cottonmouth and water moccasins abound.

There is one interesting and endangered species of snail that can be found in only a few rivers in the country and the Weogufka is one of them. The tulotoma (*Tulotoma magnifica*) is a filter-feeding, gill-breathing snail that only grows to the size of a golf ball. It's distinguished from other snails in the region by its ornate shell of spiral, knoblike structures. Generally the snail lives in the shoals of the river to a depth of 15 feet. The snail, which can also be found in our trips in the Coosa River and Hatchet Creek, was first listed as an endangered species by the government in July 1990.

Trip Information

Contact

Coosa County Constable Chris Culver
Mount Moriah Road
Weogufka, AL 35183
(256) 245–1942

Wet sand and dense trees line the banks of the Weogufka.

Season
Year-round, but the water is highest in the spring.

Fees/Permits
There are no permits or fees required for paddling the river or putting in or taking out.

Local Information
Chilton County Chamber of Commerce
500 5th Avenue North
Clanton, AL 35046
(800) 553–0419
www.chilton.al.us

Local Events/Attractions
Verbena Trade Days (first Saturday of October)
500 5th Avenue North
P.O. Box 66
Clanton, AL 35046
(830) 553–0493, (205) 280–0600
Email: cccoc@scott.net

Accommodations

Sunrise USA
950 Lake Mitchell Road
Clanton, AL 35045
(205) 775–8360

Restaurants

Cow Pasture Café
1910 County Road 43
Clanton, AL 35046
(205) 755–4231

Jeanette's Place
404 7th Street North
Clanton, AL 35045
(205) 280–3133

Maps

USGS maps: Flag Mountain, AL.
DeLorme: *Alabama Atlas & Gazetteer:* #38, C-3.

Flag Mountain Lookout Tower

Geologically speaking Flag Mountain in the Weogufka State Forest is the southernmost mountain in the Appalachian range. The mountain itself was used as a signal relay station during the Civil War.

Atop this 1,152-foot mountain stands the Flag Mountain Lookout Tower. Built by the CCC (Civilian Conservation Corps) in 1935, the 50-foot stone tower is a unique structure. The walls are 2 to 3 feet thick. Large timbers were laid in the rock in a criss-cross pattern, which has since been replaced with inlaid stone. The 12-foot-by-12-foot cab lookout was staffed by the Alabama Forestry Commission until 1989. The tower and surrounding buildings have since been leased to the Coosa County Cooperative and are slated for extensive restoration.

22 Weoka Creek

River Specs

County: Elmore.
Start: County Road 432 (Sewell Road).
End: County Road 29 (Titus Road).
Length: 2.4 miles.
Approximate float time: One and one-half to three hours, depending on water level.
Difficulty rating: Difficult.
Rapids: Class II to Class III.
River type: white water.
Current: Moderate to fast.
Minimum level: On the Hatchet gauge, 700 to 800 cfs optimum.
Environment: Mixed forest of pines and hardwoods.
Elevation drop: 30.4 feet per mile.
Land status: Private and unincorporated.
Nearest town (or city): Wetumpka.
Other users: None.

Getting There: Put-in and Takeout Information

To shuttle point/takeout: From the intersection of Alabama 14 and U.S. Highway 231 in Wetumpka, take US 231 north 10.3 miles, and turn left onto County Road 29. Travel 2.9 miles to the takeout.

Park your car on the narrow strip of shoulder just before the bridge. There is a driveway here that has a PRIVATE PROPERTY sign, so don't block it. There is probably room for two—maybe three—cars. The takeout is on the opposite side of the bridge (this would be the right, upstream side as you head down the river). The trail to the road is butted almost directly next to the bridge and is a short 20- to 30-foot climb up a moderate hill. The path is about 1 foot wide and brushy. You'll have to paddle through some water lilies to get to the takeout.

To put-in from takeout: Head back the way you came on CR 29 1 mile, and turn left onto Spiegner Road. Travel 1.6 miles, and turn left onto County Road 432 (Sewell Road). Travel 1.1 miles, crossing over the river. There will be a dirt road to the left. (You may want to travel to the first house on the right after the bridge, make a U-turn, and head back toward the bridge. The dirt road will be easier to see on the right from this direction.) Follow the road 0.1 mile to just near the river.

The put-in is on a moderate mud/sand slope but is not too difficult of a climb as you slide your boat into the river. The flow is fairly slow here, so access is easy.

Weoka Creek

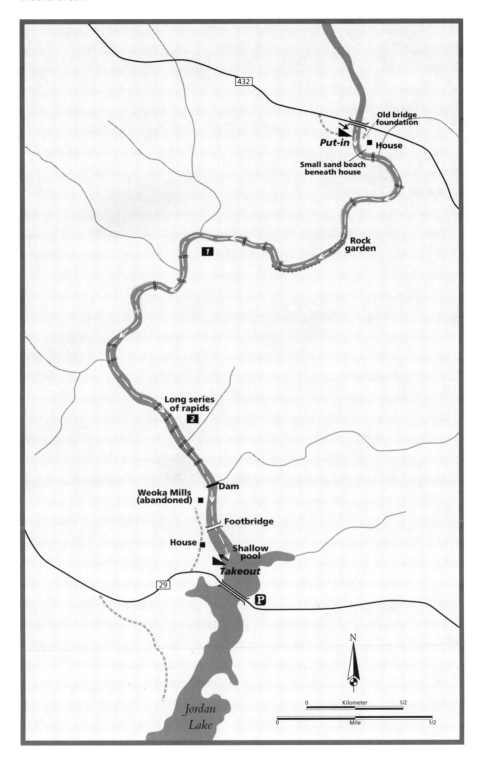

432

Old bridge
foundation

Put-in

■ House

Small sand beach
beneath house

Rock
garden

1

Long series
of rapids
2

Weoka Mills ■
(abandoned)

Dam

Footbridge

House ■

Shallow
pool

Takeout

29

P

N

*Jordan
Lake*

0   Kilometer   1/2

0   Mile   1/2

Trip Summary

Here's a pretty nice run if you're short on time. The current starts out very slow, but by the end of the trip, you'll have passed (either floating or walking, depending on current rainfall amounts and the water level) over a series of ledges and an old dam close to Weoka Mills.

Trip Description

Through summer and fall, good rainfall is required to keep this creek decently runnable. Keep your eye on the Hatchet gauge, which currently will give you the closest approximation of the Weoka's level. Unfortunately the last 10 years or so have not been very good for floating the Weoka. It's easier said than done, but try to catch this one no more than one day after a good rain.

This short section of Weoka Creek starts off due south from the Elmore CR 432 bridge. Just after putting in, you'll float slowly past a house on the left and rock cairns from an old bridge on both sides of the river. A thick overhanging canopy of trees darkens the view. The bottom starts out sandy. Just around the first left bend is a rapid with a 1-foot drop that can be hectic fun, even approaching Class III at the right water level. Quickly the sandy bottom turns to rock, and large, smooth granite boulders project low off the surface, with rock ledges seaming across the width.

Headed east, there is a stream entering on the left about 6 feet in width, just as you begin a 180-degree turn to the right to head back west. Along the inside of the curve, there is a large sandy beach, and the bottom turns sandy. Being just a few minutes into the trip, you probably won't be needing a rest yet, but in lower water this is a nice place to stop. Continuing around the right bend, the sand suddenly changes, and you're immediately into a nice rapid of large, smooth granite boulders. As you finish the right bend, you'll see the contrast of the two sides of the river. The left bank is a 30-foot high cliff of jumbled granite, and off to the right side is a sand bank. The width increases to about 50 feet, and you'll float a couple more sets of rapids consisting of perpendicular granite ledges across the river's width.

After a southwest straightaway, the river cuts hard to the right, then left again. Here again you'll see the interesting contrast between the sand and boulders on the left and the right. As you head west there is a long set of rapids. We ran at pretty low water and ended up walking much of this part. This would definitely be nice in higher water, as there are two good drops, one about 2 feet, then one about 18 inches.

Before bending hard to the left, there's a stream on the right that is pretty bottled up with tree trunks and limbs. At this point you're just past the 1-mile mark. To the left is a beach that would make another good stopping spot with low water. Headed south and just ahead of a hard right turn is another stream, this one flowing down about 8 feet of smooth rock. Another small rapid approaches here.

After completing the right turn and heading west, there is a small island about 8 feet in width and 100 feet long. After a couple more bends, you'll come to the final one-third of this trip—the best part. While headed southeast on a straightaway of about a mile are the largest rapids on this section. The first set begins just as you begin a southeast bearing. There's a quick 2-foot drop, it levels off for about 6 feet, then there's another 2-foot drop. After 30 feet is a chute on the left where the flow picks up fast for about 40 yards. This set of rapids was actually the only set that we ran completely without getting stuck. There's another rapid that usually flows quite well, but it is not for the faint of heart. This one extends for about 200 yards with a 15- to 20-foot overall drop. We advise that you scope this one out before running it. If you think it's too much, there's a portage path on the right by stepping down about 8 feet of rock.

From top to bottom you'll notice a pattern with the rapids—they keep getting bigger and bigger. The final set of rapids could be huge. Here is where you'll meet up with an old overflow dam. There are large rapids before the dam (described in the previous paragraph) and even larger rapids on the downstream side of it. The water's level again will determine what you'll have to do here. Too little water and you'll be forced to drag over the dam, and too much water could create a dangerous scenario. Either way you should stop around the dam to scout your path.

After finishing the largest rapids after the dam, it's an easy float to the end. You'll pass by an abandoned mill on the right—an interesting old building four stories high. There is a cable extending across the river from the mill to the opposite side. Soon after is an old shredded footbridge strung across. As the depth shallows the takeout will be in sight on the right.

Watch recent rainfall amounts—this trip can really rock at high water.

Trip Information

Contact
Southern Trails
5143 Atlanta Highway
Montgomery, AL 36109
(334) 272–0952

Season
The trip is runnable all year, but this is another one of those fickle rivers. During the summer and fall you need to watch for decent rain to run it, but it has to be almost immediately after the rain because the level drops off rapidly.

Fees/Permits
No fee or permit is required to launch or paddle the river.

Local Information
Wetumpka Chamber of Commerce
110 East Bridge Street
Wetumpka, AL 36092
(334) 567–4811
www.wetumpkachamber.com

Local Events/Attractions

Al Holmes Wildlife Museum
1723 Rifle Range Road
Wetumpka, AL 36093
(334) 567–7966
Animals such as lions, tigers, and sharks are displayed in their natural habitats.

Coosa Whitewater Festival (May and October)
c/o Southern Trails
5143 Atlanta Highway
Montgomery, AL 36109
(334) 272–0952
This is a semiannual event for kayakers. Jordan Dam is opened to 10,000 cfs and the best kayakers around test their skills on the Coosa. Call for the exact dates.

Accommodations

Fort Toulouse Historic Park/Jackson State Park
2521 West Fort Toulouse Road
Wetumpka, AL 36093
(334) 567–5147
www.alabamafrontierdays.com/index2.html
This is an excellent facility with nonprimitive camping (water and electricity). Overnight camping is only $11. This is an active archeological site of an authentic colonial French fort. The fort has been reconstructed for visitors.

Key West Inn
U.S. Highway 231 North
Wetumpka, AL 36092
(800) 833–0555, (334) 567–2227

Wetumpka Inn
8534 U.S. Highway 231 North
Wetumpka, AL 36092
(334) 567–9316

Restaurants

Ranchito Morin
5791 U.S. Highway 231
Wetumpka, AL 36092
(334) 834–7462

A nice flow of water in Weoka Creek.

Other Resources

Some 80 million years ago, Wetumpka was struck by a meteorite that left a crater 4 miles wide. Information on Wetumpka's impact crater, or astrobleme, can be found at www. auburn.edu/~kingdat/wetumpkawebpage3.htm.

USGS River Gauge Online for Hatchet Creek at Rockford:
wwwdalmtg.er.usgs.gov/rt-cgi/gen_stn_pg?station=02408540

Local Outdoor Retailer

Southern Trails, Inc.
5413 Atlanta Highway
Montgomery, AL 36109
(334) 272–0952

Maps

USGS maps: Holtville, AL.
DeLorme: *Alabama Atlas & Gazetteer:* #38, H-2, H-3.

Freestyling

An interesting and fairly uncommon aspect of paddling can be found in freestyle canoeing, sometimes called interpretive freestyle or canoe ballet. Freestyle presents paddling as an art, in which a paddler's individualism can shine.

Canoe freestyle and kayak freestyle are quite different. In a kayak a paddler frantically surfs waves, rolling, cartwheeling, dipping, and spinning. Canoe freestyle is much slower and subtler. Most often it is performed on quiet water. It is often accompanied by music, which helps the canoer convey his or her own unique style and grace. Many times it is performed at night, as spectators watch the freestyler under a blaze of light. It can be performed solo or tandem. Basic paddling classes teach strokes such as Indian, box, Canadian, bow jam, bow cut, circle, low-brace turn, and sculling draw. Freestyle is a great way to show off the efficiency of one's practiced strokes.

Expert canoe freestylers maneuver their boats in seemingly impossible ways. Leaning over the side so the gunwale is barely off the water causes the keel to come out of the water, which allows for very tight arcs and circles.

A skilled freestyler, either in a canoe or kayak, is a beautiful sight to see.

North Region

The north region provides those who want some great white water a chance to air it out. This section of our travels stretches from the Tennessee/Alabama state border near Huntsville to the state's largest city, Birmingham. Geologically the region is known as the Cumberland Plateau, a mountainous region that has seen its sandstone heights carved and weathered by the elements by the many rivers and streams that flow through the area. Throughout the region you will find spectacular gorges, cascading waterfalls, and thrills aplenty.

In the northwest section of the region you will find the state's only National Wild and Scenic River, the Sipsey. Located in the heart of its namesake wilderness area, the Sipsey River trip has some nice Class I rapids, but the beauty of the river is what makes it most spectacular. Towering canyon walls surround it, and the water ranges in color from crystal clear to turquoise. Tack on Borden Creek to the Sipsey River trip, and you have one great overnight experience in the heart of the William B. Bankhead National Forest.

Just a few short miles northeast of the Sipsey is Bear Creek. This run has recreational flows throughout the summer provided by the Tennessee Valley Authority (TVA). Spectacular Class II and III rapids are the fare on this river, with beautiful rock outcroppings and bluffs. The TVA has outdone themselves by purchasing and creating excellent canoe access points along the river, making it a joy to paddle.

To the northeast the East Fork of the Little River carves its way down to the largest canyon east of the Mississippi, Little River Canyon. Class II and III rapids are in order on this river, which many paddlers call "an attention keeper."

Also in this region is the Terrapin River. This little jewel provides lots of white water for all levels, with some nice drops. An added attraction is a crystal clear and icy cold freshwater spring near the end for refreshment.

The northern region is more prone to freezing-cold temperatures in the winter and early spring than the rest of the state. Ice and snow with considerable accumulation is possible, so keep this in mind when heading out.

Bear Creek

River Specs

County: Marion.

Start: Mill Creek on County Road 172.

End: Rock Quarry Branch takeout on County Road 172.

Length: 6.7 miles

Approximate float time: Three and one-half to four hours.

Difficulty rating: Moderate.

Rapids: Class I to Class III. Lower Factory Falls at mile 2.75 is rated Class VI. It is much too dangerous to run and requires a portage.

River type: White water.

Current: Swift.

Minimum level: 210 cfs. Highest flows (and best time to run) is during summer because of dam releases (see Season).

Environment: Mixed forest and woodland.

Elevation drop: 7.8 feet per mile.

Land status: Mostly privately owned; however, the TVA has acquired a 50-foot easement that gives the public the right to stop, walk, and fish on either side of the creek.

Nearest town (or city): Hayleyville.

Other users: Canoes, kayaks, rafts, tubes.

Getting There: Put-in and Takeout Information

To shuttle point/takeout: From Hayleyville turn right onto State Road 13 north. Cross the Don Tidwell Bridge over Bear Creek. At mile 6.7 turn left onto State Road 172 west. At mile 4.0 continue left on SR 172 west at the T. Go 1.5 miles, and the Rock Quarry takeout is on the right. There is a short road that leads to a nice graveled parking area.

The takeout is perfect because the TVA created the put-ins and takeouts with paddlers in mind. You'll find the takeout from the river after crossing under the Don Tidwell Bridge and rounding a bend for 0.5 mile. The takeout is on the right and is a cement landing. The carry is a moderate climb of about 50 feet up really wide stairs to the parking lot.

To put-in from takeout: Pulling out of the takeout parking lot, go left onto SR 172 heading east. In 1.5 miles turn right, and continue east on SR 172. Go 2.9 miles. Turn right at the intersection of U.S. Highway 241 and County Road 172 onto CR 172 east. In 0.5 mile the Mill Creek put-in will be on the right.

As with the takeout the put-in is an excellent TVA facility with a nice moderate 50-foot path to the riverbank. The parking area is wide with plenty of parking.

Bear Creek

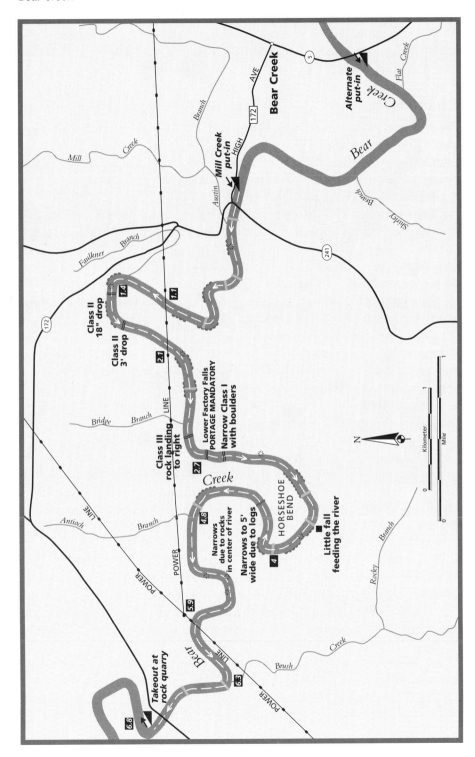

Bear Creek

Alternate put-in

Flat Creek

Creek

Bear

Shirley Branch

Mill Creek put-in

AVE

HIGH

172

Austin

241

Mill Creek

Branch

Faulkner Branch

Class II 18" drop

Class II 3' drop

1.4

1.7

2.1

Bridge Branch

LINE

Class III rock landing to right

Lower Factory Falls PORTAGE MANDATORY

Narrow Class I with boulders

2.7

Creek

Antioch Branch

LINE

POWER

POWER LINE

4.8

5.9

Narrows due to rocks in center of river

Narrows to 5' wide due to logs

HORSESHOE BEND

4

Little fall feeding the river

Rocky Branch

Bear

Creek

Brush

POWER

6.3

Takeout at rock quarry

6.8

N

Kilometer

Mile

1

1

0

0

Trip Summary

This trip is both scenic and exciting at times. The scenic portion is highlighted by scores of rocky bluffs, heavy woods, and a large, flat surface of boulders just before Factory Falls, where you can stop and stretch. Factory Falls is just around the bend from here and requires a portage around.

Trip Description

The TVA controls water release from Upper Bear Creek Dam and normally releases 210 cfs on weekends and holidays during the summer. Depending on rainfall amounts and availability of water behind the dam, the release schedule and amounts may change. Make sure you call or check the Web site listed under Schedule. During nonrelease times the flow is so low that you will carry your boat from hole to hole.

Bear Creek is unique in that the TVA has acquired the right for the public to float, fish, and swim the waterway. It has also acquired a 50-foot-wide strip of land on either side of the creek for walking, sunbathing, bank fishing, etc. (however, there is no camping allowed anywhere along Bear Creek). TVA is responsible for constructing the great public access areas and accompanying parking lots as well.

When the water is flowing at around 210 cfs, this river is as close to perfect as it gets for the beginner to intermediate paddler. A variety of flowing shoals, rapids, falls, and turns, mixed with classic northern Alabama scenery, will enthrall both paddlers and nature lovers alike. Especially during the slower portions, you'll be able to take in the beauty of the high rocky cliffs common to the area, often partially hidden in the shadows behind trees about 100 feet off the banks. The 50-foot-wide easement allows you to take a break or swim whenever and wherever you please. The banks are clean, unlike some other rivers. Paddlers seem to take pride in keeping Bear Creek beautiful by not leaving trash of their own and picking up that left by other, more careless visitors.

Bear Creek flows generally west and northwest. The water can range anywhere from crystal clear to chocolate-milk muddy, depending on the recent rainfall and water release at the dam. The bottom consists of smooth boulders and sand, just right for wading in bare feet. The depth during release time is always deep enough to float with no portaging over shallows, but stay off Bear Creek when flows are more than 700 cfs—portage routes go under water, and the creek is very dangerous.

With the correct flow the current ranges from slow to swift, and you'll encounter lots of fun, swift shoals and rapids. You can easily average more than 2 mph, but there are a couple of spots along the way that you'll want to stop and walk around.

Just after mile 2, you'll cross under power lines with a wide path cleared beneath. There's a chance you'll see some wildlife here in the open expanse—possibly a white-tailed deer or two.

One interesting spot is about 2.5 miles downriver from the put-in and a couple hundred yards before you come to Factory Falls. On the right side of a long, swift, Class III rapid with a long chute, large waves, and a pool at the end is a large, flat, collection of smooth boulders. You'd do good to stop on the right before you continue, for two reasons: one, to scope out your route through the rapids; and two, to stop for a break and look around.

Once you are through this section, within a hundred yards or so is a required portage before a section known as Factory Falls. Do not attempt to go down Factory Falls! They are extremely dangerous and must be portaged. Fortunately the falls are well marked, and several warning signs precede the falls, reminding paddlers that a portage on the large, smooth boulders to the right is required. Pull your boat up on the right just before the river takes a hard bend left to the south, and carry your boat about 50 yards on the right of the falls over smooth rock with a couple of rather large step-downs.

Just a couple minutes after putting in after Factory Falls and heading south toward Horseshoe Bend, there are two quick sets of rapids totaling about 200 yards. Choose your route here, and have fun. Next some of the most spectacular of the rock formations will be seen. There is a 50-foot-high giant rock jutting into the river on the left and sheer, 100-foot cliffs behind trees on the right side. You'll begin a long slow bend right around Horseshoe Bend. At the bottom of the bend are more rock formations, including an overhanging cliff with streams flowing over.

Just 0.5 mile before the takeout, at the bottom of a U, you'll float by Brush Creek, which enters on the left. Shortly after there is a long, swift shoal approximately 300 yards in length. After a couple more shoals, you'll reach the takeout on the right side. The takeout is specially designed for canoers, kayakers, and floaters. It is a 50-yard walk up to the parking lot.

Trip Information

Contact

Bear Creek Canoe Rentals
U.S. Highway 43
Hackleburg, AL 35564
(205) 993–4459

Season

Best run on the weekends from Memorial Day to Labor Day, when the TVA releases water. For release level and schedule, call the TVA Lake Information Line at (800) 238–2264, or go to lakeinfo.tva.gov. It may also be run in the spring during the rainy season. A minimum flow of 200 cfs is required.

Fees/Permits

There is no charge to put in, take out, or paddle the river.

Local Events/Attractions

Bear Creek Lakes
1111 Highway 88
P.O. Box 670
Russellville, AL 35653
(877) FOR–BCDA (367–2232), (256) 332–4392
The Bear Creek Development Authority (BCDA) manages four lakes with five campgrounds and the Bear Creek Floatway. Fishing, boating, swimming on sand beaches, miniature golf, and pavilions are available for group outings. The park is open April through October 15. The lakes are open year-round.

Dismals Canyon
901 Highway 8
Phil Campbell, AL 35581
(205) 993–4559
www.dismalscanyon.com
A secluded wilderness filled with natural phenomena tucked deep within the foothills of the Appalachian Mountains, Dismals Canyon offers a serenity so extraordinary and a location so secret that it is featured in *Reader's Digest's* "Off the Beaten Path"" as one of America's most interesting and still uncrowded places to visit. Past twilight the canyon lights up with tiny creatures called dismalites. It's one of only a few places outside New Zealand where these tiny creatures are known to exist. Dismals Canyon is not a state or national park—it is privately owned and operated. Development has been designed for tranquility and serenity. Recreation is exploration of the natural environment with an emphasis on relaxation. Visitors can shop the unique country store, swim in a natural limestone pool, hike, mountain bike, and canoe.

Accommodations

Imperial Inn
1250 11th Avenue
Hayleyville, AL 35565
(800) 233–0841, (205) 486–5205

Restaurants

Hayley Diner
812 Highway 13
Hayleyville, AL 35565
(205) 485–9412

Midway Restaurant
5303 State Highway 13
Hayleyville, AL 35565
(205) 486–6771

Don't get any big ideas . . . portaging is absolutely required at Factory Falls.

Organizations

Tennessee Valley Authority Land Resources
400 West Summit Hill Drive
Knoxville, TN 37902
(865) 632–2101

Other Resources

TVA flow information:
lakeinfo.tva.gov/htbin/lakeinfo?site=UBD&DataType=All&SUBMIT=View+data

Local Outdoor Retailer

Bear Creek Canoe Run
U.S. Highway 43
Hackleburg, AL 35564
(205) 993–4459

Maps

USGS maps: Hackleburg, AL/Phil Campbell, AL.
DeLorme: *Alabama Atlas & Gazetteer:* #23, C-6, B-6.

Tidbit

The first 911 emergency call in the United States originated on 16 February 1968, from Hayleyville, Alabama. It came thirty-five days after AT&T designated the three-digit number for nationwide, universal emergency access.

24 Borden Creek

River Specs

County: Lawrence/Winston.

Start: Forest Road 208 or Forest Road 224.

End: Sipsey Recreation Area, County Road 6.

Length: 5.9 miles.

Approximate float time: Four to five hours.

Difficulty rating: Moderate, with challenging maneuvering in higher water.

Rapids: Class I.

River type: White water.

Current: Swift.

Minimum level: 350 cfs.

Environment: Beautiful stands of hemlock, beech, mountain laurel, and holly amidst the backdrop of rock bluffs and boulders.

Elevation drop: 6.4 feet per mile.

Land status: National forest.

Nearest town (or city): Double Springs.

Other users: None.

Getting There: Put-in and Takeout Information

To shuttle point/takeout: From Jasper take Alabama Highway 195 north 25 miles to the intersection of Alabama Highway 278. Continue straight (this is now Alabama Highway 33). Travel 12.5 miles, and make a left turn onto County Road 6. (This road is marked County Road 60 on most maps. It is actually CR 6 until it crosses into the next county.) Travel 4 miles, and make a left turn into the Sipsey Recreation Area parking lot. To the right will be a parking area for hikers. Continue straight across the one-lane wooden surface bridge to the second parking area.

The parking area is a large gravel lot with plenty of parking. The river is straight ahead from where you enter the parking lot and to the left of a national forest information sign.

You will cross under three bridges during the trip. The second bridge is the CR 6 bridge that runs next to the Sipsey Recreation Area. One hundred feet past that bridge, you will cross under the third bridge. That is the single-lane recreation bridge. The takeout is about 10 yards past this bridge to the right.

The takeout is a moderate 50-foot climb up a wide path that is a combination of dirt and gravel with railroad tie supports used to prevent erosion.

To put-in from takeout: Turn right from the recreation area onto CR 6, and travel 4 miles. Turn left onto County Road 33, and head north 1.4 miles. Make a sharp left turn onto Forest Road 208. This is a winding dirt road to the river. In 0.3 mile you will pass the Blackwater Wildlife Management Area headquarters, where you can pick up brochures. Continue down the road another 2 miles, and cross a single-lane bridge. Immediately after

Borden Creek

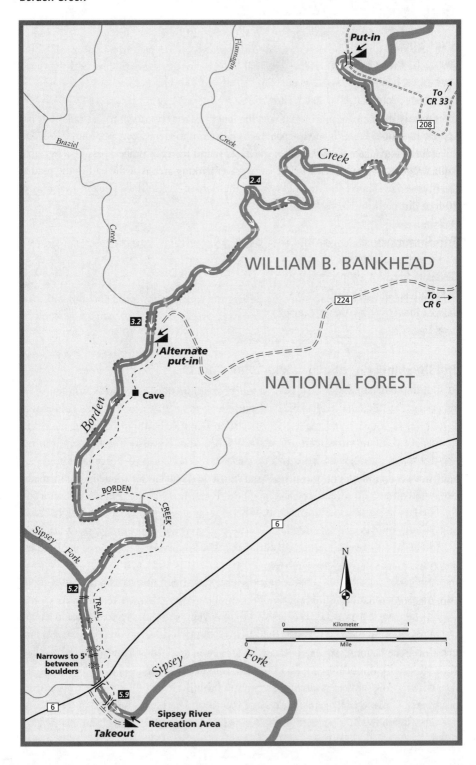

crossing the bridge is a wooden post that reads BORDEN CREEK. There is a small strip of shoulder here you can park on to the left of this sign, but it's only big enough for one car. You may be able to park other cars on the shoulder just before the bridge.

The put-in isn't the best. Across the road from where you park (the upriver side of the bridge) is a small foot trail. Follow the trail into the woods about 50 feet, and then turn right and head to the river. It may require a little bushwhacking to get there. It's steep, so be cautious.

There is an alternate put-in that cuts the length of the trip down to 2.7 miles but has a better parking and put-in area. Again, turn right from the recreation area onto CR 6, and travel 3 miles. Make a left onto Forest Road 224, and travel 2.5 miles, passing a sign that reads WARNING—ROAD CLOSED. The large gravel parking area is at the end of the road at the river's edge. This is also the trailhead for the Borden Creek Trail. The put-in is a short 20-foot dirt path to the river.

Trip Summary

Borden Creek combines beautiful scenery with challenging paddling. The creek flows through beautiful rock bluffs—not as tall as the Sipsey, but just as impressive. Along the banks waterfalls can be heard and seen carving the rocks. Wildflowers abound, and there are a few small caves you can explore off the river. The creek is narrow, with large boulders to maneuver around and a couple of Class I rapids to give some thrills.

Trip Description

Nestled within the confines of the Bankhead National Forest and the Sipsey Wilderness lies Borden Creek. This 5.9-mile trip is often overlooked by paddlers and is probably more famous for its namesake foot trail that runs alongside the river. But the creek is an excellent paddle for all who want to experience the wilderness and its beauty up close and personal.

The Bankhead Forest that surrounds Borden Creek covers more than 180,000 acres of land in two counties. The forest was established in 1918 under the name of Alabama National Forest. This was changed to Bankhead Forest in 1942 by Congress to honor former Speaker of the House William B. Bankhead. A subarea of acreage totaling 26,000 acres was designated as an official wilderness area in 1988 and was called the Sipsey Wilderness. It is the third largest wilderness area east of the Mississippi and is home to one of the last old-growth oak forests in the southeast.

Although there are no canyon walls that tower over the creek like on the Sipsey River trip, the Borden has beautiful bluffs and outcroppings that line the riverbanks. As soon as you put in, you will be greeted with bluffs to your right that jut out of the river. Many of the bluffs have interesting undercuts and small caves carved in them from the action of the creek over the centuries. Huge boulders also line the creek. We found ourselves viewing them almost like clouds, seeing images carved into the rocks.

The gray rock bluffs are accented by beautiful wildflowers in the spring and summer—there are so many that we couldn't possibly name them all here. This is a favorite area for wildflower photographers, who spend weeks at a time photographing the colors. The banks are also lined with hemlock, beech, and flowering mountain laurel.

Paddling Borden Creek is challenging in that it is narrow—20 feet or less in some areas—with boulders bottlenecking the river and providing some fast water. This creates several excellent shoals and a few Class I rapids, but also allows for some logjams, which you will have to portage around.

During times of high water, you may want to paddle up two of the feeder creeks of the Borden: the Flannagan and Brazeal. Both have clear water and sandy bottoms and more of the beautiful Bankhead scenery.

The Borden Creek Trail runs alongside the creek beginning at mile 3.2. Here—0.1 mile south of the trailhead and the alternate put-in for this trip—you may want to get out of the boat and do a little caving. The trail travels directly through a 100-foot cave just to the right of a waterfall. The cave is big enough to walk into standing up, but halfway through narrows so that you may have to crawl a bit. It gets dark as it makes a 90-degree turn to the right and comes out again directly above the river. It's lots of fun, especially if you have kids along.

This is a northern river, and it is prone to dry up in the summer. The best time to run the creek is in the winter and spring, but again, keep an eye on the gauges (see Other Resources). The severe thunderstorms of the summer often spike the flow and make it runnable during these dog days. It's safe to say that a flow of less than 200 cfs is not runnable at all.

Being in a national forest, camping is permitted anywhere along the river with only a few guidelines set down by the Forest Service. As a matter of fact, an excellent weekend trip would be to combine the Borden and the Sipsey, which merge at 5.2 miles into the trip, for a wonderful 16-mile adventure.

When it comes to camping, keep the following in mind: Although the Forest Service allows you to camp anywhere in the forest, they ask that you pitch your tent at least 100 feet from the river or foot trail. Use fire rings for campfires, and be sure that your fire is completely out before leaving. Some campers have already cleared campsites and established fire rings, sometimes near the rivers, despite what the Forest Service requests. If you see these, use them. It is better to reuse a campsite than to disturb the forest by creating a new one. And remember to use the "no-trace" policy—leave the forest better than when you arrived.

Also keep in mind that hunting is allowed in national forests. Contact the USDA Forest Service for dates and restrictions on access to the river and camping during the hunting season.

Thick vegetation colors the crystal-clear water of Borden Creek during a lull in the action.

Trip Information

Contact

USDA Forest Service, William B. Bankhead District
Main Street
Double Springs, AL 35553
(205) 489–5111
The office is open Monday through Friday, 7:30 A.M. to 4:00 P.M.

Season

The creek is best run in winter and spring. In the summer the level becomes very low. but sudden heavy summertime thunderstorms can give you an unexpected trip. Check the river gauge (see Other Resources) for flow conditions. Any reading below 200 cfs would not be floatable. Also during certain months in the fall and winter, hunting season is open. Contact the Forest Service for exact dates and restrictions.

Fees/Permits

There is no fee to put in or paddle the river. If you choose to use the Borden Creek Trail-head as a put-in, there is a $3.00 day-use fee. There is also a $3.00 day-use fee at the take-out. Camping is allowed anywhere in the forest at no cost (refer to the text for restrictions).

Local Information

Alabama Mountain Lakes
25062 North Street
Mooresville, AL 35649
(800) 648–5381
www.almtlakes.org

Lawrence County Chamber of Commerce
14220 Court Street
Moulton, AL 35650
(205) 974–1658

Winston County Chamber of Commerce
P.O. Box 147
Double Springs, AL 35553
(205) 489–5026

Local Events/Attractions

Looney's Tavern/Entertainment
22400 Highway 278
Double Springs, AL 35553
(800) 566–6397
This tavern, dinner theater, and entertainment center first opened in the 1800s with a lit-tle play called *Incident at Looney's Tavern,* which depicted the story of Winston County's Union sympathizers during the Civil War. Various musicals, including those of Rogers and Hammerstein—and, of course, *Incident at Looney's Tavern*—play throughout the year.

Accommodations

Free State Inn
15757 Highway 278
Double Springs, AL 35553
(205) 489–0056
This bed-and-breakfast inn is located within the Bankhead National Forest on AL 278 just west of Looney's Tavern.

Restaurants

Looney's Tavern/Entertainment
(See Local Events/Attractions)

Organizations

Alabama Environmental Council
2717 7th Avenue, Suite 207
Birmingham, AL 35233
(205) 322–3126
www.aeconline.ws

Other Resources

USGS Stream Gauge Online for the Sipsey and Borden Creek:
wwwdalmtg.er.usgs.gov/rt-cgi/gen_stn_pg?station=02450250

Local Outdoor Retailer

Wild Alabama
11312 Alabama Highway 33
Moulton, AL 35650
(256) 974–7678
Wild Alabama rents canoes and has arts and crafts in their store as well.

Maps

Brochures: Available at the ranger office or by writing to the district ranger office (see Contact).
USGS maps: Bee Branch, AL/Grayson, AL.
DeLorme: *Alabama Atlas & Gazetteer:* #23, B-10.

A Yankee Holdout

Winston County, Alabama, is not only known for the beautiful Sipsey Wilderness, but also for a bit of history as well. It was here that an uprising of sorts took place in the midst of the Civil War.

The residents of the county owned land but were poor enough not to be considered plantation owners and couldn't afford to own slaves. Because of this they were not permitted representation at the southern secession proceedings to decide if the Confederacy should be created. Winston County felt that their economic survival was more closely linked to northern assistance, and they therefore opposed secession.

So in 1861 the county took it upon itself to send schoolteacher Chris Sheets to the secession conference to argue their point. The schoolteacher was thrust into a name-calling session that almost led to a brawl. Sheets refused to sign a declaration of allegiance to the Confederacy, shouting, "I am an American and an Alabamian. I don't need to sign anything to prove who I am!"

Sheets found himself in jail, which infuriated the citizens of Winston County. The county became divided amongst itself on the issue for a time as war neared, causing the end of friendships and the separation of church congregations. Finally on 4 July 1861, a neutrality meeting was held at Looney's Tavern where the idea for the county to secede from Alabama was hatched. Realizing that a simple county could not survive on its own, a declaration was created and signed affirming the citizen's allegiance to the United States but requesting that the North and the South recognize the county's "free state" declaration. To this day the play *The Incident at Looney's Tavern* recalls the day when Winston County nearly became the Free State of Winston.

25 Flint River

River Specs

County: Madison.
Start: Oscar Patterson Road/Patterson Baptist Church.
End: Winchester Road/Flint River Canoe Rentals.
Length: 5.4 miles.
Approximate float time: Two and one-half hours.
Difficulty rating: Easy to moderate.
Rapids: Class I.
River type: White water.
Current: Moderate to swift.
Minimum level: 200 cfs.
Environment: Mixed forest, deciduous forest, evergreen forest.
Elevation drop: 2 feet per mile.
Land status: Mostly privately owned.
Nearest town (or city): Huntsville.
Other users: Anglers.

Getting There: Put-in and Takeout Information

To shuttle point/takeout: From Huntsville take I–565 from the I–65 exit 19 miles east to U.S. Highway 231/431. Take US 231/431 north 4.3 miles. Turn right onto Winchester Road, and travel 6.2 miles. Flint River Canoe Rentals and the takeout is on the right just before the bridge that crosses the Flint.

The takeout is immediately after you float under the Winchester Road bridge on the right. It is a somewhat steep, muddy, 100-foot climb to the parking area. There are some fairly swift shoals and some rocks lying just under the water's surface here, so watch them or you could broadside them. Flint River Canoe Rentals charges $10 to takeout from their lot. (See Local Outdoor Retailers for more information).

To put-in from takeout: From the takeout, turn left onto Winchester Road and travel 50 feet. Turn right onto Riverton Road and travel 4.6 miles. Turn right onto O. Patterson Road, and continue 1 mile. Make a right onto Rube Robertson Road, and head down the road 0.1 mile. The Patterson Road Baptist Church will be on the right. Turn in here. A gravel parking area is located to the left almost immediately after the turn.

The put-in is a very nice, level bank in a small cove in the river. There is plenty of parking in the grass parking lot here.

Trip Summary

The Flint River runs almost exactly 50 miles, with its headwaters beginning in Tennessee around David Crockett Highway and emptying into the Tennessee River in Madison County, Alabama. The river's water may be clear or muddy, depending on recent rainfall

Flint River

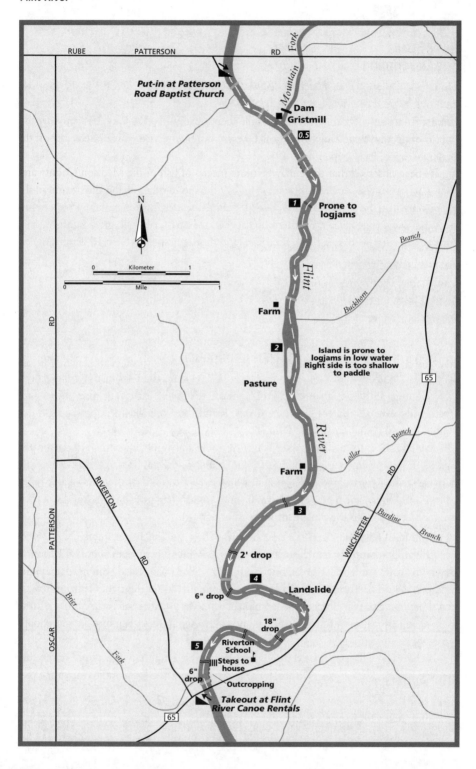

Put-in at Patterson
Road Baptist Church

Dam
Gristmill
0.5

1
Prone to
logjams

Flint

Farm

2

Island is prone to
logjams in low water
Right side is too shallow
to paddle

Pasture

River

Farm

3

2' drop

4

Landslide

6" drop

18"
drop

5   Riverton
School

Steps to
house

6"
drop

Outcropping

Takeout at Flint
River Canoe Rentals

RUBE   PATTERSON   RD
Mountain Fork

N

Kilometer   1
Mile   1

Branch
Buckhorn

65

Branch
Lollar

RD

Burdine
WINCHESTER

Branch

RIVERTON

PATTERSON   RD

OSCAR   RD

Brier Fork

65

amounts. Generally its depth ranges from 2 to 5 feet, and its width averages about 40 feet (ranging from about 15 to 150 feet in places). The banks are muddy, with abundant green foliage, including parrotfeather, pondweed, and riverweed.

Trip Description

Hunstville was once known as the "Watercress Capital of the World." It lost that primary "distinction" in 1958, when a group of German scientists launched Explorer I, America's first Earth-orbiting satellite, here. Huntsville then became "Rocket City." As you float this stretch of river, you probably won't notice watercress, but be assured it is there, just off the banks.

It's been observed that there may be more species of fish in the Madison County area than can be found in some entire states. Some of the species that inhabit the streams in the vicinity are the large-scale stone roller, striped shiner, scarlet-fin shiner, flame chub, blunt-nose minnow, white sucker, northern hog sucker, rock bass, bluegill, green sunfish, long-ear sunfish, rainbow darter, black-fin darter, and the Tennessee snub-nosed darter. Anglers will enjoy their catches of large- and smallmouth bass, spotted bass, and bream, along with garfish, panfish, and crappie.

The put-in is just 12 miles from the center of Huntsville and only 7.5 miles south of the Tennessee-Alabama state line. You'll begin the trip on the west side of the Flint River, near the Patterson Road Baptist Church, a one-room building built in 1936. Just half a mile downriver, there is a floatable stream entering from the left called Mountain Fork. A few hundred yards up this fork is a dam with water flowing through its center. You can paddle a ways up into the fork but will probably need to stop short of the dam. You'll want to get out and walk around a little bit here. The water is clear and cool, and fish abound.

To the left of the dam and through the trees you will see the remains of an old grist-mill. Stay clear of the structure. It is extremely old and dangerous.

Continuing southward down the Flint, you'll encounter many pretty wildflowers, including black-eyed Susan. Within fifteen minutes or so, on the left you'll see Buckhorn Branch, a perennial stream originating near Buckhorn, a town just about a mile northeast of this point. Just after this branch you'll encounter two small islands that are prone to log-jams. The easy path for us was to the left. In this small stretch grow brilliant wildflowers of purple and pink.

After another mile or so of heading due south, another perennial stream, Lollar Branch, enters in from the left. Lollar originates about 3 miles northeast of this point, close to where Buckhorn Branch begins. Just after passing Lollar Branch, as the river bends toward the southeast, Burdine Branch enters from the left. You'll take a hard right into a narrow, swift-flowing portion of water with close and overhanging trees, then into a swift, choppy shoal. At this point you're about halfway through your float.

By now you will have floated through several shoals but no rapids or drops. From here to the takeout, however, the ride becomes more exciting, with several rapids for you to pick your way through.

While heading in a southwesterly direction, the first rapid you'll come to has a 2-foot drop and is about three-quarters of a mile past Burdine Branch. Just after the rapid on the right is a small stream and a shoal to pass through. The river now takes a sharp left, heads generally east, then begins heading back to the right. As the Flint begins a bend right back toward the southwest, Winchester Road parallels the river on the left for a few hundred yards. After completing this near circle of forested woodland, you'll bend left, putting you on a southerly bearing once again. You'll pass Finlen Road on your left, and you're now just a couple thousand feet from the takeout.

But there's one last scenic view, just before you pull out your boat. Brier Fork, a wide flowing stream, enters from the right, just before Winchester Road bridge. Interestingly Brier Fork begins in Tennessee, just 15 miles west-southwest of the beginning of the Flint River, and meanders southeasterly until it flows into the Flint.

The takeout is on the right (west) side of the river, right after you cross under the Winchester Road bridge.

Trip Information

Contact
Flint River Canoe Rentals
See Local Outdoor Retailers for contact information.

Season
There is usually enough water to make a paddle of it, but the best time is winter and spring. Summer rains can get the river up enough to make a decent run. Contact the outfitter listed below for current flow information.

Fees/Permits
No fee to paddle and put in. Flint River Canoe Rentals charges $10 to park and take out (see Local Outdoor Retailer).

Local Information
Chamber of Commerce of Huntsville/Madison County
225 Church Street
Huntsville, AL 35804
(256) 535–2000, (256) 535–2028
www.hsvchamber.org

Local Events/Attractions
U.S. Space and Rocket Center
1 Tranquility Base
Huntsville, AL 35807
(256) 830–4987
www.spacecamp.com

Joe at the dam.

Von Braun Astronomical Society
Huntsville, AL 35807
(256) 539–0316
www.vbas.org.
A wonderful attraction high atop Monte Sano Mountain is the Von Braun Astronomical Society and their observatory/planetarium. Twice a month, the club (which was founded by Dr. Werner Von Braun) hosts a show for members and the public. A brief look at the sky in the planetarium is followed by a guest speaker and then, if the skies are clear, a spectacular look at the night sky through their telescopes. Admission is $2.00 for adults, $1.00 for children ages 6 to 11, children under 5 are free. Check the Web site for dates and times of shows.

Accommodations

Cochran House Bed and Breakfast
5529 Winchester Road NE
New Market, AL 35761
(256) 379–4529
An award-winning B&B, this inn has graced the pages of such notable magazines as *Southern Living*.

Monte Sano State Park
5105 Nolen Avenue
Huntsville, AL 35801
(800) ALA–PARK (252–7275), (256) 534–3757
A wonderful park with plenty of trails and the Von Braun Observatory (see Local Events/Attractions). Camping is $10.00 for primitive, $15.75 for sites with water and electricity.

Organizations
Flint River Conservation Association (FRCA)
P.O. Box 275
Brownsboro, AL 35741
www.geocities.com/frca2000

Local Outdoor Retailers
Flint River Canoe Rentals
107 Michael Drive
Huntsville, AL 35811
(256) 858–2280
Shuttles are available for $15 per canoe. Rentals are $30. There is a $10 charge to park and take out at their site. Camping is permitted at the put-in if you rent or shuttle with the outfitter (they own property near the put-in).

Tee's Bait and Guide Service
5008 Lumary Drive
Huntsville, AL 35810
(256) 859–1465
Guide service specializing in largemouth bass on Lake Guntersville and Wheeler Lake.

Maps
USGS maps: New Market, AL/Maysville, AL.
DeLorme: *Alabama Atlas & Gazetteer:* #19, B-9, C-9.

26 Lower Locust Fork of the Black Warrior River

River Specs

County: Blount.

Start: U.S. Highway 231 bridge.

End: Swann Bridge/Swann Bridge Road.

Length: 3.7 miles.

Approximate float time: Three hours.

Difficulty rating: Moderate to difficult.

Rapids: Class II to Class III.

River type: White water.

Current: Fast.

Minimum level: 2.0 feet (river stage).

Environment: Beautiful limestone bluffs accentuating the froth of the rapids with pines.

Elevation drop: 15.3 feet per mile.

Land status: Private and unincorporated land.

Nearest town (or city): Cleveland.

Other users: None.

Getting There: Put-in and Takeout Information

To shuttle point/takeout: From just north of Warrior take exit 287 from I–65 and take U.S. Highway 31 north. Travel 6.2 miles, and turn right onto County Road 9 south. Travel 6 miles and come to a stop sign. Turn left onto Alabama Highway 160 east, and travel 7.8 miles to a stoplight. Turn left, and head north on County Road 79. After 0.7 mile turn left onto Swann Bridge Road (it isn't marked). Continue for 1.1 miles, and arrive at Swann Bridge. Parking is a large wide dirt area on the opposite side of the bridge.

The takeout is on the right upstream side of the old Swann Covered Bridge. The path is actually a dirt road and is a moderate 100-foot climb to the roadway and the parking area. Tougher vehicles than the little compact cars we use might be able to drive to the riverbank and a medium-sized grassy parking area. The parking area on the road is a wide strip of shoulder to the immediate right after you cross the bridge.

You can park on a *very* narrow shoulder large enough for only one vehicle just before crossing the bridge on the left side of the road. In this case when paddling the river, the takeout would be on the left upstream side of the bridge. The path is a moderate 50-foot climb to the roadway on a dirt and rock path. If you use this side for the takeout, you need to move fast to get your boat across the road and onto your car because of traffic coming through the bridge, which is on a bend.

To put-in from takeout: Head back the way you came from the bridge to CR 79. Turn left, and head north on CR 79. After 2 miles, just before the bridge over the Locust Fork, veer left off of the highway and down a dirt road that leads to the river.

Lower Locust Fork of the Black Warrior River

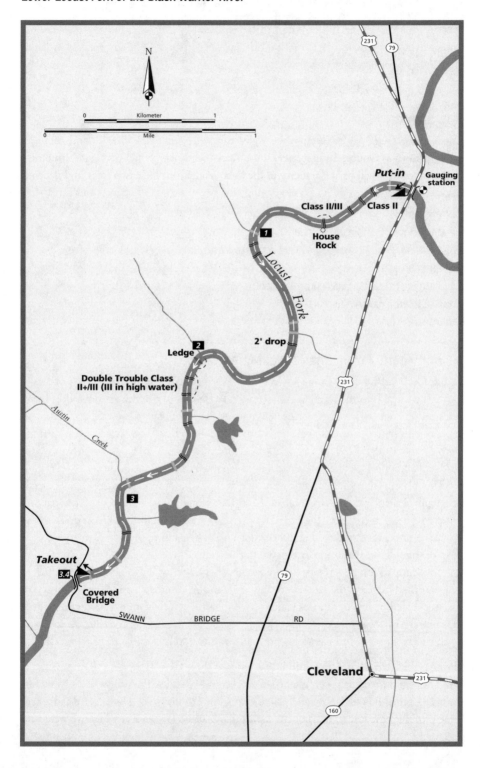

The put-in is on the left side of the bridge on this dirt and sand road. It heads down to the riverbank a good 0.2 mile and ends at a large sandbar. When we were here a pickup truck with locals picking berries blocked the road, so we decided to portage down to the river, leaving our car next to US 231. This may be the best bet anyway because the landing itself is a popular party area.

The beach to the river is low and an easy put-in.

Trip Summary

Challenging? *Very!* An excellent white water run with some very difficult and technical rapids known as Double Trouble and House Rock. Beginners should portage around these two areas or they will be at the mercy of the river. Aside from these two areas, and depending on the river level, this is a good learning river for supervised beginners and intermediates. Beautiful limestone bluffs accent the froth of the rapids.

Trip Description

Alabama is truly blessed with some of the best rivers in the country, and one of the best in the state is the Locust Fork of the Black Warrior River. The National Park Service uses cultural heritage, fisheries, scenic beauty, geological interest, historical significance, recreational value, and wildlife criteria to determine the rivers they feel represent the best in the country. The Locust has been placed in the top 2 percent of that list.

To add to the accolades, American Rivers placed the river on its "Outstanding Rivers" list in 1991, and American Whitewater named it an outstanding white water river in 1990.

The Locust Fork begins its 90-mile journey just west of Gadsden near Snead and Walnut Grove and flows southwestward to just west of Birmingham as it merges with the Mulberry and into the Black Warrior. There are many different sections to paddle that offer a different view of the river and scenery. The two most popular include the Upper Locust (a 10-mile run from County Road 1 near Cleveland to US 231, which features some Class I rapids) and the more popular run we describe here from US 231 to Swann Bridge.

The scenery is typically beautiful for this region. The banks are frequently lined with high limestone bluffs. The river itself, from start to finish, is boulder strewn. The face of the Locust changes, however, depending on the water level. With levels higher than 3 feet, the Class II rapids described here become Class III to III+ and a real problem for beginning paddlers. So keep in mind that we are describing the river at a level of 2.2 to 2.3 feet. Above that expect the level of experience needed to navigate the river to increase exponentially and become extremely dangerous for the inexperienced.

From the beginning the trip is full of fast water as you head off from the sandy put-in. Immediately the strong current of the first shoal will hit you. And, okay, we'll admit it: We weren't quite prepared for this first set, and ploosh, over we went. And as soon as you get through this, you immediately run into a series of three Class II rapids.

The first of two really tough rapids is reached at 0.6 mile. It is House Rock, so named because of the huge rock on the left bank that some say resembles a house. We had a hard time picturing the house, but not the rapids. Even at the low level at which we were running the Locust, the water flowing is powerful as it rounds the bend. It is floatable by staying close to the right bank; otherwise, there is a possibility of being swept into the rock. If you feel uncomfortable with the run or are a beginner, there is easy portage over large rounded rocks to the right. Also, in higher water, watch for a big eddy at the end of the bend to the right. After House Rock there are three shoals and two more rapids—and this is all within the first mile!

Just before the second trouble spot is a rock ledge that spans across the river. Again, this is a tricky and possibly dangerous run. Portage is fairly easy to the left side of the ledge.

And then comes Double Trouble, and it is just that. It comprises two sets of powerful Class II+/III rapids (probably up to IV with water above 3 feet). Inexperienced or novice paddlers should just portage around this section on the left. Even the more experienced should scout this section before running it, because different river stages present different faces of the run.

The first set of rapids in this section comes up on you out of nowhere as you round the bend. A pointed rock awaits you at the bottom of the rush of water that would be a bone-jarring, and possibly boat-crushing, jolt if hit. There is a short pool that follows this, and then the second rapid comes up, which ranges from a 1- to 2-foot drop on the left side to a 3-foot fall on the right.

Generally the remaining rapids and shoals are fun and are pick-your-own-route, but again, beginners should be supervised and have safety in mind before venturing out.

This section of the Locust ends at Swann Bridge, one of the few remaining covered bridges in the state. Built in 1933, the bridge makes a beautiful picture from the river with some low bluffs surrounding the banks. In the fall when the leaves are turning color, the image is reminiscent of an autumn in New England.

The run can be extended an additional 2 miles to State Road 160. The takeout here, however, is extremely steep and brushy.

Trip Information

Contact

Birmingham Canoe Club
P.O. Box 951
Birmingham, AL 35204
www.birminghamcanoeclub.org

Season

This river is best run during winter and spring. Again, watch for late summer storms to spike the river for some excellent warm-weather white water.

Fees/Permits

There are no fees to launch, take out, or paddle the river.

Built in 1933 and spanning 324 feet, Swann Bridge is one of the oldest surviving covered bridges in Alabama.

Local Information

Dodge City Town Office
130 Howard Circle
Hanceville, AL 35077
(256) 287–0364

Local Events/Attractions

Locust Fork River Festival
550 Red Maple Road
Blountsville, AL 35031
(256) 429–3090
www.dease.net/flfr/fest2u.htm
A fun day of arts, crafts, music, and food, plus canoe rides on the river. Call for dates.

The Maize
County Road 13
Locust Fork, AL 35097
(877) 787–6293
www.cornfieldmaze.com

A phenomenon occurring around the country in which plots of corn are grown and then a giant maze is cut out in the field for people to explore and try to find their way out. It's a blast, but only available for a short time. This one in Locust Fork runs only in mid-October to the first week of November.

Accommodations
Motel I-65
14466 Highway 91
Hanceville, AL 35077
(256) 287–1114

Restaurants
Wayne's Bar-B-Que
36721 Highway 79
Cleveland, AL 35049
(256) 625–4635

Organizations
Friends of the Locust Fork River
P.O. Box 245
Hayden, AL 35079
(256) 466–3858
www.flfr.org

Other Resources
USGS Stream Gauge Online for the Lower Locust Fork:
wwwdalmtg.er.usgs.gov/rt-cgi/gen_stn_pg?station=02455000

Local Outdoor Retailer
Blount Outdoor Supplies
227 1st Avenue East
Blountsville, AL 35079
(256) 429–2668

Maps
USGS maps: Blountsville, AL/Cleveland, AL.
DeLorme: *Alabama Atlas & Gazetteer:* #25, F-8.

Water, Water Everywhere . . .

So you're paddling down the crystal clear waters of the Sipsey, or the Yellow, or any other river for that matter. The water sure looks inviting. You see deer drinking it. It must be OK to drink, right? (Where's the buzzer?) Wrong! Even the purest-looking stream or river can carry a variety of diseases, the most common being giardiasis.

Giardiasis is an intestinal bacteria that can cause diarrhea, gas, loss of appetite, abdominal cramps, bloating, and weight loss. While not pleasant, it is rarely life threatening. You may not even know you have it until weeks after you drank the water, and then it will reoccur intermittently until treated.

If you are taking a short trip, pack along your water from the house, convenience store, water spigot from the state park, etc. For longer trips purify water in one of three ways:

- The best method is to boil the water before using it for three to five minutes.
- Use a water-purifying pump or filtered water system. (Check the instructions for exactly what it filters. Some may not do the job in the wilderness.)
- Use water-purifying tablets, such as iodine or chlorine.

Lower Mulberry Fork of the Black Warrior River

River Specs

County: Cullman/Blount.

Start: Old U.S. Highway 31 bridge.

End: Birmingham Canoe Club Landing/White Water Drive (Whitewater Bend Road).

Length: 3.1 miles.

Approximate float time: Two hours.

Difficulty rating: Moderate.

Rapids: Class II+ to Class III.

River type: White water.

Current: Fast.

Environment: Rocky cliffs with many overhanging pines and oaks.

Elevation drop: 12.5 feet per mile.

Land status: Private and unincorporated land.

Nearest town (or city): Garden City.

Other users: None.

Getting There: Put-in and Takeout Information

To shuttle point/takeout: From exit 287 off I–65 take U.S. Highway 31 north toward Garden City. After 7.8 miles turn left on to Philpot Road, and travel 0.2 mile to a Y. Veer right at the Y (White Water Drive, or Whitewater Bend Road), and then go 0.7 mile until the road dead-ends. From the river the takeout is a nice sandbar to the left as you make your way around the horseshoe bend of the river. To your right will be a 50- to 60-foot bluff, and the "Hawaii Five-O" wave will be reached right at the bend. After hitting the wave, the takeout is immediately on the left.

You will have to portage your boat a good 100 yards up a path through the woods to the parking lot, but the walk is easy. There is a bathhouse, so you can change if you don't make the wave here.

The residents here on White Water Drive apparently have no patience for paddlers. So be courteous, park in the designated areas, follow the rules posted by the Birmingham Canoe Club, and perhaps we can change their opinions.

To put-in from takeout: From Philpot Road, turn left to head north on US 31. After 1.9 miles, just before the bridge over Mulberry Fork, veer right off the highway, and follow a paved road 0.2 mile to the old US 31 bridge. This bridge is blocked off on one side and impassable, so no traffic flows here. Park on the left side of the road before the bridge, but don't park on the bridge. It is not in any shape for that. On the left (downstream side), there is a set of steep steps leading down to the gauging station platform, but it may be easier to carry your boat down a cement runoff culvert on the left about 50 feet farther up the road from the bridge, then onto a moderate dirt path for another 10 feet. The river is less than 100 feet away once you make it down the steep part.

Lower Mulberry Fork of the Black Warrior River

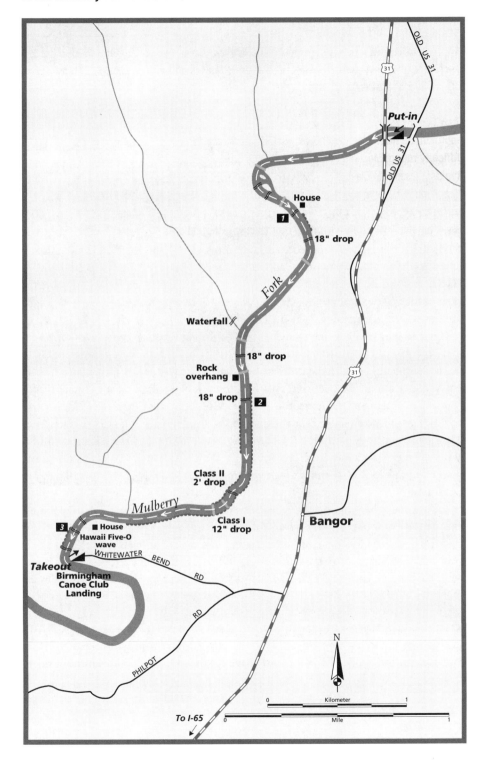

Trip Summary

Mulberry Fork is a typical river for the region. That said, it has individual characteristics. As always, for all rivers in this region, the water's level plays an important role in how the river will affect your run. The rating of II+ means that at very high water levels, some of the rapids turn into Class III. The run is capped at the end by the infamous "Hawaii Five-O" wave at the takeout.

Trip Description

This section from the old US 31 bridge is usually called the Lower Mulberry, because there are two other sections of the river above this point (sometimes known as the Upper Mulberry and the Upper Upper Mulberry), which also provide excellent runs. The Lower Mulberry would be classified somewhere between the Upper Upper, which is a mellower ride with lots of pools and eddies, and the Upper, which offers a somewhat wilder ride. Mulberry Fork is the dividing line between Cullman and Blount Counties.

Just after putting in, head west to cross under the US 31 bridge. Within five minutes of putting in, heading westward for about a half mile, you'll encounter gorgeous horizontally striated rock formations off to the right, then a large flat boulder rising just above the surface. Right here you'll realize that this is a scene both typical of the region and unique in its own spectacular beauty. Here the flow slows.

Overhanging trees growing by and into the rock complete the picture. Five or ten minutes after that, you'll become more engaged with the river, as a small drop comes into sight when you round a bend to the left. Finishing out the long bend you'll encounter a small rapid, then a shoal. The river continues bending left, and a series of three small islands approaches. You can take a shortcut to the left side of the islands, where the width narrows and the current speed increases, or you may choose to continue to the right of the islands. The right-side path is probably the wilder side, where you'll ride down a long rapid with about a 3-foot drop in elevation over its length. Whichever route you choose, take a few minutes to paddle back upstream a little ways to see what you missed on the path that you didn't take.

When you're back under way, you'll be heading southeast for about a third of a mile, encountering four or five shoals through the stretch, some high rock bluffs off to the left, then a Class II rapid with an 18-inch drop and lots of rocks to maneuver around as the river begins turning back to the south, then southeast. You are just past the 1-mile point. After the bend to the right, you'll now be heading southwest for about a half-mile, where there are lots of large boulders projecting above the water surface, but with plenty of space to easily maneuver through. Just where the river begins a turn due south, there is a small perennial stream flowing over large flat rocks on the right—a beautiful sight. If you take a few minutes and stop to climb the rocks of the waterfall, you'll get to see the stream flowing down more rocks and into a pool, all out of sight from the Mulberry's level. Ferns and rich foliage along with black-eyed Susan and other colorful wildflowers abound here.

Back on the water you'll be heading due south for another half-mile. This stretch is full of rock bluffs and overhangs on the banks. There are a few shoals through here, two 18-inch drops, then a Class II 24-inch drop. At the end of the southerly stretch is mile 2.3, where the river bends to the west as you travel through a Class I rapid, with lots of rocks to traverse.

Now heading west is a 1-foot rock ledge expanding across the width of the river, about 80 feet. Some flat grassy banks suitable for stopping and eating lunch appear in this area; otherwise there is the usual scenery of many rocks and overgrown muddy banks of about 2 to 5 feet in height. There's a flat rocky ledge on the right with a NO TRESPASSING sign posted, and you'll pass an intermittent stream about 3 feet in width on the right.

At this point you are within a half-mile of the takeout, but the fun isn't over just yet. A long set of rapids approaches as you round the turn back toward the south, and a pretty, rocky bluff comes into view on the right. The last rapid is called "Hawaii Five-O" and is known for ending a paddler's trip in a very soggy fashion. The wave formed here is also a favorite play spot mainly for kayakers. Whether you make it through upright or over-turned, the takeout is on the left.

Trip Information

Contact
Birmingham Canoe Club
P.O. Box 951
Birmingham, AL 35204
www.birminghamcanoeclub.org

Season
Year-round. Keep your eye on the level gauge.

Fees/Permits
There are no fees to launch, take out, or paddle the river.

Local Information
Cullman Area Chamber of Commerce
211 2nd Avenue NE
P.O. Box 1104
Cullman, AL 35056
(800) 313–5114
www.cullmanchamber.org

The old U.S. Highway 31 bridge as seen from the put-in.

Local Events/Attractions

Mulberry Fork Canoe and Kayak Race (annually in March)
c/o Birmingham Canoe Club
5620 9th Avenue South
Birmingham, AL 35212
(205) 987–2826
The Mulberry Fork Canoe and Kayak Race draws hundreds of visitors and contestants each year.

Accommodations

Motel I–65
14466 Highway 91
Hanceville, AL 35077
(256) 287–1114

Restaurants

Top Hat BBQ
U.S. Highway 31
Blount Springs, AL 35079
(256) 352–9919
Serving tender, delicious BBQ and fried catfish fillets, Top Hat is a favorite among paddlers.

Organizations

Friends of the Mulberry Fork River
489 Starnes Chapel Road
Blountsville, AL 35031
(256) 429–4504
or
P.O. Box 1161
Hanceville, AL 35077
(256) 625–4745
www.ag.auburn.edu/grassroots/fmfr
Friends of the Mulberry Fork River are committed to establishing and keeping public access points for recreation, and maintaining the water quality in and around Mulberry Fork River.

Other Resources

USGS Stream Gauge Online for the Mulberry Fork near Garden City:
wwwdalmtg.er.usgs.gov/rt-cgi/gen_stn_pg?station=02450000

Local Outdoor Retailer

Blount Outdoor Supplies
227 1st Avenue East
Blountsville, AL 35031
(256) 429–2668

Maps

USGS maps: Blount Springs, AL.
DeLorme: *Alabama Atlas & Gazetteer:* #25, F-6, G-6.

Tidbit

The Alabama Music Hall of Fame is overflowing with residents who have made a mark in the world of music with their various styles. Members include Lionel Richie and the Commodores, Hank Williams, Bonnie Raitt, Jimmy Buffett, Tammy Wynette, Emmylou Harris, and Nat King Cole.

28 **Sipsey River**

River Specs

County: Winston.
Start: Sipsey Recreation Area.
End: W. T. Mims Public Access area.
Length: 10.1 miles.
Approximate float time: Five to six hours.
Difficulty rating: Moderate, with considerable maneuvering around boulders.
Rapids: Class I.
River type: White water.
Current: Swift.
Minimum level: 350 cfs.
Environment: Wildflower-laden river with magnolia, oak, southern yellow pine, hemlock, and muscadine trees lining the banks. The scenery is accented with towering bluffs and turquoise water.
Elevation drop: 3 feet per mile.
Land status: National forest.
Nearest town (or city): Double Springs.
Other users: None.

Getting There: Put-in and Takeout Information

To shuttle point/takeout: From Jasper take Alabama Highway 195 north 25 miles. Come to the intersection of Alabama Highway 278. Continue straight (this is now Alabama Highway 33). Travel 5.2 miles, crossing over the Sipsey. There will be a white sign on the right that reads W. T. MIMS PUBLIC ACCESS POINT. Turn onto the gravel road here, and travel downhill about 30 yards to the large gravel parking area.

There is a gravel/dirt/rock road that heads down to the riverbank for 0.5 mile. The road begins with very large ruts that may be impassable by small cars. The hill is also rather steep here, so getting back up in a small car could be a problem. In 0.2 mile, the road levels off and there is a large secondary parking area. To the left the road heads downhill again steeply for 0.1 mile and is definitely impassable unless you have an SUV. The road ends at a small cement landing on the river.

As you near the end of your trip, the cement takeout ramp is easily found as you cross under the only bridge on the trip, the AL 33 bridge. The takeout is 0.1 mile beyond the bridge on the left bank.

To put-in from takeout: Turn right from the W. T. Mims Public Access area and travel north on AL 33 for 7.3 miles. Make a left turn onto County Road 6. (This road is marked CR 60 on most maps. It is actually CR 6 until it crosses into the next county.) Travel 4 miles, and make a left turn into the Sipsey Recreation Area parking lot. To the right will

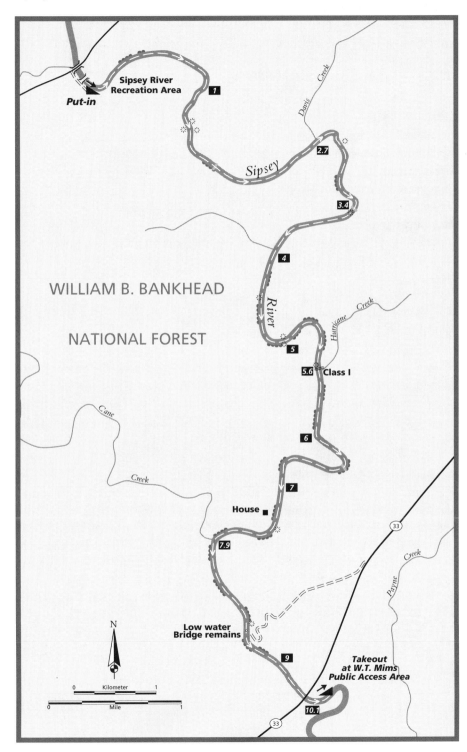

Sipsey River
Recreation Area
Put-in
1
Davis Creek
2.7
Sipsey
3.4
4
WILLIAM B. BANKHEAD
River
Hurricane Creek
NATIONAL FOREST
5
5.6 Class I
Cane
6
Creek
7
House
33
7.9
Payne Creek
N
Low water
Bridge remains
9
Takeout
at W.T. Mims
Public Access Area
10.1
33

0   Kilometer   1
0   Mile   1

be a parking area for hikers. Continue straight across the one-lane wooden-surface bridge to the second parking area.

The parking area is a large gravel lot with plenty of parking. The river is straight ahead from where you enter the parking lot to the left of a national forest information sign.

The put-in is a moderate 50-foot climb and is a combination of dirt and gravel with railroad tie supports used to prevent erosion.

Trip Summary

A standout river in the northwest, the Sipsey is the epitome of wilderness paddling in the state with a fun Class I rapid around large boulders. It also boasts beautiful towering limestone canyon walls, waterfalls after a good rain along the banks, hundreds of varieties of wildflowers, and clear turquoise water.

Trip Description

All of the rivers in Alabama are unique and beautiful in their own way, but none stand out like the Sipsey. The river is the only National Wild and Scenic River in the state, and for good reason.

The Sipsey begins its flow deep within the William B. Bankhead National Forest where the waters of Thompson and Hubbard Creeks converge. From here the river travels 61 miles through its namesake wilderness area and eventually into Smith Lake.

The water of the Sipsey is beautiful in itself. It is crystal clear for most of the trip until it flows into deep pools, where the color turns to a beautiful turquoise. The bottom for the most part is sandy, with rocks and boulders strewn about. The clarity of the water makes it easy to avoid the rocks and to see—and catch—a variety of fish, such as largemouth bass and bluegill.

The gray canyon walls are accented with brilliant wildflowers in the spring and early summer. There are too many varieties to name, but the many wildflower photographers who spend weeks at a time in the wilderness will be more than happy to talk to you about them.

What makes the river so spectacular is the canyon itself, which has been carved by the river over the centuries. The limestone walls jut skyward 300 feet in some places. Huge overhangs protrude where we float by. Many small caves that have been formed by the river invite exploration. And after a rain the sight and sound of waterfalls cascading off the walls and into the river prove that this is still a work in progress.

Like Borden Creek, the Sipsey is best run with levels greater than 350 cfs. Anything below 200 cfs and you might as well wear your walking shoes and prepare to carry your boat. The best times, as with many northern rivers in the state, is during the winter and spring, but keep an eye on the gauge (see Other Resources). There are always some good spikes in water flow during the summer after a good thunderstorm.

Overall the trip is loaded with fast shoals that make it fun for beginners and has one nice Class I rapid located at mile 5.6. It's an easy run to either side of the large boulder in

Besides being a National Wild and Scenic River, the Sipsey is a wildflower lover's dream come true, with hundreds of varieties lining the banks throughout the year.

the center of it, but keep a distance from the rock. Some paddlers have wrapped their canoe around it. One standing wave is found at the end of the run.

The put-in is located easily enough at the Sipsey Recreation Area on CR 6 (Cranal Road). The takeout, however, is another story. Some people will tell you to take out at the AL 33 bridge, but high, vertical canyon walls along both banks surround the river here. Our recommendation is the W. T. Mims Public Access Area 0.75 mile north of the Sipsey Bridge on AL 33. The road down to the river isn't the best, but it provides an excellent landing (see Getting There).

When you paddle the Sipsey, you may want to make it an overnight trip by running Borden Creek to the Sipsey Recreation Area and then the Sipsey to the takeout at the Mims Public Access Area. The Borden merges with the Sipsey 0.7 mile before reaching the recreation area. Although camping is not allowed at the recreation area itself, it is allowed anywhere in the forest with only a few guidelines. The Forest Service asks that campers camp at least 100 feet from a riverbank and off of trails. There are no designated camping areas, which means it's your choice, so remember to practice "no-trace" camping and leave the forest better than when you arrived.

Other campers have already set up fire rings and cleared tent areas, sometimes near the rivers, despite what the Forest Service requests. If you find one of these, use it. It's better to reuse an already cleared campsite than to disturb more forest.

And as with all national forests, hunting is allowed. Be sure to contact the ranger office for dates and restrictions placed on camping and traveling in the forest during hunting season.

Trip Information

Contact

USDA Forest Service, William B. Bankhead District
Main Street
Double Springs, AL 35553
(205) 489–5111
The office is open Monday through Friday, 7:30 A.M. to 4:00 P.M.

Season

As with Borden Creek the Sipsey is best floated in the winter and spring. In the summer the level becomes *very* low. Check the river gauge (see Other Resources) for flow conditions before heading out, or you could be walking the river. Any flow below 200 cfs would not be floatable. Also, during certain months in the fall and winter, hunting season is open. Contact the forest service for exact dates and restrictions.

Fees/Permits

There is no fee to take out or paddle the river. There is a $3.00 day-use fee required at the put-in at the Sipsey Recreation Area. Camping is allowed anywhere in the forest at no cost (refer to the text for restrictions).

Local Information

Alabama Mountain Lakes
25062 North Street
Mooresville, AL 35649
(800) 648–5381
www.almtlakes.org

Lawrence County Chamber of Commerce
14220 Court Street
Moulton, AL 35553
(205) 974–1658

Winston County Chamber of Commerce
P.O. Box 147
Double Springs, AL 35553
(205) 489–5026

Local Events/Attractions

Looney's Riverboat
22400 Highway 278
Double Springs, AL 35553
(800) 566–6397
A two-hour dinner cruise is the offering aboard the paddle-wheel boat *Free State Lady.* The cruise takes you down the lower Sipsey River to Lewis Smith Lake.

Accommodations

Free State Inn
15757 Highway 278
Double Springs, AL 35553
(205) 489–0056
This bed-and-breakfast inn is located within the Bankhead National Forest on AL 278 just west of Looney's Tavern.

Restaurants

Cardinal Drive-In
15240 Court Street
Moulton, AL 35650
(265) 974–9065

John's Bar-B-Que
15165 Court Street
Moulton, AL 35650
(265) 974–7721

Organizations

Alabama Wilderness Alliance
P.O. Box 223
Moulton, AL 35553
(205) 265–6529
www.wildlaw.org/awa-wild.htm

Wild Alabama
11312 Alabama Highway 33
Moulton, AL 35650
(256) 974–7678

Other Resources

USGS Stream Gauge Online for the Sipsey and Borden Creek:
www.dalmtg.er.usgs.gov/rt-cgi/gen_stn_pg?station=02450250

Local Outdoor Retailer

Wild Alabama
11312 Alabama Highway 33
Moulton, AL 35650
(256) 974–7678
Wild Alabama rents canoes and has arts and crafts in their store as well. They currently do
not have shuttle service.

Maps

Brochures: Available by mail from the USDA Forest Service.
USGS maps: Bee Branch, AL/Houston, AL/Grayson, AL.
DeLorme: *Alabama Atlas & Gazetteer:* #23, B-10, C-10.

America's Wild and Scenic Rivers

Late in the 1960s as the world had their first pictures of their fragile blue planet beamed
back to them from the gray surface of the moon, Americans realized that the nation's outdoor wonders were disappearing rapidly. Rivers in particular were the dumping ground for
industry and were being dammed and dredged at an alarming rate. If not protected, the
wild rivers of the United States would vanish.

It was this awakening that forced Congress to create the National Wild and Scenic
River System in 1968. This legislation set up a set of guidelines so that selected rivers
could be preserved. To be selected a river must have remarkable scenic, recreational, geo-
logic, fish and wildlife, historic, or cultural value. The act has been a huge success, with
rivers like Alabama's Sipsey and its beautiful canyon scenery being preserved for generations to come.

29 Terrapin Creek

River Specs

County: Cherokee.
Start: County Road 8 at the Frank Stewart Memorial Bridge.
End: County Road 175 at Alabama Highway 9.
Length: 7.3 miles.
Approximate float time: Four to five hours.
Difficulty rating: Easy. Class I for beginners to intermediates.
Rapids: Class I.
River type: White water.
Current: Swift with intermittent deep, slow pools.
Minimum level: 600 cfs.
Environment: Oak-, magnolia-, and evergreen-lined river with picturesque outcroppings and the Appalachian foothills as a backdrop.
Elevation drop: 6.4 feet per mile.
Land status: Mostly unincorporated, some private property.
Nearest town (or city): Piedmont.
Other users: Anglers.

Getting There: Put-in and Takeout Information

To shuttle point/takeout: Take Alabama Highway 9 north from the junction with U.S. Highway 278 in Piedmont. Travel 7 miles. Turn right onto County Road 175 (this is a hairpin turn). Head down the road 0.1 mile. The river will be on your left. There is a small, 5- to 6-foot gravel shoulder on the left where you can park.

The takeout is a steep 50-foot bank from the river to the road. The good news is that the footing is excellent. As you near the end of the trip, be on the lookout for the takeout 0.5-mile after crossing under the power lines on the left side of the river.

To put-in from takeout: Travel 0.1 mile back up CR 175 to AL 9. Make a left turn, and head north 3.2 miles. Turn left onto County Road 8. Continue on CR 8 for 1 mile. The put-in is just before the Frank Stewart Memorial Bridge, which crosses the river on the left side of the road.

The put-in is a moderate 200-foot climb to the riverbank. This is a dirt road that is possible to drive down, but the turnaround at the bottom is small to nonexistent. It would be best to carry your canoe. There is ample parking on the grassy shoulder on CR 8.

Trip Summary

The Terrapin is an excellent Class I river. Around almost every bend there is a shoal or drop, requiring rapid careening around the rocks. The banks are lined with interesting rock formations, and the foothills of the Appalachians provide a breathtaking backdrop. The trip

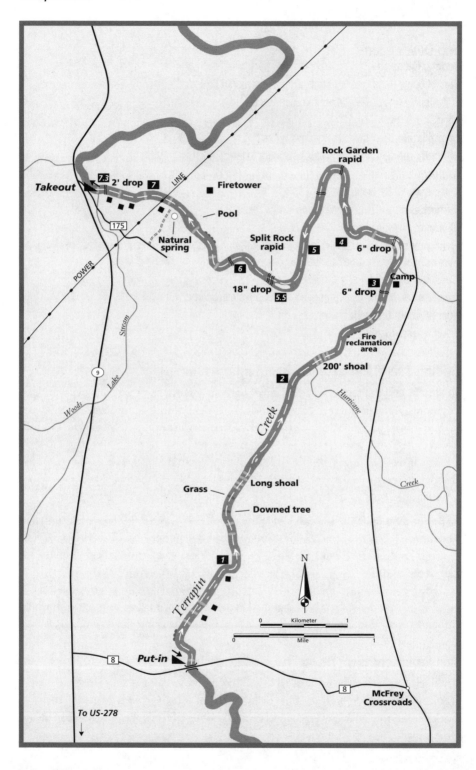

Rock Garden rapid

Takeout

7.3 2' drop **7**

LINE

■ Firetower

175

— Pool

Natural spring

Split Rock rapid

5

4

6" drop

POWER

6

18" drop

5.5

6" drop

3

Camp ■

Stream

Fire reclamation area

9

200' shoal

2

Woods

Lake

Hurricane

Creek

Creek

Grass —

Long shoal

Downed tree

N

1

Kilometer
0 — 1

Terrapin

Mile
0 — 1

8

Put-in

8

McFrey Crossroads

To US-278

comes to an end with a wonderful freshwater spring flowing through the ground into the river. It's icy cold and delicious on a hot day.

Trip Description

Terrapin Creek is one of those "secret" little rivers you find in Alabama. Secret in that not many people know about the river or what a great ride it will provide.

Overall the river is 400 miles in length, originating in Georgia, heading into Alabama, and eventually merging with the Coosa. The water is fairly clear, offering good views of turtles and lots of fish, including bass, panfish, and gar.

Some locals say the minimum flow to paddle the river is 600 cfs, but we have paddled it during midsummer with a flow of around 300, and it was still superb. It is a beautiful and picturesque river. Floating it you will see many rock outcroppings jutting from the riverbanks, providing a stark contrast to the lush Appalachian foothills in the background. There are a good ten or fifteen shoals and three good-size Class I rapids on the river. The shoals are pretty much the pick-your-own-way type with no wrong way. Two of the most notable rapids are what are known as the Rock Garden and Split Rock.

The Rock Garden makes its appearance 4.5 miles into the trip. It is literally an area strewn with large rocks. We found the best path to the right. There is a nice 2-foot drop toward the end of the run.

The Split Rock rapid is at 5.5 miles and is identifiable by a 3-foot rock split down the middle in the center of the run. Again the best path we found was to the right. There is a 1.5 foot drop here.

One of the highlights of the river isn't the white water but a freshwater spring that bubbles up through the ground to the left of the river 0.25 mile from the end of the trip. You can't miss it, as the clear water pushes the slightly muddy water aside. It's icy cold and delicious to drink. Just before the spring there is a nice, deep pool perfect for swimming (and there's a swing here).

If you want you can extend the trip 2.5 miles by floating past the takeout to the State Road 9 bridge. After one last set of shoals at the listed takeout, the river pretty much turns into a flat float trip all the way to the bridge.

We need to mention the folks at the Terrapin Outdoor Center. A family-owned business located just before the takeout, they have a large selection of canoes and kayaks for sale and rent as well as accessories. The staff is very friendly and very knowledgeable about the river. They also have shuttle service for those with their own boats.

Like many rivers around the country, the Terrapin is in the midst of an environmental battle of dire consequence. The river and the watershed around it provide drinking water for much of the area. According to health officials, the river is virtually free of toxic metals at this time. However, several mining companies have been given the go-ahead to begin strip-mining operations for precious metals near the river's banks, which threatens the quality of the water. You can keep up with the battle by visiting the Friends of the Terrapin Web site (see Organizations).

Trip Information

Contact

Terrapin Outdoor Center
4114 County Road 175
Piedmont, AL 36272
(256) 447–6666

Season

Best in winter and spring with a minimum flow of 600 cfs. Can still be run at 300 cfs in the summer.

Fees/Permits

No fee to put in, take out, or paddle the river.

Local Information

Anniston/Calhoun County Convention and Visitor Bureau
1330 Quintard Avenue
Anniston, AL 36201
(800) 489–1087
www.calhounchamber.org

Local Events/Attractions

Rabbittown Harvest Moon Festival (mid-October)
P.O. Box 187
Anniston, AL 36202
(256) 237–3536
Local artists, craftsman, and farmers gather for this three-day event and sale along the banks of the Terrapin Creek with music and plenty of food. No admission charged.

Piedmont Museum
North Center Avenue
Piedmont, AL 36272
(256) 447–6904
Artifacts from the region found at this museum date back to 1828. The museum is housed in the Selma, Rome, and Dalton railroad depot.

Accommodations

Lamont Motel
U.S. Highway 278 East
Piedmont, AL 36272
(256) 447–6002

You can see why they call the rock in the middle of this photo Split Rock.

Restaurants

Gateway Restaurant
806 North Main Street
Piedmont, AL 36272
(256) 447–9920

Organizations

Friends of Terrapin Creek
39150 County Road 49
Piedmont, AL 36272
(205) 447–7143
www.geocities.com/Athens/Rhodes/5980/fotc.html

Other Resources

USGS River Gauge Online:
wwwdalmtg.er.usgs.gov/rt-cgi/gen_stn_pg?station=02400100

Local Outdoor Retailer

Terrapin Outdoor Center
4114 County Road 175
Piedmont, AL 36272
(256) 447–6666
www.microxl.com/toc/toc.htm
Shuttles are available for $10 for one to two canoes. Rentals are $30 for a canoe, $15 for a kayak. Reservations are required. Open Saturday and Sunday, 9:00 A.M. to 5:00 P.M.

Maps

USGS maps: Piedmont, AL.
DeLorme: *Alabama Atlas & Gazetteer:* #27, F-7, G-7.

Appendix A
Resources and Information

General State Information

Alabama Gulf Coast Area Chamber of Commerce
3150 Gulf Shores Parkway
Gulf Shores, AL 36547
(251) 968–6904
www.alagulfcoastchamber.com

Alabama Mountain Lakes
25062 North Street
Mooresville, AL 35649
(800) 648–5381
www.almtlakes.org

Alexander City Chamber of Commerce
120 Tallapoosa Street
Alexander City, AL 35010
(256) 234–3461
www.alexandercity.org

Andalusia Chamber of Commerce
1208 West Bypass
Andalusia, AL 36420
(334) 222–2030
www.alaweb.com/~chamber/city.html

Anniston/Calhoun County Convention and Visitor Bureau
1330 Quintard Avenue
Anniston, AL 36201
(800) 489–1087
www.calhounchamber.org

Atmore Area Chamber of Commerce
501 South Pensacola Avenue
Atmore, AL 36502
(251) 368–3305
www.frontiernet.net/~atmoreal

Central Baldwin Chamber of Commerce
22913 Highway 59 South
Robertsdale, AL 36567
(251) 947–5932
www.cbchamber.org

Chamber of Commerce of Huntsville/Madison County
225 Church Street
Huntsville, AL 35804
(256) 535–2000, (256) 535–2028
www.hsvchamber.org

Chilton County Chamber of Commerce
500 5th Avenue
Clanton, AL 35046
(800) 553–0419
www.chilton.al.us

Cullman Area Chamber of Commerce
211 2nd Avenue NE
P.O. Box 1104
Cullman, AL 35056

Dadeville Chamber of Commerce
185 South Tallassee Street #103
Dadeville, AL 36853
(256) 825–4019
www.dadeville.com

Dauphin Island Chamber of Commerce
1011 Bienville Boulevard
Dauphin Island, AL 36528
(877) 532–8744, (251) 861–5524
dauphinisland.cc

Dodge City Town Office
130 Howard Circle
Hanceville, AL 35077
(256) 287–0364

Eastern Shore Chamber of Commerce
327 Fairhope Avenue
Fairhope, AL 36532
(251) 621–8222
www.siteone.com/towns/chamber

Enterprise Chamber of Commerce
553 Glover Street
Enterprise, AL 36330
(800) 235–4730
www.enterprisealabama.com

Evergreen/Conecuh County Chamber of Commerce
100 Depot Square
Evergreen, AL 36401
(251) 578–1707
www.evergreenal.com

Flomaton Area Chamber of Commerce
307 Ringold Street
Flomaton, AL 36441
(251) 296–3454

Florala Chamber of Commerce
405 South 5th Street, Suite 100
Florala, AL 36442
(334) 858–6252

Greater Geneva Chamber of Commerce
517 South Commerce Street
Geneva, AL 36340
(334) 684–6582
www.genevaalabama.com

Huntsville/Madison County Convention and Visitors Bureau
700 Monroe Street
Huntsville, AL 35801
(256) 551–2230
www.huntsville.org

Lawrence County Chamber of Commerce
14220 Court Street
Moulton, AL 35553
(205) 974–1658

Mobile Chamber of Commerce
P.O. Box 2187
Mobile, AL 36652
(251) 433–6951, (251) 431–8608
www.mobcham.org

North Baldwin Chamber of Commerce
301 McMeans Avenue
Bay Minette, AL 36507
(251) 937–5665
www.northbaldwinchamber.com

South Baldwin Chamber of Commerce
104 North McKenzie Street
Foley, AL 36535
(251) 943–3291
www.southbaldwinchamber.com

Sylacauga Chamber of Commerce
17 Fort Williams
Sylacauga, AL 35150
(256) 249–0308
www.sylacauga.net

Wetumpka Chamber of Commerce
110 East Bridge Street
Wetumpka, AL 36092
(334) 567–4811
www.wetumpkachamber.com

Winston County Chamber of Commerce
P.O. Box 147
Double Springs, AL 35553
(205) 489–5447

National Paddling/Outdoor Information

American Whitewater
1424 Fenwick Lane
Silver Spring, MD 20910
(866) 262–8429
www.americanwhitewater.org

Bon Secour National Wildlife Refuge
12295 Highway 180
Gulf Shores, AL 35603
(251) 540–7720
bonsecour.fws.gov

USDA Forest Service, Conecuh National Forest District
P.O. Box 310
1100 South Three Notch Street
Andalusia, AL 36420
(334) 222–2555

USDA Forest Service, William B. Bankhead District
Main Street
Double Springs, AL 35553
(205) 489–5111

Weeks Bay National Estuarine Research Reserve
Alabama Department of Economic and Community Affairs
11300 U.S. Highway 98
Fairhope, AL 36532
(251) 928–9792

Outfitters/Tour Guides

Bear Creek Canoe Rentals
U.S. Highway 43
Hackleburg, AL 35581
(205) 993–4459

Blount Outdoor Supplies
227 1st Avenue East
Blountsville, AL 35031
(256) 429–2668

Bulldog Bend Canoe Park
3224 Bulldog Bend Road
Brierfield, AL 35035
(205) 926–7382

Camp Coleman
Riviera Centre Outlet Mall
2601 South McKenzie Street, Suite RC-1
Foley, AL 36535
(251) 970–3500

Coosa River Adventures
415 Company Street
Wetumpka, AL 36092
(334) 514–0279
www.coosariveradventures.com
Escatawpa Hollow Campground and Canoe Rental
15551 Moffett Road
Wilmer, AL 36587
(251) 649–4233

Fairhope Boat Company
702 Section Street North
Fairhope, AL 36532
(251) 928–3417

Flint River Canoe Rentals
107 Michael Drive
Huntsville, AL 35811
(256) 858–2280

Limestone Park Canoe Rentals
RR 1
Centreville, AL 35042
(205) 926–9672

Southern Trails, Inc.
157 East Magnolia Avenue
Auburn, AL 36109
(334) 821–6249

Spoke 'N Trail, Inc.
4453 Old Shell Road
Mobile, AL 36608
(251) 341–1712

Sunshine Canoe Rentals
5460 Old Shell Road
Mobile, AL 36608
(251) 344–8664

Tensaw EcoTours
3807 Battleship Parkway
Spanish Fort, AL 36577
(251) 625–0339

Terrapin Outdoor Center
4114 County Road 175
Piedmont, AL 36272
(256) 447–6666

Wild Alabama
11312 Highway 33
Moulton, AL 35650
(256) 974–6166

River Gauges/Flow Information

Bear Creek:
   lakeinfo.tva.gov/htbin/lakeinfo?site=UBD&DataType=All&SUBMIT=View+data
Big Escambia Creek: waterdata.usgs.gov/al/nwis/uv?02374950
Choctawhatchee River near Newton: waterdata.usgs.gov/al/nwis/uv?02361000
Conecuh River: waterdata.usgs.gov/al/nwis/uv?02372422
Elkahatchee Creek, Hatchet North, Weoguka Creek:
   wwwdalmtg.er.usgs.gov/rt-cgi/gen_stn_pg?station=02408540
Lower Locust Fork: wwwdalmtg.er.usgs.gov/rt-cgi/gen_stn_pg?station=02455000
Lower Mulberry Fork near Garden City:
   wwwdalmtg.er.usgs.gov/rt-cgi/gen_stn_pg?station=02450000
Pea River at Elba: wwwdalmtg.er.usgs.gov/rt-cgi/gen_stn_pg?station=02364000
Sipsey River and Borden Creek:
   wwwdalmtg.er.usgs.gov/rt-cgi/gen_stn_pg?station=02450250
Styx River: wwwdalmtg.er.usgs.gov/rt-cgi/gen_stn_pg?station=02377570

Tallapoosa River near New Site (Horseshoe Bend):
waterdata.usgs.gov/al/nwis/ uv?02414715

Terrapin Creek: wwwdalmtg.er.usgs.gov/rt-cgi/gen_stn_pg?station=02400100

State Government Organizations

Alabama Division Wildlife and Freshwater Fisheries
64 North Union Street
Montgomery, AL 36130
www.dcnr.state.al.us/agfd/wildsec.html

Alabama Environmental Council
2717 7th Avenue, Suite 207
Birmingham, AL 35233
(205) 322–3126
www.aeonline.us

Choctawwhatchee, Pea, and Yellow Rivers Watershed Management Authority
(CPYRWMA)
400 Pell Avenue, Collegeview Building
Troy, AL 36082
(800) 652–2019, (334) 670–3780

Florida Department of Environmental Protection
3900 Commonwealth Boulevard MS 49
Tallahassee, FL 32399
(877) 822–5208
www.dep.state.fl.us

Forever Wild
Alabama Department of Conservation/Alabama Division of
    Wildlife and Freshwater Fisheries
64 North Union Street
Montgomery, AL 36130
(334) 242–3465
www.dcnr.state.al.us/agfd/forever.html

Tennessee Valley Authority Land Resources
400 West Summit Hill Road
Knoxville, TN 37902
(865) 632–2101
www.tva.gov

State Paddling/Outdoor Organizations

Alabama Black Bear Alliance
P.O. Box 26
Leroy, AL 36548
www.alawild.org/abba.html

Alabama River Alliance
2027 2nd Avenue North, Suite A
Birmingham, AL 35233
(205) 322–6395
www.alabamarivers.org

Alabama Water Watch
203 Swingle Hall
Department of Fisheries
Auburn University, AL 36849
(334) 844–4785
www.auburn.edu/aww

Alabama Whitewater
www.alabamawhitewater.com

Alabama Wilderness Alliance
P.O. Box 223
Moulton, AL 35650
(205) 265–6529
www.wildlaw.org/awa-wild.htm

Alabama Wildlife Federation
P.O. Box 1109
Montgomery, AL 36104
(800) 822–WILD (9453)
www.alawild.org

Bama Environmental News (BEN)
2617 11th Avenue South
Birmingham, AL 35205
(205) 226–7739
www.bamanews.com

Birmingham Canoe Club
P.O. Box 951
Birmingham, AL 35201
www.birminghamcanoeclub.org

Coalition for the Preservation of Hatchet Creek
P.O. Box 583
Sylacauga, AL 35150
(256) 245–5635
www.alabamarivers.org/dirabc.htm

Coastal Land Trust
P.O. Drawer 7414
Mobile, AL 36670
(251) 470–0902

Conecuh/Sepulga Watershed Alliance
P.O. Box 2792
Brooklyn, AL 36429
(251) 867–2445
www.ag.auburn.edu/grassroots/cswa

Coosa River Paddling Club
5143 Atlanta Highway
Montgomery, AL 36109
(334) 272–0952

Coosa River Society
908 Walnut Street
Gadsden, AL 35999
(256) 546–4429

Fellows and Advocates of the Little Cahaba
P.O. Box 1000
Brierfield, AL 35035
(205) 665–5650

FRCA—Flint River Conservation Association
P.O. Box 275
Brownsboro, AL 35741
www.geocities.com/frca2000

Friends of Perdido Bay
2233 Club House Drive
Lillian, AL 26549
(251) 962–2360

Friends of Terrapin Creek
39150 County Road 49
Piedmont, AL 36272
(256) 447–7143
www.geocities.com/Athens/Rhodes/5980/fotc.html

Friends of the Locust Fork River
P.O. Box 245
Hayden, AL 35079
(256) 466–3858
www.flfr.org

Friends of the Mulberry Fork River
P.O. Box 1161
Hanceville, AL 35077
(256) 625–4745, (256) 429–4504
www.ag.auburn.edu/grassroots/fmfr

Huntsville Canoe Club
www.huntsvillecanoeclub.org

Lake Watch of Lake Martin
P.O. Box 72
Alexander City, AL 35011
(256) 825–9353
www.lakewatch.org

Mobile Bay Canoe and Kayak Club
Gene Boothe at boothecg@bellsouth.com

Mobile Bay Watch
3280 Dauphin Street, Building C-124
Mobile, AL 36606
(251) 476–0328
www.mobilebaywatch.org

Sierra Club—Coastal Alabama Chapter
P.O. Box 852102
Mobile, AL 36685
(251) 540–7496
alabama.sierraclub.org/coastal.html

Sierra Club—Mobile, Alabama Chapter
P.O. Box 852102
Mobile, AL 36685
(251) 655–3090
alabama.sierraclub.org/mobile.html

South Alabama Birding Association
1040 Fort Dale Road
Greenville, AL 36037
(800) 382–2696
www.alaweb.com/~kenwood/saba/index.html

Southern Trails, Inc.
5143 Atlanta Highway
Montgomery, AL 36109
(334) 272–0952

Stroker's Paddling Club
P.O. Box 2285
Tuscaloosa, AL 35403

Weeks Bay Reserve Foundation
P.O. Box 731
Fairhope, AL 36533
(251) 990–5004
www.weeksbay.org

West Florida Canoe Club
P.O. Box 17203
Pensacola, FL 32522
(904) 932–3756
www.pcola.gulf.net/~jimgoff/index.html

Wildflowers of Escambia County
c/o Darryl Searcy
HC–62, Box 36E
Range, AL 36473
206.202.10.48/wildflowers

Weather Information

National Weather Service:

North Alabama Forecast: www.srh.noaa.gov/bmx
South Alabama Forecast: www.srh.noaa.gov/mob
South Alabama Marine Forecast Online: www.srh.noaa.gov/mob/marine.htm
South Alabama Tidal Information Online: www.co-ops.nos.noaa.gov/tab2ec4.html#106
Weather Channel: weather.com

Appendix B
River Recipes

Beef Stroganoff for Two

Ingredients:
4½ cups water
⅔ cup instant powder milk
1 package sour cream mix
1 package Stroganoff mix
2 cups egg noodles
½ cup dried beef (any type)
2 teaspoons salt
Optional: 4 tablespoons margarine

Mix 1½ cups water and ⅔ cup powder milk. In pot, add milk to sour cream mix and Stroganoff mix. Heat until sauce thickens. Place noodles, beef, salt, and 3 cups of water in second pot. Bring to boil and simmer 15 minutes. Stir in sauce, add margarine, and serve.

No-Bake Brownies

Ingredients:
⅓ cup water
3 tablespoons skim milk powder
6 ounces semisweet chocolate chips
¼ cup shredded coconut
¼ cup nuts (walnut, pecan, etc.)
1¼ cups graham cracker crumbs

Combine water and milk powder. Add chocolate chips and heat and stir until they are melted. Add coconut, nuts, and graham crackers. Mix well and pat into a greased 8 inch pan. Let sit 30 minutes to 1 hour until solid and cool.

The Old Standby: Turkey Tetrazzini

Ingredients:
3 cups water
3 servings dry mushroom soup mix
5-ounce can turkey
1 package Ramen oriental noodles (use only the noodles!)

Mix water and soup mix. Add in the can of turkey and noodles. Cook for 2 minutes and serve. Serves two.

Goulash

Ingredients:

12 ounces of noodles
1 beef stick, 1 hot dog, or 1 slice of ham—your choice
1 package sour cream mix
¼ teaspoon salt
¼ teaspoon garlic powder
Dash of pepper
4 tablespoons bell pepper flakes
2 tablespoons celery flakes
1 tablespoon paprika

Cut up meat into serving sizes. Cook noodles in 2 quarts of boiling water. Cook until done. Drain the noodles and add the meat, sour cream mix, and spices. Simmer covered 5 to 10 minutes. Serves two.

Shepherd's Pie

Ingredients:

1½ cups dehydrated hamburger (soak it for 15 minutes)
2 chopped onions
1 cup mixed dried vegetables
1 package onion soup mix
½ cup dehydrated tomato soup
1½ cups instant potatoes
2 tablespoons margarine
1 teaspoon salt
½ teaspoon pepper
½ cup cheddar cheese, grated
6½ cups water

Combine the meat, soup, and mixed vegetables into salted water and bring to a boil. Simmer 30 minutes or until tender. Meanwhile, sauté onions in the margarine and set aside. Mix the instant potatoes with water as per package instructions; season to taste. Put the meat and vegetables into a greased fry pan. Cover these with the potatoes, and sprinkle on the grated cheese. Bake in a reflector oven until the cheese is melted and the pie is heated through. Serves two.

Appendix C
Other Resources

Canoe and Kayak magazine (Editorial Offices: 10526 NE 68th Street, Suite 3, Kirkland, WA 98033; (425) 827–6363, canoekayak.about.com)

The Complete Book of Canoeing: The Only Canoeing Book You'll Ever Need. Third Edition. I. Herbert Gordon, Guilford, Conn.: The Globe Pequot Press, 2001.

The Essential Whitewater Kayaker: A Complete Course. Jeff Bennett. McGraw-Hill Professional, 1999.

Hike America: Alabama. Joe Cuhaj. Guilford, Conn.: The Globe Pequot Press, 2001.

Introduction to Paddling: Canoeing Basics for Lakes and Rivers. American Canoe Association. Birmington, Al.: Menasha Ridge Press, 1996.

Kayak Cookery: A Handbook for Provisions and Recipes. Linda Daniel. Menasha Ridge Press, 1997.

Kayaking Made Easy: A Manual for Beginners with Tips for the Experienced, Second Edition. Dennis O. Stuhaug. Guilford, Conn.: The Globe Pequot Press, 1998.

Path of the Paddle: An Illustrated Guide to the Art of Paddling. Bill Mason, Paul Mason. Toronto, Ont.: Firefly Books LTD., 1999.

Glossary
Paddling Lingo from
Canoe & Kayak Magazine

Amidships: The area roughly in the center of the canoe lengthwise.

Beam: The width of a canoe or kayak measured at the widest point.

Bent-shaft paddle: A canoe paddle with a bend in the shaft, usually at its throat. Increases efficiency (power), with varying compromise in control.

Blade: The wide, flat area of a paddle, used for propulsion.

Bow: Front of the canoe or kayak.

Bulkhead: Sealed compartment fore or aft in a decked canoe or kayak. Primarily required for flotation but also used as storage area.

Canoe: An open craft with pointed ends that is propelled with a single-blade paddle. Also called an "open boat."

Chine: The edge of the kayak; transition area between hull and deck.

Class I–VI: International standard classification system for rating the difficulty of fast-moving water.

Coaming: See *Cockpit.*

Cockpit: The opening in the deck of a kayak or closed canoe where the paddler sits. The curved lip around its edge, used to secure a spray skirt, is the coaming.

Deck: Closed-in area over the bow and/or stern of a canoe or kayak. Sheds water and, on a canoe, adds strength to the gunwales.

Depth: Vertical measurement from the hull's lowest point to its highest, usually from the top of the gunwale amidships to the floor of the canoe.

Directional stability: Used to describe tendency of a boat to hold its course.

Draw stroke: Used to move the boat sideways. Performed by placing the paddle into the water parallel to the boat at an arm's reach away, then pulling boat over to it.

Feathered paddle: A kayak paddle in which the blades are set at an angle to each other in order to present the edge (rather than the surface) to the wind.

Ferry: A maneuver used to cross a current with little or no downstream travel. Uses the current to move the boat laterally.

Final stability: Also called *secondary stability.* Describes a boat's resistance to tipping once the boat has been leaned to a point beyond its initial stability.

Flare: Term used to describe a hull cross section that grows wider as it rises from the waterline toward the gunwales.

Freeboard: The vertical distance measured from a boat's waterline to the lowest part of its gunwale.

Grab loop: Short rope or grab handle threaded through bow/stern stems of a kayak or canoe.

Gradient: Refers to the steepness of a riverbed over a specified distance, usually per mile. See *Class I–VI.*

Grip: The end of a canoe paddle opposite from the blade.

Gunwales: Structural supports that run end to end along the top of the hull. Inside strips are *inwales;* outside, *outwales.*

Hatch: Access port on front and/or rear deck of a touring or sea kayak.

Hull: The body of a canoe or kayak; the area that has the greatest impact on how the boat and water interact.

Hull configuration: Shape of the hull, or that part affected by water, wind, and waves.

Initial stability: Term used to describe a boat's resistance to leaning (tippiness).

Keel: A strip or extrusion along the bottom of a boat to prevent (theoretically) sideslipping. Adds rigidity or hull support.

Keel line: The longitudinal shape of the canoe's bottom looking from the side.

Lay-up: Manner in which layers of fiberglass or Kevlar matting are placed to make a fiberglass or Kevlar canoe or kayak.

Life jacket: Personal buoyancy vest required by law for every passenger of all watercraft. See PFD.

Offside: Side of boat opposite the paddle.

Onside: Side that you're paddling on.

Paddle: Primary tool for propelling canoes/kayaks. See *Blade, Shaft, Throat.*

PFD: Personal flotation device. See *Life jacket.*

Portaging: Traditional term for carrying boats and gear, usually around a rapid or between lakes.

Pry stroke: Turning stroke in which the paddle blade is turned sideways alongside the gunwale, then pried outward.

Put-in: The starting point of a paddling trip; where the boats are launched into the water.

Ribs: Pieces of material spaced on the inside of a canoe hull to form its frame.

River-left: On the left side of the river facing downstream.

River-right: On the right side of the river facing downstream.

Rocker: Upward curvature of the keel line from the center toward the ends of a boat. Lots of rocker means quick, easy turns.

Roll: A self-rescue technique used to right an overturned kayak or canoe in the water without leaving the boat.

Rudder: Typically a foot-controlled steering device on touring or sea kayaks.

Scouting: Walking ahead on shore to inspect a rapid or other stretch of river.

Secondary stability: A hull's tendency to stabilize as it's leaned to one side. See *Hull configuration, Initial stability.*

Shaft: The area of a paddle between the upper grip and the blade.

Skeg: Fixed rudder.

Stern: The back end of a boat.

Sweep stroke: Used to turn the boat to the offside by reaching out and ahead, then sweeping in a wide arc fore to aft.

Takeout: The ending point of a paddling trip; where the boats are finally taken from the water. See *Put-in.*

Tandem: Two-person canoe or kayak.

Throat: Junction of paddle shaft and blade.

Thwart: A cross-brace between the sides of a canoe. The center thwart should be the balance point of the canoe.

Tracking: The ability of a boat to hold a straight course as a result of its hull design.

Trim: A trim boat is level side to side and end to end. Achieved by shifting the load or position of the paddlers.

Tumblehome: Term used to describe a hull cross section that curves inward from the waterline toward the gunwales.

Volume: Used to describe overall capacity of a given hull shape.

Waterline: A line reached by the water along the hull of a boat. The shape of the waterline and the handling characteristics of the boat change as the load changes.

Yoke: A padded, modified thwart used as a shoulder rest to carry the canoe overhead.

Glossary courtesy of *Canoe & Kayak* magazine (800–MY–CANOE)

ABOUT THE AUTHORS

Curt Burdick grew up in Michigan but has lived his adult life in Daphne, Alabama. Growing up near Lake Michigan in the "Land of Lakes," and then moving to south Alabama, Curt has never lived more than a mile from the water. He lives with his wife and two sons and is employed as a programmer at a local software company.

Paddling Alabama is his first venture into authoring.

Joe Cuhaj hails from Mahwah, New Jersey, where his family denies any association with him. He moved to Alabama with his wife, who is from Mobile, and currently lives in Daphne, Alabama. After a career in radio broadcasting and applying endlessly to be on *Survivor*, Joe became a full-time systems programmer for a local company.

Joe has a deep love for the outdoors and nature in Alabama, and he has written the book *Hike Alabama* for The Globe Pequot Press.

WHAT'S SO SPECIAL ABOUT UNSPOILED, NATURAL PLACES?

Beauty Solitude Wildness Freedom Quiet Adventure

Serenity Inspiration Wonder Excitement

Relaxation Challenge

There's a lot to love about our treasured public lands, and the reasons are different for each of us. Whatever your reasons are, the national **Leave No Trace** education program will help you discover special outdoor places, enjoy them, and preserve them—today and for those who follow. By practicing and passing along these simple principles, you can help protect the special places you love from being loved to death.

THE PRINCIPLES OF **LEAVE NO TRACE**

- Plan ahead and prepare
- Travel and camp on durable surfaces
- Dispose of waste properly
- Leave what you find
- Minimize campfire impacts
- Respect wildlife
- Be considerate of other visitors

Leave No Trace is a national nonprofit organization dedicated to teaching responsible outdoor recreation skills and ethics to everyone who enjoys spending time outdoors.

To learn more or to become a member, please visit us at www.LNT.org or call (800) 332–4100.

Leave No Trace, P.O. Box 997, Boulder, CO 80306